ADVANCE PRAISE

Looking for Revolution, Finding Murder

"I spent much of the decade of the 1970s with a foot, and a big part of my brain, in one underground or another, whether it was connected to the Weathermen, the Black Panthers, or Timothy Leary's clandestine network. Since then I've read much about underground groups. I have also written on the subject of fugitives, outlaws, and prisoners. Janet Landman's book, *Looking for Revolution, Finding Murder*, is the most cogent account of the radical underground of the 1970s that I have ever read. It is thoughtful, profound and thought provoking. Call it 'a meditation on the American fascination with violence' and an 'exploration of the nature of redemption'. By looking at the underground experience of Katherine Power—a bank robber who was once on the FBI's most wanted list—Landman maps the journey of one criminal/radical and at the same time illuminates a big chunk of the field of ethics. I hope that fugitives and outlaws from the past and today, too, will read this book, and that anyone who thinks that the underground life is romantic will find in its pages a sober account of what it means to be in hiding, to be hunted down, and to spend years in prison and on probation. Landman has focused a light on all the shades of gray and suggested that we hold in abeyance notions of absolute evil or absolute good."

—Jonah Raskin, Professor Emeritus of communication studies at Sonoma State University, and author of *For The Hell of It: The Life and Times of Abbie Hoffman* and *The Radical Jack London: Writings on War and Revolution*

"Years after Janet Landman's phenomenal book *Regret* comes her carefully written and researched book on conscience. It is an in-depth study of one person's conscience and ethical transformation. This book has arrived at a moment in history when a deeper look at protest, values, and conscience is more than necessary. Her subject, Katherine Power, is complex. Both Landman and Power keep in mind the tragic loss of Officer Schroeder that was the result of Power's illegal acts. But Landman's voice, both poetic and grounded in social science, is an honest one and her focus is primarily on Power. It is a book that believes in human development, in taking responsibility and making reparation. A meditation, it is also a thorough analysis of regret, forgiveness, idealism, and foolishness."

—Sharon Lamb, EdD, PhD, Professor and Licensed Psychologist, University of Massachusetts Boston, and author of *Before Forgiveness* and *The Trouble with Blame: Victims, Perpetrators, and Onlookers*

"Walter Schroeder was husband to Marie and father to nine children, a heroic police officer killed in the line of duty. Katherine Power was complicit in his murder. Some will say that no good can come from a book about her, that it would only glorify the criminal and overshadow the memory of the victim, this great and good man. *Looking for Revolution, Finding Murder* will prove them wrong, for it is a biography of a conscience, of Power's reckoning with the damage she did and what she owed for it—to the Schroeder family, to society and the state, even, as she herself put it, "to the universe." It also reflects the conscience of another woman, Janet Landman, who over years of research and hard thinking has scrupulously considered and reconsidered her appraisals of Power. Indeed, a bracing exploration of what it means to take responsibility, whoever you are, for whatever you've done or failed to do."

—Chris Walsh, Director, College of Arts & Sciences Writing Program, Boston University, and author of *Cowardice: A Brief History*

"Katherine Ann Power was a pious Catholic schoolgirl who became, over the course of her life, a terrorist, a fugitive from the law, an imprisoned convict, and finally a free woman. But her greatest transformation was an ethical one, as beautifully documented in Janet Landman's analysis of Power's twisting path to redemption. Landman draws on philosophy, psychology, and her own fine-tuned moral sensibility to shed light on a riveting life narrative forever framed in tragedy."

—Dan P. McAdams, the Henry Wade Rogers Professor of Psychology at Northwestern University, and author of *The Art and Science of Personality Development*

"*Looking for Revolution* is a powerful, well-written story. In this age of moral confusion and mass incarceration, it exposes the dilemmas we face, wherever we stand. It contains, as it says, 'supremely important wisdom about keeping one's dissent constructive, nonviolent, open, and accountable'; and, to quote more, the lesson that 'reprobates, criminals, sinners and scoundrels—that is, all of us—can re-make ourselves as good human beings—flawed', of course, but redeemable: in other words, that restorative justice is an idea whose time has come."

—Michael Nagler, Professor Emeritus of Classics and Comparative Literature at UC Berkeley, Founder and President of the Metta Center for Nonviolence, and author of *The Search for a Nonviolent Future* and *The Nonviolence Handbook*

"In her engrossing psycho-biographical immersion into Katherine Power's remarkable life, Janet Landman shows how a redemptive self comes to be. Through years of what Power called 'conscience work', she succeeded in integrating crimes, complexities, and pain into a new, deeply attuned level of moral awareness."

—Paul Wink, Professor of Psychology, Wellesley College

Looking for Revolution, Finding Murder

The Crimes and Transformation
of Katherine Ann Power

Looking for Revolution, Finding Murder

The Crimes and Transformation of Katherine Ann Power

Janet Landman

PARAGON HOUSE

First Edition 2019

Published in the United States by
Paragon House
www.ParagonHouse.com

Copyright © 2019 by Janet Landman

Permissions and Illustrations

Grateful acknowledgment is made for permission to reprint excerpts from the following copyrighted works:

Katherine A. Power, "Sestina for Jaimie" in The Best American Poetry 1996. Copyright © Katherine Alice Power. Reprinted with permission of Katherine Power.

William Stafford, excerpt from "Thinking for Berky" from *The Way It Is: New & Selected Poems*. Copyright © 1962, 1998 by The Estate of William Stafford. Reprinted with the permission of The Permissions Company, Inc., on behalf of Graywolf Press, www.graywolfpress.org

William Stafford, excerpt from "Following the *Markings* of Dag Hammarskjöld: A Gathering of Poems in the Spirit of His Life and Writings: Prologue" from *Stories that Could Be True: New and Collected Poems*. Copyright © 1977 by William Stafford. Reprinted with the permission of The Permissions Company, Inc., on behalf of The Estate of William Stafford.

Photo Credits:

Katherine Ann Power in the courtroom for sentencing, © AP
Katherine Ann Power Wanted Poster, © Getty Images/Brooks Kraf/Sygma
Walter Schroeder, © *Boston Herald*
Author photo: McGivern/Star Photography

Library of Congress Control Number (LCCN): 2019014689

ISBN: 978-1-55778-939-6

10 9 8 7 6 5 4 3 2 1
Manufactured in the United States of America
The paper used in this publication meets the minimum requirements of American National Standard for Information Sciences—Permanence of Paper for Printed Library Materials, ANSIZ39.48-1984

For our children and our children's children

CONTENTS

PROLOGUE xiii
Paying Respects

INTRODUCTION 1

CHAPTER 1 9
Meeting Inmate 9309307

CHAPTER 2 15
The Crime: Looking for Revolution

CHAPTER 3 21
Asking Why: Historical Context

CHAPTER 4 33
Circumstances That Could Help Explain Her Crimes

CHAPTER 5 79
What It Was about Her That Could Help Explain Her Crimes

CHAPTER 6 95
"I Walked Away and I Kept On": The Fugitive

CHAPTER 7 107
Showing Up: The Surrender

CHAPTER 8 129
Owning Up: The Guilty Plea

CHAPTER 9 149
Redeeming Time: The Prison Years

CHAPTER 10 177
The Parole Hearing: Making Herself a Minor Character in
Someone Else's Story

CHAPTER 11 201
"I Will Always Be Answerable": Conclusions

EPILOGUE 205
by Katherine Power

Appendix 207
Acknowledgments 209
Notes 211
Works Cited 225
Index 237

Justice will take us millions of intricate moves.
—William Stafford
"Thinking for Berky"

Rebellion, when it develops into destruction,
is illogical . . . .[Rebellion] is a force of life,
not of death. Its most profound logic is not the
logic of destruction; it is the logic of construction.
—Camus
The Rebel

PAYING RESPECTS

IT WAS A BRILLIANT DAY in May of 2003 when I rode my bicycle the few blocks from my apartment to Evergreen Cemetery in Brighton, Massachusetts, one of Boston's many neighborhoods. Evergreen Cemetery is a quiet place founded in 1848 on what was to become a major Boston thoroughfare, Commonwealth Avenue. My eyes took in a profusion of Victorian angels, obelisks, crosses of various shapes, headstones of various hues. So many souls, so many stories. Somewhere in this place, I knew, Officer Walter Schroeder was buried.

I spotted a groundskeeper mowing the grass. At my approach, he turned off the machine. Yes, he knew where I could find the grave: "I helped bury him," he murmured, pointing: "He's first in that row."

The caretaker walked me to the site in silence. I wanted to ask him about Officer Schroeder's burial, but I couldn't bring myself to break the silence. We arrived. Two rows of cherry trees in pink bloom lined a nearby path to a stone entrance across the street from Boston College. Stretching for a hundred yards on both sides stood headstones in straight rows. Out on Commonwealth Avenue, a green trolley rolled east toward the sea. After the groundskeeper left, I sat down on the grass facing the headstone.

Near the top of the salmon-hued, polished granite is carved the outline of a police badge, and inside the badge:

Boston Police Patrolman
1035

Below that in an engraved rectangle:

SCHROEDER

Someone had decorated the grave with white freesias, red roses, and pink azaleas. I had to touch them to realize they were silk. Living hostas graced the right corner, a small American flag the left.

Why was I there? It was a feeling I had, a feeling that I needed to make this visit. This feeling came with some sense of trespass. I was neither a family member nor an old acquaintance of Walter Schroeder. I had become acquainted with him through my study of someone responsible for his killing. Nonetheless, now I was involved, and I wanted to make Officer Schroeder's death as real as I could. I wanted to foreground him. I wanted to pay my respects. We all need to pay our respects. For at the still heart of this story lies a human being who was murdered. Shot in the back before he had a chance to defend himself. A murder in which Katherine Ann Power had a hand.

Officer Schroeder

I have read that two years before his murder at the State Street Bank, he had single-handedly chased down and captured three armed men who had robbed that very same bank. Nine years before his murder, Officer Schroeder had resuscitated a child, saving her life.[1] He had received every award for bravery the Boston Police Department had to offer.[2] So respected and beloved by his fellow officers was he that they later named the Boston police headquarters after him. He was a genuine hometown hero.

After he was shot, Officer Schroeder underwent hours of surgery. More than 200 people donated blood for him.[3] A neighbor told a reporter that he was always "friendly and talk[ed] to everyone" in their housing complex, where some folks were tight-lipped and wary.[4] A family friend described him as "one of the most congenial people you'd want to meet."[5]

No one has given a more intimate or more moving portrait of this man than his daughter Clare, who was 17 when she was called out of a high school class to join her mother at the hospital where her father was dying.[6] What follows is part of the victim statement Clare Schroder read at Katherine Power's sentencing 23 years later:

> Some of the press accounts of this case have ignored my father completely. Others have referred to him anonymously as a Boston police officer. Almost none of the stories has made any effort to portray him in any way as a real human being.[7] It is unfair and unfortunate that such a warm and likeable person who died so heroically should be remembered that way.
>
> One of the most vivid pictures I have of my father as a police officer is a photograph showing him giving a young child CPR and saving that child's life. I remember being so proud of my father, seeing him on the front page of the old *Record American,* saving someone's life. Years later, when I was a 17-year-old girl at my father's wake, a woman introduced herself to me as that child's mother. I was very proud of my dead father.
>
> More than anything, my father was a good and decent and honorable person. He was a good police officer who gave his life to protect us from people like Katherine Power. I do not doubt for a moment that he would have given his life again to protect people from harm. He was also a good husband and he was a good father. I have been proud of my father every single day of my life. I became a police officer because of him. So did my brother Paul, my brother Edward and, most recently, my sister Ellen.

My father had so many friends that we could not have the funeral at the parish where we lived because it was too small. On the way to the church the streets were lined with people. As we approached the church, the entire length of the street looked like a sea of blue—all uniformed officers who had come to say goodbye to my father. I saw from the uniforms that the officers had [traveled from] towns and cities all across the United States and Canada. I felt so proud but so hollow. I remember thinking that my father should have been there to enjoy their presence.

When my father died he left behind my mother, who was then 41 years old, and nine children. He wasn't there to teach my brothers how to throw a football or change a tire. He wasn't there for our high school or college graduations. He wasn't there to give away my sisters at their weddings. He could not comfort us and support us at my brother's funeral. He never had a chance to say goodbye.[8]

***

I think of Officer Schroeder's wife and all those children, ages 10 months to 17 years, left with no goodbye, left without warning to select a casket and arrange a funeral. Walter A. Schroeder happened to work as a police officer in the combustible Sixties. He didn't deserve to be murdered for that.

I think too of Katherine Power, who has lived out her life knowing that she contributed to this man's murder—and eventually living with the rest of the world knowing it. This book is about her, but I hope Officer Schroeder would understand why I went there, to that hushed spot near the cherry trees. I wish I could tell him that he stands, all 6'4" of him, always at the center of the story I am about to tell. I want him to know we will not forget him.

INTRODUCTION

KATHERINE ANN POWER was a 21-year-old dean's-list student at Brandeis University, former valedictorian of her all-girls' Catholic high school, former youth columnist for the *Denver Post*, winner of a Betty Crocker Homemaker Award[1]—and on the morning of September 23, 1970, a member of a revolutionary cell robbing a Boston bank. The proceeds of the robbery of the State Street Bank & Trust Co. were to go to the Black Panthers to support the cause of revolution.

Power sat at the wheel of the getaway switch-car half a mile from the bank, nervously running the motor. At last, three of the other four, having shot up the bank and bagged $26,000, jumped into the car, and they all took off.

Unknown to Power, the fifth member of the group, William "Lefty" Gilday, had stayed behind in his lookout car. When the alarm went out from the bank to the police station at 9:37 a.m., Gilday was watching. When two police officers arrived at the bank and bounded out of the squad car, Gilday was watching. He fired thirty rounds from a submachine gun. Officer Walter Schroeder fell to the pavement, shot in the back. His partner lifted him into their cruiser and rushed him to the hospital. Power and the others learned this when they heard it on the radio later back at her apartment. The next day, Walter A. Schroeder, 42-year-old husband and father of nine, died.

Under Massachusetts' felony murder law, everyone in the group was chargeable with murder. They all fled. Thus began, in Walker Percy's phrase,[2] the "dark pilgrimage" of Katherine Ann Power. She went underground. She changed her name and moved from place to place, remaining on the FBI's Most Wanted list longer than any other woman in history. Eventually she established a new identity in Oregon: Alice Metzinger, mother, wife, and taxpaying chef and restaurateur.

Twenty-three years later, as if out of the blue, on September 15, 1993, Power turned herself in. She waived her right to trial and pleaded guilty to manslaughter and armed robbery. The judge assigned her an 8-to-12-year prison sentence, 20 years' probation, and a "special condition" whereby, if she or her family received any "profit or benefit" from telling the story of her crimes or her life underground, she would be incarcerated for life. She was imprisoned at the Massachusetts Correctional Institution in Framingham, Massachusetts. On October 2, 1999, six years after surrendering, she completed her sentence and was released from prison.*

***

Katherine Power's story has all the drama of a true-crime book. This is not a true-crime book. I think of it as the biography of a conscience. It traces a three-decade-long evolution from good Catholic girl, to idealistic anti-war activist, to gun-toting revolutionary and unwitting accomplice to murder, to longtime fugitive, to voluntary but defiant prisoner, to woman transformed in the autumn of her life.

In 1998, after her parole hearing, a *Boston Globe* editorial distilled her stories down to two key elements: the "ability to wreak ruin through a single misdeed" and the "power of redemption."[3] In a series of interviews I conducted with Power during her prison years, she talked in detail about both matters.

Part of Power's story, her ethical fall and the ruin she wreaked, is as old as time. It, or something like it, has all happened before. But someone somewhere has never heard this ancient story, or heard it once upon a time but forgot, or—worst of all—remembered it too late. So it forever needs re-telling. Certainly this is a story for a time plagued

---

*She served six rather than the technical minimum of eight years of the sentence because she accumulated that much "good time" through work, teaching other inmates computer skills, and other positive conduct. The Schroeder family, who had input into her sentencing, were aware of the fact that she could complete her sentence in six years. (See Ford, "Power Could Be Freed in '99 with Good Behavior.")

by terrorism—for the young Katherine Power succumbed to the sinister attraction of domestic terrorism. Poet William Stafford once wrote: "What we bring back is what we derive from / our errors." From her errors Power has brought back some supremely important wisdom about keeping one's dissent constructive, nonviolent, open, and accountable.

Her ethical turnaround, this part of Power's story, is new. Sitting with her in the visiting area of Massachusetts' only women's prison, I listened as she navigated the process of remaking herself. What I heard was extraordinary, for I happened upon someone on intimate terms with her inner life and unusually good at articulating it without cliché. I listened as, bit by bit, she sought to arrive at a just accounting. The world needs to hear what I heard.

It matters, of course, who is telling the story. I am, among other things, a research psychologist who has studied the moral sentiments—regret, guilt, shame, remorse, and the like. My first book, *Regret: The Persistence of the Possible* (Oxford 1993), was published the same year Power surrendered. What I had planned to investigate next was what people do with their regrets over serious mistakes they had made. I wanted to talk with people who had found honorable ways to deal with such regrets: maybe social action, confession, apology, reparation, expiation. I wanted to know the *how* of it.

The following year, I happened across a *New Yorker* article in which Lucinda Franks interviewed Power, her family, friends, attorneys, and others.[4] What inexplicable crimes and hideous regrets, I thought as I read. To have become an accessory to murder at age 21. And what remarkable, though woefully belated, attempts by Power to contend with her crimes and regrets through confession and expiation.

Aside from my professional life, I am of course a human being with my own personal, generational, political, and cultural history. In that capacity, I was pretty sure I understood Power. I too had grown up with chalice and crucifix, confession and crown of thorns. I too had gone through my formative years in Sixties' America,* had abhorred the Vietnam War, had been young and foolish and helplessly enraged about that war. I thought I could understand this woman who had also been young once—and foolish. Worse than foolish.

If I had believed in such things, the startling conjunction of my professional interests and personal history would have convinced me I was fated to speak with this woman. I thought I was well-positioned to go and listen to Katherine Power, to document what she had already done and what, if anything, she would do next to try to move toward a moral reckoning. In the process, I hoped to understand the logic of her crimes and those decades of flight—or their non-logic, if that's how it had gone.

I wrote Power at the prison, described my work on regret, and asked whether I might interview her about how she had worked out her evident regrets. She said yes.** Following are salient excerpts of her letter:

> I would be happy to talk with you about the questions of regret, transformation, reparation, and your work . . . . I hope to be able to contribute something to thoughtful understanding of the ways people act, what constitutes responsibility, and what is owed to persons, the state, the universe as a result of acts that seriously damage . . . .[and to] pass on the wisdom-gained-from-experience which is the responsibility of the generation of elders.

And so began my rare access to this prisoner. At the end of the summer of 1995, her second year in prison, I was sitting across from Katherine Power in a small room off the prison's visiting area, audiotaping a four-hour interview with her. I was to speak with her in more than thirty visits over four of the last six years of her incarceration. My principal sources

---

*Although Katherine Power's crimes occurred in 1970, I refer throughout to "the Sixties," following the convention that the cultural period called "the Sixties" started around, say, 1965, with the passage of the Voting Rights Act, and ended around 1975, with the end of the Vietnam War.

**For those who are interested, the entirety of our initial correspondence can be found in Appendix A.

for this book are the transcripts of that first interview and notes I took from subsequent visits.

My other sources include Power's written correspondence with me from 1995 to the present; the full texts of her surrender statement and her parole statement; other writings she did in prison; archival documents from Brandeis University; phone interviews with Power's first lawyer, Steven Black; newspaper and other journalistic accounts concurrent with the relevant events; historical, biographical, and auto-biographical books on the Sixties and Sixties' radicals; a phone inter-view with Robert McNamara about his own Vietnam War regrets, in which Katherine Power was briefly discussed; scholars of emotion and ethical transformation; and a documentary film by award-winning filmmaker Helen Whitney entitled *Forgiveness: A Time to Love and a Time to Hate*, in which Katherine Power and Clare Schroeder figure prominently (and I fleetingly). *Looking for Revolution, Finding Murder* is my synthesis of these sources, digested through many rewritings over many years.

Gradually, sometime during the four years of my prison visits with Power, I came to think of myself as the friend I signed in as—although my scholar-self would not have admitted it to fellow scholars. After she got out of prison we remained friendly. Our correspondence has been sporadic and usually delivered by e-mail—typically me asking yet another belated follow-up question, occasionally a personal check-in from one of us. Soon after she wrote her epilogue for this book in 2012, I stopped ask-ing questions, feeling that the time for that was over, that she had more than fulfilled our implicit contract.

One further note about methodology: when I wrote an article or gave presentations here in the U.S. and abroad on various aspects of Power's ethical life, I would ask her to take a fact-check look at my material before it went public. When, nine years after that first interview, I realized that this material should become a book, I told her I needed independence while writing, with a fact-check reading before publication. She agreed with my assessment, and that is the procedure we used.

***

In presuming that I understood Power before I had met her, I was wrong. Partly because it took me years to recognize how wrong, this book has been long in preparation. I had always tried to let the evidence lead where it would, to see my subject in full. Even so, my analyses kept getting upended and changing shape. From romanticism to cynicism. From too soft to too hard to what seemed, over time, right. In the end my goal has been neither to praise nor to bury but only to inquire. And, after inquiring, to witness, to send Power's remarkable story out into the world.

It is important to tell this story straight. That original hagiography of mine would have forfeited something important above and beyond accuracy. So many people living with ethically blighted souls desperately want to redeem themselves but hardly know where to begin. *Looking for Revolution, Finding Murder* offers a realistic, concrete, nuanced, and original pathway.

This story lends itself almost inexorably to the journey metaphor. Unfortunately, that metaphor has had the life wrung out of it by overuse. I have alluded to a pilgrimage, a dark one. The pilgrimage metaphor encapsulates the aspects of purpose, morality, and prolonged timespan germane to Power's experience. But the word "pilgrimage" fails to capture the absence for Power of either a prescribed route or a clear-cut destination. I have at hand a better metaphor, one that she often used with me—namely, work. Usually she called it "conscience work," sometimes "soul work."

To recover her ethical footing, she was going to have to do the demanding work of looking hard at the truth—the truth of what she had done, who she had been, and the ruin she had wrought. And she was going to have to bear her crushing feelings about the truth of it all. Power's crimes had inflicted great and terrible damage on other human beings. For that reason, her conscience work had to reach beyond the private cloister of her head and heart. She had spent a lifetime lying about herself to people who trusted her, including her own son. More important, she had spent a lifetime running from the justice owed to the murdered man's family. The story of her conscience work—the repair work inside and outside—is the heart of this account.

The story of Katherine Power's reckoning, although *new* news, is not especially welcome news, at least not in our aggressively forward-facing, quick-fix, redemption-hungry culture. This is no tale of a knocked-off-your-horse epiphany. Power's conscience work was, well, *work*—thirty years of it, hard, probing, relentlessly painful work. At the same time, much of it, arguably the better part, was a kind of *non*-work—simply opening herself, unarmored, to whatever or whoever might put back together another piece of the wreckage. Most unwelcome of all, this story lacks the Hollywood ending of a protagonist who achieves full, unalloyed redemption. For the hard fact is: the murder of Walter Schroeder cannot be undone.

***

I have related parts of Power's story to a number of audiences, and I am always struck by how deeply it speaks to all sorts of people. Perhaps we can all read it as our own story. For who among us has never done anything awful enough to warrant regret, guilt, shame, or remorse? And who has not longed to find a path forward from their worst acts?

The story of the long moral reckoning of Katherine Power shows that reprobates, criminals, sinners and scoundrels—that is, all of us—can re-make ourselves as good human beings—flawed and laudable, scarred and repaired, and something like redeemed.

CHAPTER 1

MEETING INMATE 9309307

THE TAXI LET ME OUT AT MCI-Framingham around 8:00 a.m. on August 30, 1995. A low brick building sprawled before me. With its land-scaped entrance—petunias, geraniums, begonias, shrubs, evergreens—it could have been a suburban medical clinic.

On either side of the entrance stood two very high brick walls, an outer wall and another one set maybe ten feet inside. Atop these walls gleamed two rows of razor wire in the morning sun, spiraling like sil-ver curly-ribbon bedecking a gift. This was no clinic and, by most lights, no gift. MCI-Framingham is short for Massachusetts Correctional Institution, a medium security prison in Framingham, a city 25 miles west of Boston.

Inside, a reception area was appointed with several rows of plastic chairs, short lockers along two walls, and a wall phone. Signs warned in English and Spanish: "All Visitors Are Subject to Being Searched" and "All Persons Entering are Subject to Video Surveillance." A pocket-sized, bullet-proof check-in area enclosed two police officers, one male, one female, both with heavy guns strapped to their belts. Using the small cir-cular speaker, I signed in and seated myself in one of those chairs waiting to be called.

While I waited, I wondered: Who exactly was I about to meet? Just who was this Katherine Ann Power?

The information I had to go on at that time came from press accounts, many laudatory, some hostile; the *New Yorker* article by Lucinda Franks; the seven paragraphs of Power's surrender statement; and her letter to me agreeing to be interviewed. Depending on the source, it seemed she could be any of these: (a) a phony penitent: more interested in "personal growth" or self-forgiveness than making amends; (b) a genuine penitent; (c) a genuine penitent driven by neurotic "Catholic guilt"—a reflexive residue of childhood religious instruction. I inclined toward the third explanation. In any case, I wanted to see Katherine Power with my own eyes and listen to her with my own ears.

At around 8:30, a sturdy female guard called my name, sorted out a key from a loaded key ring, and unlocked a heavy metal door to the left of the office/cage. The door shut behind us with a resounding clank. After thoroughly wanding me, she led me into the visiting area, a room furnished with orange Formica tables and chairs. Behind a door topped with wire-embedded glass stood another guard—and the woman whose photograph I had seen in so many newspaper and magazine articles. Katherine Power. The guard led Power and me into a small, narrow, windowless room off the visiting area. The guard informed us that she'd be sitting just outside the door throughout my visit with quote/unquote "the inmate."

What first struck me was how short Katherine Power is—barely 5'. She wore black Bermuda shorts, a black sweatshirt, sneakers, and unfashionably large plastic eyeglasses ("prison-issue," as I later learned). A compact woman in early middle age, Power had a short sandy bob, unlined face, strong jaw line, open and direct gaze, confident bearing, and ready smile. Her demeanor, simultaneously serene and crackling with energy, remained a near-constant. She didn't look like a violent revolutionary— whatever a violent revolutionary might look like. But that's what she had been. So there we were sitting together in this prison bombarded with a cacophonous din: strident walkie-talkies, loud male voices, ringing phones, harsh yelling, and strident singing.

Once Power began talking, it didn't take me long to realize that she was not about to be anyone's passive specimen. She spoke from the heart, and she spoke directly to the issues of concern to both of us: regret, guilt, shame, confession, reparation, and ethical reconstruction. She never needed to be nudged back on topic or beyond the level of empty cliché. What she had to say was never not interesting.

Afterwards, sitting on the curb outside waiting for my taxi, I realized that my tape-recorder had taken in hours of rich material. Had I been an anthropologist, I might have said that I had happened upon one of the world's best informants on the subject of interest to me.

***

Years later Power told me more about why she had consented to talk with me. During a March 1999 prison visit, she mentioned that she had just turned away still another person who had tricked his way in to talk to her in hopes of writing her biography. I asked her why she had agreed to talk with me and not those others. It was crucial to her, she told me, that my interest stemmed from my own work, that I wanted to write my "*own* story," not hers. Plus, she said, she felt that I was someone she could trust to get it right. Much later, I came to believe that, in addition, she may have hoped, consciously or not, to find something in my work of use to her in her quest for ethical transformation.

I left the prison after that tape-recorded interview believing I would not be back, as the Department of Corrections had green-lighted only one interview. But for reasons completely unrelated to this project, a year later I would move across the country for a faculty position at Babson College in Wellesley, Massachusetts. At that point, I was just a seven-mile drive from Framingham. Hoping against hope, I again phoned the Director of Public Affairs for the Massachusetts Department of Corrections to request permission to do follow-up taped interviews with Power. Hadn't I heard him the first time? he asked testily. *One* tape-recorded visit. Period.

When I wrote Power about this, she suggested that I visit her as a "friend"—sans tape recorder, sans written interview questions, sans writing implements or paper. By then I had read the transcripts of the first interview, and they gave me a taste of something that Paula Scharf, Power's former co-owner of the restaurant, had said about her: "Every once in a while, you meet someone who changes your life. Alice [Katherine Power's fugitive alias] is one of those people. She's a rare person, an exceptional person."[1] Of course I would visit.

I spoke with her in prison extensively between 1995 and October 2, 1999, two days before her release. Usually we would have two to three hours together, sitting at one of those Formica-topped tables in the visiting room.

To prepare for those later visits, I would formulate one or two project-related questions in my head. After visiting hours I would head out to my car in the prison parking lot and write down as faithfully as possible anything relevant to this project.

Little by little, Power and I spent part of our visits discussing other things. I asked what a typical day was like for her there in MCI-Framingham. Among other things, I learned that she had a cell-mate. Power taught computer applications (spreadsheet, word processing, etc.), developed curricular materials for prison classes, and served as a teacher's assistant. This work earned "good time" and money—$3.75 a week. She—this former cook, chef, and restaurateur—told me that if cafeteria workers skimped on meting out vegetables, she would hold up the cafeteria line until they gave her the full regulation serving.

We talked about our children, our husbands, and later her first grandchild. She told me about her small prison-yard vegetable garden and how, because the inmates had no hose, they lugged five-gallon buckets back and forth some distance to water the garden. She explained to me what purslane was, and sorrel. I caught in her voice how much pleasure she took in tending that garden, and, months later, how she savored the harvest.

Often we talked about our shared passion for writing, and especially the making of poems. Yes, this woman, accessory to murder, is also a poet. "Sestina for Jaime," a poem Power created in prison, was selected for inclusion in the anthology *The Best American Poetry:1996*.[2] Taking the highly structured form of a sestina,* it expresses, among other things, her love for her son, who was 14 when she told him her real name and that she would shortly be leaving for prison. This is a woman of layers—as we see in later chapters, some less than edifying and some brutally unpoetic. This poem reveals a more enlightened layer of Katherine Power's sensibility. I include it in its entirety:

Sestina for Jaime

The woman and the boy look back at the years
They have spent together. At what she will leave: the river,
The Santiam that flows cold
From the mountains over its bed of rock
Into the wide Willamette, warm in the summer;
And the sound roof and sturdy walls of their house.

Now that they have more or less deserted this house—
He only sleeps in it; she plans to return in some years—
Now that she will not plan their summer
Around work whose reward is to lifeguard at the river,
Now that she is walled behind an official sort of rock,
And he has come to find the water uninvitingly cold,

He remembers her holding back, afraid of the cold
Water, reading instead on the boat dock; how the house,
A few hours each day, got painted; and the rock
Cliff with its rope where for years
His friends had swung out over the river
Into the deep pools of summer.

---

*A sestina has a lot of rules. It must have six six-line stanzas and must end with a three-line stanza. The same six words that end the lines in the first stanza must end the lines in the other stanzas (in a particular sequence in each stanza). The concluding three-line stanza must end in three of those six words and must include the other three words midline in that stanza (Nims, *Western Wind*, 338).

She remembers him in the freedom of summer,
And his friends, teeth chattering from the cold
Plunge into the green flow of the June river,
When he alone could coax her from the house
Where she hid out, from what, for years,
He did not know. Their life was like the rock

Walls of the Santiam Canyon, he thought: rock,
River, Mother, Son, sun, swimming, living for the summer.
She thought they had all the years
Of their lives to buy pizza and cold
Drinks for his friends, pay for painting the house
When they swam too well to need her at the river.

She dreams she has become the flow of the river;
And basking in sun, that she has always been rock;
That she once tried to keep house,
Baking cookies for a human boy. He dreams it is summer;
That he still has a mother holding back from the cold,
And watching, watching him. It has been years

Since he painted the house in summer.
He loads another log into the stove against the cold.
He's added a Zen garden of plants and river rock. It took him years.

CHAPTER 2

THE CRIME: LOOKING FOR REVOLUTION

THE BANK ROBBERY THAT set in motion Walter Schroeder's killing was a vicious business from start to finish. While Katherine Power waited half a mile away in the getaway switch car,* Susan Saxe, Stanley Bond, and Robert Valeri—all heavily armed—burst into the State Street Bank in the Boston neighborhood of Brighton. Saxe, wearing a purple dress, brandished a semiautomatic weapon capable of firing thirty rounds at a time, and shouted: "This is a hold-up!"[1] Bond fired several shots into the ceiling and barked at the tellers to stuff the cash into the bags faster.[2] Valeri stood guard at the door with a sawed-off shotgun. As a Boston newspaper reported, when the three tore out of the bank, they "let loose with a thunderous barrage of gunfire, pumping .45 caliber bullets from a submachine gun into the bank and a nearby house."[3] In all, the group fired 18 shots in and around the bank, including 10 that "pierced the living room" of the house next to the bank.[4] Most vicious of all, William Gilday gratuitously and fatally shot Officer Walter Schroeder in the back.

***

---

*The crime involved two getaway cars. Bond, Valeri, and Saxe used one to exit the bank and then, in order to hide their tracks, switched to a second vehicle driven by Power.

Who were these people, what exactly did they think they were doing, and what became of them?* Briefly: the group included Katherine Power and Susan Saxe, enrolled at Brandeis University and roommates (whom the newspapers of the day referred to as "coeds")—and three male ex-convicts. For short, I call them the gang of five. The ex-cons—Stanley Bond, William "Lefty" Gilday, and Robert Valeri—were participating in a Boston-area parole-release education program designed to help promising offenders re-enter the community.

Susan Saxe became Power's friend, roommate, comrade, sister-in-crime, lover, and fellow fugitive. Saxe majored in literature and was active in Brandeis's Women's Rights Organization. In June of 1970, Saxe graduated magna cum laude, but continued working with a protest organization in the sociology department that summer. (Power was to begin her senior year that September.) After the robbery, murder, and flight by the gang of five, police found a purple dress and money bags marked "State Street Bank and Trust Co." in a trash bin at Boston's Logan airport.[5] For four years Saxe and Power eluded the FBI by hiding out with members of the antiwar movement and women's groups.[6] In 1974 Saxe and Power split up. Saxe was caught in Philadelphia in 1975 after she decided to take her feminist activism aboveground[7]—and after the U.S. had left Vietnam for good.

Saxe's first trial in 1976, for murder, ended in a hung jury. In a retrial the following year she pleaded guilty to manslaughter. She completed her sentence after serving almost seven years in prison.

By the time he was 25, **Stanley Bond** had been incarcerated for 20 armed robberies committed after his return in 1965 from Vietnam. Just before he came into Power's life, he was imprisoned at the Walpole

---

*For the most part I refrained from asking Power questions about matters extraneous to my investigation into her process of ethical evolution. When I did venture questions about the other four members of the group, Power declined to discuss anyone except Bond. I obtained almost all of the information about the other members of the group from newspaper and other media accounts.

maximum-security prison south of Boston, serving an 8-to-12-year sentence for two armed robberies. As a participant in the parole-release education program, the 26-year-old Bond enrolled as a second-semester freshman at Brandeis early in 1970. That summer, Bond hung around the protest organization in the sociology department, which is where Power met him. A Brandeis worker who knew Bond as a fellow employee at the university library reported that after the Kent State killings in May, Bond began frenetically "collect[ing] money and recruit[ing] people to react to Kent State"[8] with national student strikes. He elected himself steward of the money the group collected and stole; there is no evidence that he passed any of it on to the Panthers or any other antiwar organizations.

Reportedly Bond kept a gun in his dorm room on campus and had threatened the life of a dean and other Brandeis faculty.[9] At one point, Bond said, "It's such a beautiful day. It makes you want to kill someone."[10] More than one Brandeis official, including the dean of students, who had met him, viewed Bond as a dangerous psychopath.[11]

"'Brilliant' Bond Seen as Founder of Gang." This headline appeared on the front page of a Boston newspaper three days after the crime.[12] The "brilliant" part, though perhaps exaggerated, was probably close. A fellow student later reported being "very impressed with Stanley," observing that "in a classroom with about twenty kids he stood out. He had a real veneer of brilliance."[13] No doubt, like most sociopaths,* he had more than his share of people smarts and, like many ex-cons, more than his share of street smarts. The "founder" part of the headline is accurate. Bond started the group. Power, however, has always emphasized her own

---

*I follow the convention among most psychologists, using the words "sociopath" and "psychopath" more or less synonymously. Sociopathy/Psychopathy falls under the rubric of a personality or character disorder (antisocial personality). As such, it is not a "mental illness" and is therefore excluded from the definition of legal insanity; sociopaths are "crazy like a fox." They show no signs of having a conscience; they may intellectually understand relational emotions and often come across as quite charming, but they do not connect emotionally or empathically with other people. Sociopaths use, abuse, manipulate, and sometimes kill others with no feelings of guilt or remorse.

agency, insisting that she freely chose to join him in what she viewed as a revolutionary action cell.

Following the bank robbery/murder, Bond was caught within the week in Colorado, having bragged to a woman on a plane that he had committed the robbery (true) and the killing (not true).[14] The woman called the police. When Bond was arrested, he said that he had planned to kill the woman the next morning.[15] Nineteen months later (in May 1972), Bond was in prison awaiting trial when he was killed making a bomb for an escape.[16]

At the time of the 1970 crimes, **Robert Valeri**, 21, was on parole from a four-year sentence for attempted bank robbery. Through the same prisoner education program that Bond and Gilday participated in, Valeri had been accepted at Northeastern University in Boston for the Fall 1970 term.[17] Twelve hours after the bank robbery and murder, Valeri was taken into custody at his mother's home near Boston. He named the other four and told the FBI that the group was a "revolutionary action cell," whose mission was to finance the antiwar movement by purchasing weapons for the Black Panthers and to "disrupt the military"[18] by, for instance, purchasing thermite to fuse military trains to their tracks.[19] That summer, he said, the group had pulled off a number of bank robberies and had firebombed an armory north of Boston, stealing weapons and uniforms. The ultimate goal was to commit numerous acts of domestic terrorism, which when multiplied coast-to-coast would ignite a massive uprising on the part of students, blacks, and workers— eventually bringing down the U.S. government.[20] Valeri testified for the prosecution and got a 25-year sentence. He was released after serving a short sentence.

At 41, **William "Lefty" Gilday** was by far the oldest of the five. His nickname came from a stint as a left-handed pitcher for a minor-league baseball team. First arrested at age 18, he accumulated a string of arrests and convictions, including a 12-to-25-year sentence for armed robbery.

Fellow inmates viewed him as a bright "jailhouse lawyer," and he told people he planned to become an attorney. At the time of the crimes, his application for admission to Northeastern University was pending.[21]

After fatally shooting Officer Schroeder, Gilday sped north to New Hampshire. He gave away his whereabouts by drunkenly waving around rolls of money in a bar and, according to the *Washington Post*, yelling, "I'm going to kill some pigs!"[22] Within ten days he was caught, after a wild 100-mph chase in which he kidnapped at gunpoint first an elderly woman and later another driver, forcing them to drive him through the massive police manhunt. He was sentenced to life for the murder of Walter Schroeder. At age 82, 41 years after the murder, Gilday died in prison, expressing "condolences" to the Schroeder family for the first time, but still denying that he was the trigger man.[23]

***

At first the Boston newspapers reported that the bank robbery had been carried out by "'Bonnie and Clyde' style bandits,"[24] referencing the fact that a woman had accompanied the men in the stickup—or "desperados,"[25] possibly because of those 18 bullet holes. After Valeri sang, the tune changed. Now the world knew that this was no "ordinary decent crime" (a phrase coined by the Irish during the Troubles to distinguish politically motivated crimes ["indecent" ones] from other crimes). On September 26, 1970, the *New York Times* ran this headline on page 1: "Students Hunted in Police Killing: Four Sought in Boston Case Are Linked to Radicalism."[26]

When Boston Police Commissioner Edmund McNamara found out that it was students who had been involved in the killing of a police officer, he called a press conference. As reported in the *Washington Post*, he announced that the "coeds" were "allegedly involved with a revolutionary campus organization," and less professionally he barked: "I'd say they were damned radical and damned revolutionary."[27] Perhaps partly to show solidarity with students from a sister university also located along

the Charles River, the *Harvard Crimson* condemned McNamara's out-
burst as breaking "all rules on pre-trial publicity."[28]

***

Power told me virtually nothing about the inner workings of this
group. Only that "it all emerged." I take this to mean that one thing led to
another, as it did for another antiwar activist turned radical and fugitive,
Jane Alpert.

Alpert wrote in her memoir about how taking up with an unbal-
anced male radical led to her withdrawing a large sum of money from
her own bank account to purchase plane tickets for two Québecois terrorists who she knew were going to force the plane at gunpoint to land in
Cuba, which led to her complicity in stealing dynamite, which led to her
allowing the dynamite to be hidden in her own refrigerator, which led,
in a mere year's time to her setting off bombs (fashioned from that dynamite) in eight government and corporate buildings in New York City.
The bombings led to her arrest in 1969, then to her escape and life on the
lam for over four years.[29]

It all emerged.

CHAPTER 3

ASKING WHY: HISTORICAL CONTEXT

How DID IT ALL EMERGE? How did Katherine Power come to such a pass that she was chargeable with felony murder?

Whenever anyone asks "why" questions about people and their behavior, the answers fall into two categories: internal (personal) and external (situational). Research has established, however, that we in Western cultures[1] strongly favor personal explanations. We tend to greatly overestimate how much of an effect individuals have on the way their lives go, and greatly underestimate the impact of external factors—forces wholly or partially outside of the control of the individual: circumstances, situations, and sheer luck. So potent and so pervasive is this tendency that in psychology it is called the "*fundamental* attribution bias" or, where warranted, the "fundamental attribution error."[2] Typically it is referred to as a cognitive tendency or bias. To give it its full due, in America it's virtually an ethos and an orthodoxy. But let's leave it at *worldview*.

An example. A man and a woman are seated together at a café. The man is talking on his phone. An onlooker might think: What an inconsiderate ass, ignoring the woman he's with in favor of talking on the phone. With this thought, the onlooker has just committed the fundamental attribution *bias*—presuming that something internal to the man, his abysmal character—explains his behavior. Trouble is, the observer has no idea what external factors, in his situation or circumstances, might better explain things. Maybe the gentleman was answering an urgent phone call he's been waiting for from a sibling telling him his mother is dying and it's time for him to get on a plane. Maybe he was calling a towing service to come fix a flat that has just disabled their car. Maybe the woman he's with asked him to make that particular call for her. If any of these is the case, then the watcher has not only shown the bias, they've committed the fundamental attribution *error*. The observer was mistaken in deploring the man's conduct on the grounds of a rotten character.

This example illustrates as well another especially important category nested within the fundamental attribution error. The penchant for ascribing people's conduct to the person is stronger for bad behavior (or, as in my example, behavior that we wrongly assume to be bad) than for good or neutral behavior. Which is not logical. Logical or not, Western culture swears by this austere dogma. Some people live their lives certain that in the case of bad deeds, paying attention to external factors is the same as excusing the bad deeds.* Because our questions about Katherine Power's crimes are specifically "why" questions about unambiguously bad behavior, we need to keep this phenomenon in mind.

I consider the outing of the fundamental attribution worldview one of the great gifts of social psychology. Having recognized that error, we do well to enlarge that rigidly narrow worldview. The *person-in-circumstances* standpoint affords a more expansive and more accurate outlook on human behavior. In this explicitly both/and way of thinking, human conduct almost always stems from an intertwined network of personal and external forces. The individual never acts outside of the particular world in which she lives and breathes; we all get shaped by our time, place, and pure luck. Nevertheless, apart from cases of extreme duress, external circumstances do not erase personal agency.

Another Vietnam War personage about whom many have asked "why" questions affords a real-world example of what is meant by

---

*Obversely, some frown on taking personal credit for good deeds.

person-in-circumstances thinking. This personage (who will also figure rather prominently in Katherine Power's story) is Robert McNamara.

In his role as Secretary of Defense from January 1961 to February 1968, Robert McNamara oversaw such a massive escalation of the Vietnam War that it became known, with his approval, as "McNamara's War." Thirty years later, for the first time, he publicly expressed regret about the war and his part in it, writing in his 1995 Vietnam memoir, *In Retrospect: The Tragedy and Lessons of Vietnam*: "We were wrong, terribly wrong."[3] There he enumerated and analyzed specific mistakes that he believed had unnecessarily prolonged the war. Many read McNamara's book with derision and contempt, as too little and decades late. I, however, along with others, found his admission of mistakes worthy of admiration. The intense reactions to his memoir inspired me to write an essay about McNamara and Power, "The War Maker and the War Resister." That essay led to a phone interview with Mr. McNamara.[4]

The morning of that interview (January 13, 1999), Mr. McNamara happened to be reviewing the page proofs for his second post-Vietnam book, *Argument without End: In Search of Answers to the Vietnam Tragedy*.* Preoccupied with this book, McNamara wanted my informed opinion of those who held that the regret and sense of responsibility McNamara expressed were simply irrational—because social and historical forces are so powerful that they fully determine a leader's actions. (Such extreme social determinism is, of course, the direct opposite of the fundamental attribution worldview.) "And," McNamara fairly thundered, "I totally disagree with that, and in the book I refute it." **

He asked me whether I was a historian or a philosopher and ethicist. When I said a personality/social psychologist, he responded that he

---

**Argument without End* is based on face-to-face meetings that McNamara set up in Vietnam to discuss these mistakes and missed opportunities with his Vietnamese counterparts (notably General Giap, former commander of the North Vietnamese forces).

**In my anxiety about this early morning interview, I neglected to turn on the tape recorder until some minutes into the interview, limiting what I am able to quote.

didn't quite know where that located me on questions of determinism. I explained the person-in-circumstances perspective in which everyone always acts from within a web of powerful social forces, and yet that fact does not nullify the individual's personal agency and responsibility. "*Absolutely*!" exclaimed McNamara. "I just couldn't agree with you more! Not only responsibility but he *has* responsibility because he has *opportunity* to act against the social forces. And with wisdom he [the leader] would do so" [emphases are McNamara's]. "With wisdom," he repeated.

It appears that over the years Robert McNamara had arrived at rueful insight into the person-in-situation nature of human conduct. On the one hand, external factors had to have influenced his decisions as war maker. One such factor was public pressure. During his tenure as Secretary of Defense the majority of Congress, the press, and the American people supported our intervention in Vietnam—and he knew it. Doubtless exerting greater pressure on McNamara was the fact that he was working for a strong-willed president, Lyndon Johnson, who was quoted in 1966 declaring: "I'm not going down in history as the first American President who lost a war."[5] On the other hand, better than anyone else, he knew of specific opportunities he had had to act counter to those powerful forces. A personal deficiency of his, a dearth of wisdom, Robert McNamara all but explicitly told me, meant he bore a hefty weight of responsibility for the tragedy of Vietnam.

The next two chapters show Katherine Power's early fumbling attempts to arrive at a similarly two-pronged understanding of how she came to wreak ruin occasioned by this same war. These chapters are based mainly on the initial interview I conducted with Power two years into her prison sentence. As later chapters demonstrate, Power's early accounts were to develop quite dramatically over her last four years in prison.

In an effort to modulate the overwhelming power of the fundamental attribution bias in explaining odious deeds, I am opening the inquiry into Power's crimes by probing external forces. I will get to personal factors in Chapter 5 and beyond.

***

In Power's first letter to me, she wrote that "we owe our children the story of the events of Viet Nam." For the benefit of those too young to have experienced it, I present here a thumbnail history of that highly charged time.[6] With respect to the history, per se, I am not trying to be especially neutral. For one thing, I am accenting certain elements of the history (e.g., the Panthers and Weathermen) because they are deeply intertwined with Katherine Power's story. With respect to the questions central to this inquiry, however—how Power went wrong and then right—I try to be as neutral as possible.

It is a historical fact that during Power's undergraduate years (1967-1970), Presidents Johnson and then Nixon were waging what we in America call the Vietnam War and the Vietnamese call the American War. The architects of the Vietnam War were operating under the sway of the "domino theory," which President Eisenhower had articulated and named in 1954. Regarding Vietnam specifically, the belief was that if South Vietnam were allowed to fall to Communism as had the north, then, like dominoes, so would the other countries of southeast Asia, one by one. It was further assumed that Ho Chi Minh, the Communist leader of North Vietnam, was a puppet of Communist China, the U.S.S.R., or both. Proponents of the domino theory were convinced that if all of Vietnam went Communist, Communism would move closer to attaining world domination—a truly alarming thought during the Cold War. Regrettably, the domino theory and the assumptions about Ho Chi Minh proved to be mistaken (or at minimum overstated).* But because of the clout of these beliefs among decision makers, 58,000 Americans and three- to four million Vietnamese died.

---

*A quarter of a century later, in *In Retrospect,* Robert McNamara listed as the first of eleven "major causes for our disaster in Vietnam" the fact that the "United States had misjudged ... the geopolitical intentions of ... North Vietnam and the Viet Cong [who valued independence and nationalism above all—decidedly not an alliance with China or the Soviet Union], ... and we exaggerated the dangers to the United States of their actions" (321).

Throughout the war, our presidents, their generals, and their defense secretaries were deceiving the American people about the Vietnam War. Based on what they were being told by the government, the majority of the American populace supported the war in its early years. In 1969 the public began to learn about the My Lai massacre, the slaughter by American soldiers of over 500 Vietnamese women, children, and old men. With that knowledge, it was much harder for Americans to think of themselves as gallant protagonists in a heroic narrative. In part because of revulsion over My Lai, by 1969 over half of the U.S. populace had come to oppose the war, either privately or in public protest.[7]

Protest against the Vietnam War was a global phenomenon. It rocked cities in Japan, Indonesia, Italy, France, England, Ireland, West Germany, Sweden, Belgium, Czechoslovakia, Turkey, Mexico, Uruguay, and Brazil, among other countries. Most, but not all, of the protesters were college students. As some antiwar dissent grew increasingly violent, so did the reactions of the authorities to dissent, whether violent or nonviolent. This toxic chemistry first detonated on the streets of Chicago during the Democratic National Convention in August 1968.

Young people went to Chicago in droves to protest the war. They were loud and unruly. But being unarmed, they posed no threat to life and limb. Nonetheless, Mayor Richard J. Daley (the first Mayor Daley) unleashed 28,000 police officers to teargas and severely beat protesters. He posted National Guardsmen armed with machine guns and grenade launchers on rooftops and in jeeps fortified with barbed wire.[8] Tanks rolled through the streets with gun turrets aimed at protesters. Mind you, this was Chicago, Illinois in the United States of America—not Tiananmen Square in the People's Republic of China.

After the cataclysm, an impartial group, the Walker Commission appointed by President Johnson, investigated what had happened. Based on 20,000 pages of witness statements and 180 hours of film, the Walker Commission termed the Chicago events a "police riot" authorized and paid for by the mayor.[9]* Nonetheless, eight of the protesters—Tom Hayden, Dave Dellinger, Abbie Hoffman, Jerry Rubin, Rennie Davis, John Froines, Lee Werner, and Bobby Seale—were put on trial the next year for inciting riot and conspiracy. Judge Julius Hoffman presided over the trial.

Bobby Seale, co-founder of the Black Panthers, was the only black defendant, the only defendant denied the lawyer of his choice, and therefore the only one serving as his own lawyer. Or trying to. Whenever Seale would try to address the court to level an objection or ask to cross-examine a witness, Judge Hoffman ordered him to be silent. When Seale continued to try to defend himself, Hoffman ordered Seale to be bound, gagged, and shackled in the courtroom, and eventually hauled him off to prison for four years for contempt."[10] At that point, the group, which had briefly been known as the Chicago Eight was reduced to the Chicago Seven, and activists immediately took up the cause to "Free Bobby Seale!"

On April 30, 1970, President Nixon announced that he had sent U.S. troops into neutral Cambodia. In doing so, he was illegally expanding the war, which he had claimed during his presidential campaign to have a "secret plan" to end. Reaction was instant, massive, and enraged. All over the country, students responded with protests, walk-outs, and strikes. Even students who described themselves as "middle-of-the-road" came out to protest the invasion of Cambodia.[11]

Then the powers-that-be blew up their use of force to an unthinkable degree. On May 4 and May 14, 1970, respectively, six unarmed students protesting the war were shot to death, four at Kent State University in Ohio and two at Jackson State College in Mississippi. In both cases the

---

*That didn't stop a large segment of the U.S. population from blaming the protesters for the police riot. In a parallel manner, fellow clergy had earlier condemned Martin Luther King's "actions, even though peaceful, . . . because they precipitate[d] violence." In "Letter from Birmingham Jail," King answered the charge as follows: "Isn't this like condemning a robbed man because his possession of money precipitated the evil act of robbery?" (271). I have to wonder whether so much of the populace would have done so much victim-blaming in 1968 and later had they read King's legendary letter.

authorities were confronting belligerent students; for example, at Kent State students had burned down the ROTC building two days before. In response, the state turned campuses into battlegrounds. In Ohio, Governor James Rhodes stationed a small army of National Guard soldiers on the Kent State campus. On May 4, 100 members of the National Guard amassed on campus and fired into a crowd of students as many as 67 shots from M1s, weapons designed for military combat. Four protesters lay dead.[12] Ten days later, at historically black Jackson State College in Mississippi, 75 state and local police riddled a women's dorm with 400 bullets, killing two.[13] The shockwave from these attacks convulsed the antiwar movement.

The violence being perpetrated by the U.S. government against the people of Vietnam, the police violence in the streets of Chicago and elsewhere, the judicial violence against dissidents in the courtrooms, the expansion of the Vietnam War into Cambodia, the slayings of students on campuses—it was all too much for a lot of disaffected youth. As Sixties' scholar Todd Gitlin put it, in May 1970 "the dam broke."[14]

By that time, the Black Panthers had eclipsed the nonviolent Civil Rights movement. Founded in Oakland in 1966 as a group that armed itself in "self-defense" against very real police brutality, soon the Panthers adopted the early slogan of the by-then-slain Malcolm X, "Freedom by any means necessary." In fact, the Panthers were not of one mind about this. Eldridge Cleaver wanted violent revolution to be the Panthers' sole mission, but Huey Newton, co-founder of the Panthers, wanted service to the black community (e.g., free breakfasts for schoolchildren and free medical clinics) to come first.*[15]

In the middle of the night on December 4, 1969, the deputy chairman of the Panthers, Fred Hampton, was murdered in his bed by the police. Soon after, the Panthers pronounced 1970 "The Year of the

---

*Cleaver was later expelled from the party and became one of the leaders of the extremely violent Black Liberation Army.

Revolution."[16] "Nothing," writes Gitlin, "made the idea of revolution more vivid to the white Left than the Black Panther Party."[17] Vivid and thrilling and perilous.

Mirroring the changeover of the nonviolent Civil Rights movement to the Panthers, SDS (Students for a Democratic Society), which was explicitly founded on principles of nonviolence,[18] had by the spring of 1970 been toppled in a coup by outspokenly violent groups like the Weathermen.[19]* The Weather Underground would taunt wavering SDS-types like Tom Hayden (the co-founder of SDS) with rhetoric about how Armageddon was coming and "would have to be met with attacks on property, disruption of the repressive government, formation of an underground, and *armed conflict*"[20] [emphasis is mine]. The Weather Underground instituted a campaign to "bring the war home"[21]—employing armed conflict, mostly bombings, to give a complacent American populace a taste of what America had been doing to the Vietnamese people with bombs bombs bombs. (It is a fact that America "dropped three times more ordnance over Vietnam, Laos and Cambodia than all sides did" during all of World War II.)[22] The ultimate goal of the Weathermen was to provoke a great upswelling of blacks, whites, students, and workers, all banding together to overthrow a racist, capitalist, imperialist system. In a word: revolution.

A leader of the Weather Underground rammed home the message in this piece of bombast intended to shock: "We're against everything that's 'good and decent' in honky America. We will burn and loot and destroy. We are the incubation of your mother's nightmare."[23] Mirroring the magnetism of the Panthers for many radicals, the Weathermen, Hayden writes, had "an attraction about them, a sinister one, for many radicals. The mystery of what was out there, beyond normal experience, had the

---

*By and large the Weathermen became known as the Weather Underground, both to signify its clandestineness and to include its female members, such as Cathy Boudin, Cathy Wilkerson, Diana Oughton, and most conspicuously Bernardine Dohrn, one of its most ruthless and effective leaders.

pull of a powerful magnet for some from bourgeois backgrounds."[24]

In fact, most of the Weathermen themselves came from bourgeois backgrounds, as one of their first leaders, Mark Rudd, acknowledged in his memoir, *Underground:* "I and most of my comrades were middle-class white kids trying to prove ourselves in the world of black, working-class, and international revolution."[25] The Weathermen sought out connections with the Panthers, to "share the cost."[26] After all, the Panthers had suffered serious casualties at the front lines of the "armed struggle."

Although they have since tried to sanitize it, the agenda of the Weathermen during the early months of 1970 went far beyond normal experience. "It is a period, bluntly put, when Weathermen set out to *kill people*," writes Bryan Burrough in his well-researched *Days of Rage.*[27] People targeted for killing were the police and the military. It is also, not coincidentally, a "period whose details few Weathermen have wanted to discuss publicly," adds Burrough.

Bill Ayers, a co-founder of the Weathermen, briefly states in his memoir, *Fugitive Days,* that the Weathermen formed alliances with other underground groups when they shared a specific goal. They joined forces, for instance, with the Black Liberation Army (BLA), writes Ayers, for the purpose of doing "all kinds of insurgent mischief."[28] No further explanation. Hidden behind this coy phrase lies the fact that, unlike the Panthers, the Black Liberation Army (BLA) had one *raison d'etre*: to kill cops. Which they did.* Evidently preferring not to discuss this, Ayers euphemizes it as "insurgent mischief." In a scathing review of Ayers's memoir, Brent Staples writes that the Weathermen "fetishized [blackness]. Not just any blackness, mind you, but . . . blackness that tended toward violence and criminality."[29]

The social movements of the Sixties (most of them) rightly hoped to

---

*Probably the best-known instance of a Weatherman/BLA merger is the 1981 armed robbery of a Brinks truck in New York, in which Weathermen Kathy Boudin and Dave Gilbert drove the getaway truck and six BLA gunmen shot a Brinks guard and two policemen dead. All together nine children were left without a father.

change the world for the better. Then some of them went bad. The combination of horrific measures on the part of "The Man" and decisions to respond to those measures with violent and criminal acts transformed the "good Sixties" (1960-1967) of the Civil Rights and antiwar movements into the "bad Sixties" (1968-1970+) of the Weathermen and the Black Liberation Army.

Allowing SDS to be commandeered by and replaced with the Weathermen "was probably the single greatest mistake I've made in my life," writes Mark Rudd. More than a mistake, Rudd calls it a "crime."[30] He should have helped use the size and power of SDS to keep the focus on antiwar activity, he writes, rather than tear off half-cocked into the "fantasy of revolutionary urban-guerrilla warfare."[31] The tsunami arising from this mistake extended far and wide, and some who had initially just wanted to stop the war got swept up in the surge.

So it was that in a *Time* magazine survey conducted in 1971, over one million students described themselves as revolutionaries.[32] So it was that from early 1969 until the spring of 1970 over 5000 bombs exploded in the U.S., an average of six bombings every day carried out for political purposes.[33]

For those who didn't live through it, it must seem unreal. Six political bombings every day. It was real all right. Real enough that even Henry Kissinger has observed that the "very fabric of government was falling apart. The executive branch was shell-shocked. After all, their own children and their friends' children were themselves participating in antiwar demonstrations"[34]—and worse. Robert McNamara's children, along with his loving and loyal wife, were publicly opposing "McNamara's War."[35] So intense was the student upheaval that President Nixon established a "President's Commission on Campus Unrest."

So widespread was the unrest that I felt its rumblings even at my hotbed-of-*rest* campus. I remember that senior year at Purdue when I was young and foolish and formulated what I thought was a morally airtight principle of resistance to that endless, expanding war—namely, that violence against property was morally defensible, but never violence against persons. Certain lesser wrongs might be necessary to arrest a greater wrong—the wholesale murder that an unjust war is. My own fantasies had something to do with a ROTC building I knew was around there somewhere and with homemade Molotov cocktails fashioned from whiskey bottles stuffed with gasoline-soaked tampons. Or did it have to be kerosene? I wasn't sure.* As luck would have it, being timid and without comrades, my fantasies stayed safely confined in my head. I thought my violence-only-against-property idea was brilliant. And I thought it was my own. It was neither. It was detonating all over the land in those mad, mad times. And it ended in more than one unintended killing.

When I read about Power at her surrender, I knew that in different circumstances I might have gotten swept up, might have gone too far— and something terrible might have come of it. Knowing how very sorry I would have been, I was moved by the remorse I saw at Power's surrender.

I was not alone. Over the years, people from my generation, so many that I have lost count—conventional, respectable people; women and men; people whose worst run-ins with the law have consisted of parking infractions—have confessed to me, often in these exact words, that, regarding Katherine Power's story, "There but for the grace of God . . . ." When I first read about Power, that was my feeling exactly.

I tell you this in the interest of transparency when it matters. To let you know who this person is telling Power's story. Or who she *was*, for that was four or five lifetimes ago, and I am not the same person I was in 1970.

Once again, attending to the role of circumstances in bad deeds should not be misinterpreted as exonerating anyone. To understand is not necessarily to forgive.

---

*Even sans comrades, I would have known about Molotov cocktails and ROTC buildings from the media, who as always assiduously disseminated sensational news of violence. "If it bleeds, it leads," and so forth.

CHAPTER 4

CIRCUMSTANCES THAT COULD HELP EXPLAIN HER CRIMES

IT ALL BEGAN—WHERE ELSE?—in childhood. Early aspects of the world that we are born into—such as family, social class, and religion—start out as external forces, inasmuch as the child has no choice in the matter. In fact, such things are simply a matter of chance (for many people the most troubling and troublesome sub-category of external forces). Over time, some facets of one's early life become integral parts of the self, or internal forces.

Katherine Ann Power was born to Winfield and Marjorie Power on January 25, 1949, in Denver, Colorado. Kathy was the third child and oldest daughter of six children in a middle-class Roman Catholic family. Her father worked in a bank, and her mother worked as a nurse part time—full time when additional income was needed to send the children to parochial schools. Power summed up the family's economic status by saying: "We had enough calories but no luxury." Was there anything about her **family** that could help explain why in 1970 she was driving a getaway car in that armed robbery?

Power thought so. At our first interview she wanted me to know, for example, that she had had lessons in nonconformity at home. I'll start, as she did, with the "ice-cream truck" vignette:

KP: There . . . was an explicit teaching in my life, in my home, and that is the culture of civil disobedience. The culture of nonconformity. My mother did deliberate . . . teaching of nonconformity to us. You know, the popsicle truck came down the street, we did not run out with all the other kids on the block to get popsicles.

JL: Because?

KP: Because, because that's part of thoughtless, reflexive, manipulated consumption. It's, it's, you know, it's wrong. She didn't object to us having popsicles. We went to the ice cream store and brought home a package of popsicles which stayed in the freezer, and we could have a popsicle. But it was the mindless, mass activity of going out to the ice cream truck . . . . She codified it in words.

To bolster her claim that she had learned nonconformity at home, Power told me how her parents had bucked the system at her high school. To get accredited, Mercywood High School had to add a guidance program. The principal, Sister Sheila, hired a non-Catholic to set up the program and work as the guidance counselor the first year. There was "some resistance to him because he was not Catholic," said Power, but her parents spoke up to support hiring him. As she put it, her parents were "the activists in support of him."

Many activists of the Sixties had a pedigree of political dissent, parents who espoused beliefs ranging from left-wing to card-carrying Communist,[1] including red-diaper babies such as Angela Davis, and Michael Klonsky, Katherine Boudin, and most of the founding members of SDS[2] and the Weathermen. Power had no such pedigree. Her parents were not politically engaged.

Power also told me about an older brother who had communicated nonconformist values to her—values specific to the moral emergency of their youth, the Vietnam War. This brother, two years older than she, was attending Loyola University in New Orleans, a Jesuit university. In discussing the war, which they both opposed, her brother furnished her with a compelling moral framework for how to think about it. "The language he gave me that always made sense is: 'Augustine says that if something is wrong, it's not enough just to not participate.'" She and her brother took Augustine to mean that not only must you not participate in a wrong but also, Power said, that "you have to try to stop it or repair the damage it causes. His idea of what to do was to enlist as a medic and in his off hours provide what he called a medical mission to Vietnamese people. My idea of what to do," she said, "was to try to stop the war."[3]

The most powerful figure by far in the family was the father, who suffered from depression and was prone to what Power often referred to as "homicidal rage." He would yell at the kids in fury, thrusting his hands in his pockets to restrain himself from going too far. In a prison visit on June 17, 1998, Power told me she and her siblings grew up constantly afraid of dying at the hands of their father. She said that her mother used to fear, when she left for her 3-to-11 shift, that she would come home to find that he had murdered them all.

Kathy's own "place in the family constellation was to be perfect,"[4] she said. Both parents had great expectations for this daughter, so much so that they regularly had her stand up in the corner of the living room and deliver impromptu half-hour Rotary Club-type talks. This assignment, not uncommon for the bright and pliable child in families, originated from deep within her father's psyche, something she learned only when she and her parents did family therapy in prison. She explained the poisonous core of it:

> KP: I was the carrier of my father's betrayed dreams. I was the lost life for him. That was my place in the family.
>
> JL: His dreams were . . . ?

KP: He didn't get to go to college. His father refused to send him.

Kathy's father was grooming her from childhood to realize his own might-have-beens.

In her father's vision of this perfect daughter's future, a college degree was to be the start of something big. She told me that in family therapy "one of the most important things that happened is my father sat across from me and said in pain and accusation and a sense of betrayal: 'You were supposed to be Hillary Clinton. Or better.'"

This revelation helped her understand a key dynamic within herself. She said: "I didn't know that my whole life, that this drive of mine, that I, God I hated it, I hated how it drove me, I hated being driven, and I couldn't stop."

Oh, but she *did* stop. Rather than starting her senior year in September, 1970, she was out firebombing an armory and robbing banks. From her father's perspective, when she dropped out of college, Power told me: "I stepped outside of prestige and success . . . . I *threw away my life*" [Power's emphasis*]. But for the young Katherine, that was the point, or part of the point. She even framed that decision as a holy act: "I made a myth about [it]," she told me. "I said I *have* to do [it], God calls me to do [it], the holiest thing I can do is throw away my life." To young Katherine Power, a member of a generation righteously disgusted with bourgeois careerism and materialism, making revolution was worlds more important than making money.

Consciously or unconsciously, dropping out might also have seemed like a way to free herself from unbearable ties with her father. The problem is that connection, however unwanted, however painful, lives on within every father's child. It is not uncommon for child victims of parental aggression to become perpetrators themselves. For Katherine

---

* Throughout, italics are used to indicate whenever Power used a vehement tone of voice in the interviews.

Power, engaging in violent activities could have represented an unconscious attempt to overcome early helplessness by standing up to a terrorizing father—simultaneously making herself his replica.

Early psychological wounds do not, however, fully explain what Katherine Power did. Two years into her prison sentence, Katherine Power was still a walking parable of unresolved regret. This showed itself in her propensity to explain her crimes through historical, familial, and several other external factors to be addressed next.

***

As Power's father dominated the internal family dynamics, **Roman Catholicism** dominated the family in countless other ways. Her parents made sure that Katherine had 12 years of Catholic education. She attended all-girls' Marycrest High School in Denver, run by Franciscan nuns, graduating as valedictorian of her class.

The first Catholic president, John F. Kennedy, with his legendary ability to stimulate idealism, was elected when Katherine Power was the impressionable age of 11. Like so many, she had been inspired by Kennedy's call for young people to live their lives altruistically, which resonated, she said, with values she had imbibed in her religious education.[5] Linda Carroll, the therapist Power found just before she surrendered, phrased the resulting values accurately, if broadly: "Katherine Power had been a young Catholic trained to seek a higher purpose."[6] *

Faced with the Vietnam War, Katherine Power, this good girl with an Augustinian sense of responsibility to resist evil, felt torn, as she explained:

---

* Catholicism will figure prominently in Power's story, and some readers may wonder whether Power (and I) remained practicing Catholics as adults. In some sense we both continue to be Roman Catholic to the bone: "Once a Catholic, always a Catholic." Power's adult practice has been highly eclectic. She incorporates whatever she finds spiritually nourishing from a variety of religious and other traditions, including the Catholic, the Christian-but-not-Catholic, the Buddhist, the Mennonite, and the 12-Step approach. I am a reluctant agnostic.

KP: I've always been "good" .... I'm "nice." It's like I'm a joke to the inmates here, because I don't break the rules. I don't do things that are going to make the grownups mad.

And there I was [at age 21 in 1970] feeling morally compelled to break the rules. There was this discomfort—it felt so disturbing, so not *me*. I was violating something, but I was feeling that I had to do it; I had to do this to be an OK person."[7]

When she said she didn't "do things that are going to make the grownups mad," I hear how careful that child had been not to anger a wrathful father. I also hear her obscuring with her language what exactly she was doing in 1970. She wasn't simply "breaking rules"; she was breaking laws—inhumanely, violently. That nebulous "something" she was violating was common decency.

By way of explaining why she felt compelled to break the law "to be an OK person," Power offered this: "I have another piece of background . . . to complete the picture of Catholic culture as a source of the posture, the mandate, to civil disobedience." This piece of background came from Power's fugitive years when a town meeting focused on the 1991 Iraq War. She and her husband attended this meeting during the run-up to that war. A panel made up of a priest and staff aids to three U.S. congressmen from Oregon spoke against military intervention in Iraq. Here Power connects something said at the town meeting with her compulsion two decades earlier to do things she knew were wrong:

KP: Somebody from the audience . . . said to the priest, a direct question to the priest: "If according to the Catholic criteria for a just war, this Iraq invasion is not just, would I be morally justified in withholding my taxes from supporting this?" And the priest's answer was: "You'd not only be morally justified, you'd be morally obligated . . . ."

And when he said that, I felt as if a huge piece of something I always knew, but didn't have words for, fell into my awareness at that moment, and I said: God, *that* is the voice that said to me not it's *okay* to break the law—you must become an outlaw.

It is true that Catholic Just-War theology may mandate civil disobedience, which the priest at the town hall meeting was encouraging. But it is one thing to refuse to pay the portion of your taxes that supports war. And it is another thing to hold up banks with ex-convicts blasting assault rifles. In conflating armed robbery with civil disobedience, Power's 1991 epiphany can look like a back-door way of retroactively palming off responsibility for her earlier criminal violence onto "Catholic culture."

In addition to conflating armed robbery with Church-approved civil disobedience, at one point Power ticked off, almost in bullet-point form, five elements of that Catholic culture of her Catholic background that she thought had predisposed her to become an outlaw:

KP: So one of the things that you have here is a tradition of martyrdom, a tradition of glorifying outsiderness, a tradition of mandate to civil disobedience and of nonconformity, a tradition of being comfortable being an outsider in a society. It's a set-up if ever there was one. [She grins.]

There is another dimension of "outsiderness" to her history that warrants a brief mention. In the time and place of Power's childhood, White Protestantism was the mainstream, default, virtually national religion in much of 1950s America (with some notable exceptions, mostly in urban centers). Anything else could evoke reactions ranging from bewilderment to suspicion to discrimination to persecution. Simply being a Catholic meant being an outsider.

Being taught not to dance to the tune of the ice cream truck may or may not do much to explain Power's predisposition toward being a nonconformist and outsider. Of all the items in her summary, she always stressed most strongly the "tradition of martyrdom" and its glorification. Soon after her surrender, Power had described this aspect of her Roman

Catholic education in her characteristically vivid way: "I grew up on stories of the saints—the ones who got their heads chopped off. I always imagined how glorious that kind of sacrifice would be."[8] The Church did glorify martyrdom, canonizing as saints those who got their heads chopped off.

Those unfamiliar with such socialization may want to pause for a moment to take in what Power is talking about here—a *child* cheerfully daydreaming about how positively glorious it would be to die for her beliefs. If this seems farfetched, think of other terrorists, more recent ones, raised with similar views about the glories of dying while fighting a holy war.

The young Katherine Power chose, consciously or not, to figuratively "throw her life away." At an entirely conscious level she also thought she might be literally throwing her life away. In her mind, she was going to war, and that entailed putting her *life* on the line. "*Her* life?!!" you may well object, recalling, as we must, who exactly got killed. Yes. At some point that summer, Power says, she realized that two of the ex-cons in the gang of five posed possible dangers to her life (though, stunningly enough, she says, no one else's).

But this can't be right—all the emphasis Power put on Catholicism as the wellspring of her social conscience and her opposition to what she saw as an unjust war. John F. Kennedy's gift for inspiring self-sacrificing action touched the hearts of people of any and all or no religious stripe. And there have always been individuals of any and all or no religious stripe who understand that sometimes Caesar's laws have to be broken. Thoreau was no Roman Catholic; nor was Gandhi, King, or Mandela. Then too, entirely aside from Catholicism, the zeitgeist of the early- and mid-Sixties encouraged young people to reject lives of material success in favor of living idealistic lives as Peace Corps volunteers, small-money hippies, or dedicated antiwar activists.

This can't be right either—Power's emphasis on Catholicism as the wellspring of her bad behavior, her crimes. It can sound like: What I did wasn't so bad—and anyway the Church made me do it.

Both Jane Alpert and Mark Rudd wrote in their memoirs that they knew they might die for the revolution. Alpert and Rudd happen to be Jewish, however, not Catholic. The idea held such a conspicuous place in the revolutionary worldview that it had an honorific: Huey Newton dubbed it "revolutionary suicide." All this undermines Power's imputing her crimes to Catholicism's glorification of martyrdom.

Later, not in the context of her words about martyrdom, which sounded awfully "prepared," Power brought something else into the picture, something closer in time to her crimes than those early stories of saints and martyrs—or the town meeting that occurred 21 years *after* her crimes. Just as Katherine Power was trying to figure out what she could do to stop the war, an opportunity opened up to her. A group of high-profile antiwar activists, whom Power preferred not to name, invited her to take on the role of a high-profile antiwar spokesperson. She discussed this in the next two passages, whose formal deficiencies perhaps suggest some uncharacteristic verbal struggle.* She told me:

> KP: I was articulate and I was passionate and I was in the process of sort of discovering a place for myself here. I had been invited to Cuba to speak with the Vietnamese . . . . and then to come back and to, to do . . . speaking tours here . . . .
>
> I met with them in Atlanta. They wanted me to "deliver the troops" of the student militants so that they could continue to be the generals in their campaign. And I looked at them, and I felt slimed. [She chuckles ruefully.] "Don't you get it?" [she thought

---

* Here I have retained the original pauses (indicated with ellipses), repetitions, and *uh*s from the transcript because I think they indicate something important. When such elements are merely distracting, my policy is to eliminate them and indicate with ellipses that something nonessential is missing.

at the time.] "They're not mine to deliver. I don't *want* them to be mine to deliver . . . ." They offered me grandiosity because their egos is what they were about.

Without question, she loathed their big egos. Besides, the feminist in her had to chafe at the prospect of being used as a mere second lieutenant in a war where the dudes were the generals. But none of that was the main sticking point for her. Her next words reveal what was:

KP: They offered me grandiosity because their egos is what they were about . . . and . . . uh God . . . . I was . . . I was very . . . I use this word quite literally, *tempted* to do that . . . . Grandiosity was a real . . . . potential . . . in my personality, and I knew it, and it felt like for me to choose action where I had to stay hidden, where I could not be *known,* was morally superior because it would remove me from the temptation to grandiosity. You'll know what I mean* when I use this Catholic language which I think is really useful: You are responsible to remove yourself from the "near occasions of sin." [emphases are Power's]

Yes, she was disgusted by the big egos of the generals. But she was at least as disgusted by her own ego, which she pejoratively referred to as "grandiosity." She despised in other people what she most despised in herself. It was those speaking tours that she stumbled over in this exchange. In Power's formative religious training, to hanker after celebrity would be a sin. Having recognized within herself the pull of grandiosity/egotism/

---

* That phrase "you'll know what I mean . . ." wasn't the only time a complicitous "you know" cropped up. Could she have been (consciously or unconsciously) trying to oblige her interviewer or, worse, exploiting our shared socialization to make a case for herself? Evidence disconfirms these interview effects. Two years before she had ever heard from me, Power was already highlighting her Catholic upbringing—implicitly in her surrender statement and quite explicitly in the *New Yorker* piece by Lucinda Franks (which led me to take up the "Catholic-guilt" hypotheses). She has told me that she had no idea whether Franks was Catholic when she was interviewed by her.

pride, she apparently felt duty-bound to avoid the "near occasions" of that sin.*

Speaking of sin, Power used the word "conscience" 14 times in our initial morning's interview—almost always in the context of explaining her crimes. However, as scholar of conscience Louisa Thomas has argued, conscience can act as a morally problematic force, justifying harming others, for instance, as the cost of safeguarding one's own moral purity. In Power's telling, her decision to go *clandestine* was in significant part driven by the wish to avoid defiling herself with the sin of pride. To protect her own virtue, she chose "low-profile" action with the potential to do great harm. She was not going to be what she called one of those "jet-set radicals" in it for the fame. *Her* revolution would not be televised.

In her haste to flee this opportunity, the speaking tours, Power turned down a form of activism to which she, with her considerable gifts of mind and tongue, was wondrously well suited. In choosing the "purer" path of clandestine action, where she "could not be known," she chose violent, criminal activities that caused a man's death.

Given Power's stiletto-like focus on the role of Catholicism, it certainly appears that she thought then and wanted others to believe that her religious socialization had played an enormous—perhaps the deciding—role in propelling her down the path to her crimes. I believe that Katherine Power's socialization as a Roman Catholic was a factor, one among many, that helps explain why she went so wrong. Her emphasis on it was spin. But also deeply true.

***

---

* Power had been exposed to this phrase in the *Baltimore Catechism*. Comprised of 421 questions and answers, at the time it was *the* textbook of religious training in which virtually all Catholic school children were drilled to the point of perfect recall. The entry for "near occasions of sin" in the *Baltimore Catechism*, #207, reads thus: *Q. What do you mean by the near occasions of sin? A. By the near occasions of sin I mean all the persons, places and things that may easily lead us into sin.*

In addition to her family and her religion, Katherine Power's **educational** choices proved significant. So how did this good Catholic girl end up at Brandeis University, a Jewish-sponsored nonsectarian institution, anyway?

For one thing, Power's high school guidance counselor—yes, the non-Catholic her parents had fought to keep—had encouraged her to look into schools he considered intellectually more demanding than the list of Catholic schools preferred by the nuns and her father. She explained it to me this way: "He [her guidance counselor] told me that his sense was that I could've gone to any of these other provincial places and been a big fish in a small pond. Or I could've stepped into this other league. That's how he saw it." Brandeis was on his list of places in that other league.

Her choice ultimately came down to the two universities where the acceptance letters came with full scholarships: the University of San Francisco (a Jesuit school) and Brandeis University near Boston. Katherine was leaning toward Brandeis. Its attraction, she has told me, stemmed both from her conscious desire to escape a Catholic world she was experiencing as "suffocating" and a then-unconscious identification with Jews as outsiders.[9]

At decision time, the senior class at Marycrest happened to be on a three-day retreat. An older priest, Father Brody, was supposed to have led it. As fate would have it, a new young priest showed up instead. Something critical to Katherine Power's future transpired during the retreat:

> KP: One of the things in the retreat is spending this time with the priest to, you know, talk about issues, and he said: Is there anything in your life? And I said, Well, you know there *is* something. I said I really don't know what to do about this decision about where I'm going to go to college. I said, you know (and I was at that time, as I continue to be, a deeply spiritual person, and these spiritual responsibilities were the foundation for your decisions in life . . . more so than those of comfort . . .) and I

said I really don't know what to do. I said I really want to go to Brandeis. I really want to, and I don't know if that's right. His answer to me was: You belong at Brandeis. Your spiritual work is to be in the world and not ghettoized with Catholics.

JL: That's incredible. Did he know you?!

KP: He'd never met me—except you can tell a lot by the questions you ask that concern you and the issues you raise and your reasons. Father Brody would've said go to the University of San Francisco, and I'd have gone.

By sheer chance, one priest was replaced by another, an event that reinforced her personal inclination to escape Catholicism. She chose Brandeis.

She was a college freshman in 1967-1968. In the *annus horribilis* of 1968, the two most effective leaders of nonviolent opposition to the war, Martin Luther King and Robert Kennedy, were both murdered.

While those who preferred nonviolent dissent surely felt bereaved, they were not completely orphaned. Notably, the Catholic Left was continuing to head up acts of mostly nonviolent resistance against the war. Daniel Berrigan (a Jesuit priest) and his brother Philip (a former priest) led countless raids on draft boards, often destroying draft records (using fire or chicken blood) to protest the war.[10] As leaders of the Catonsville Nine, the Berrigans, along with seven other Catholic protestors, were incarcerated for destroying hundreds of draft files in the Catonsville, Maryland draft board in 1968—setting them on fire with homemade napalm "to symbolize the devastating effects of the war."[11]

At one point, I asked Power this open-ended question: "Looking back on those options that you had at the time, is there a particular one that you think, you wish, you had taken instead of the course you took?" She responded with a nod to the nonviolent Catholic Left. What follows is part one of Power's two-part response to my question:

KP: There were erratic nonviolent acts about Vietnam being taken by the Catholic Left.

JL: The Berrigans?

KP: Yeah. Somebody said to me at one point, I can't even remember when, certainly since my surrender: "Why *weren't* you doing those things with the Catholic Left?" And I have to say that rampant and *disgusting* sexism of the Catholic Left is why; that when you shut people out by demeaning their humanity ... they're shut out in your vision of God and right action. They were the only concerted, active nonviolent resistance. [emphases are Power's]

She fairly spat out the word "disgusting." In light of the allergic reaction to all things Catholic that led her to Brandeis, it would not be surprising that she would want to keep her distance from the Catholic Left. If that's how she had answered my question, without the uncharacteristic intensity in her voice, I'd leave it at that. The vehemence, however, suggests defensiveness.

Her answer indicates that I was not the first person to have asked her about the Catholic antiwar movement, and it appears that her earlier questioner had taken a somewhat accusatory tone: "Why *weren't* you ... ?" If the charge had been eating away at her, this would explain why she assumed, wrongly, that I was asking the same question.

Power's expressed anger about the misogyny of the Catholic Church is real enough. But I think her ire extended beyond the Church. The National Organization for Women was founded in 1966. By the late Sixties, many activist women could no longer abide a movement in which white males were habitually relegating to their female comrades the tasks of making the coffee and peanut butter sandwiches, serving as disposable bedmates, and mimeographing the macho manifestos paraded by the men.[12] Some of these women ended up replicating the more hotheaded machismo of their male colleagues. According to Mark Rudd, for instance, that "the Weatherwomen outdid themselves to prove they were revolutionary fighters,"[13] adopting as a slogan: "Vietnamese Women Carry Guns!"[14]

In any event, Power went on to finish addressing my question about alternative options she might have chosen—by essentially blaming other nonviolent movements for her failure to join them:

> KP: Many people who are deeply committed to nonviolence ended up in wishy-washy, namby-pamby policy places . . . . Dave Dellinger has said some very—he comes to visit me [in prison]—he's said some really interesting things about the nonviolent: the people committed to nonviolence in the antiwar movement did not actively enough create a powerful nonviolent way to act. If they had, I would have found it . . . . I was looking.

It sounded here like Power was dissing nonviolence as "wishy-washy [and] namby-pamby." When I asked her about this, she said that what she had objected to was the ineffectiveness not the nonviolence.[15] So ineffective were the Berrigans, according to her, that she claimed not even to have been aware of them when she was in college. This seemed less than plausible, as the high-profile trial of the Catonsville Nine took place in the first semester of the sophomore year of this politically engaged young woman. On the other hand, it corresponds to her repudiation of the Catholic Left. And it corresponds to her increasing weariness at the time with the seeming futility of demonstrations and other nonviolent actions.

Finally, it could also be that Power, a college junior in 1969, was ripe for embracing the macho dynamic described by Rudd. When Katherine Power rejected the civil disobedience of the Catholic Left as erratic, namby-pamby, and impotent, opting instead to embark on an "explosive career"[16] of violent crime with heavily armed ex-convicts, she may have been enacting her own form of female machismo.

***

The national and international upheavals outlined in the previous chapter coincided with Katherine Power's undergraduate years. Any university worth its endowment encourages critical analysis, from the right and the left, about matters in and outside of the classroom. Brandeis happened to be one of only a few universities with a history of left-wing political critique going back as early as the Fifties.[17] Not that long before Katherine Power first ventured up the green hills of its campus, Brandeis had added to the ranks of its tenured professors Herbert Marcuse, a known Marxist (1954-1965);[18] and it had recently educated and graduated Abbie Hoffman and Angela Davis, in 1959 and 1965, respectively. The authors of the *Newsweek* cover story about Power that appeared after her surrender characterized 1970 Brandeis this way: "True, it wasn't Berkeley . . . or Madison, or . . . Ann Arbor, but it was clearly on the map of student activism."[19] In considering what her crimes might owe to where she went to college, I am making a point about context: Katherine Power was attending a university with a significant activist presence. The point is of course *not* about causality: Brandeis cannot be held responsible for her criminal activities.

It appears that, like Catholicism, Brandeis had suffocations of its own, as suggested by Allen Grossman, a poet who also taught there during those years:

> Impossible moral burdens were put on students. They were told that legitimate sources of money for the movement had dried up. Students like Katherine Power, in their enormous desire to be good, took it all as a personal mandate . . . . The liberal system and legitimate action within that system were denounced, with no thought about where this could lead.[20]

In line with Grossman's statement, which appeared in the *New Yorker* article, Power told me at our first interview that "there were a lot of radical professors" at Brandeis who were regularly holding forth on revolution. Jacob Cohen, who was a professor of American Studies at Brandeis while Power was there and who says that he had "closely observed the activities" of Brandeis radicals, put it at "a professor or two."[21] Whether there were a lot of radical professors or just a couple, it seems only natural that the increasing militancy outside would have filtered through to some of the faculty on this left-wing campus.

Almost immediately after it was learned that three of the bank robbers had recently attended Brandeis, a Boston newspaper quoted officials at Brandeis stressing that "there was no required reading that might have prompted [Power or Saxe] to become part of a revolutionary movement."[22] Brandeis may have felt it had reason to be defensive. The author of an article provocatively titled "Brandeis: School for Terrorists?" points out that in 1970 the FBI's Ten Most Wanted List featured three former Brandeis students—Angela Davis, Susan Saxe, and Katherine Power, a fact rendered even more startling since they were three of only seven women who had ever made that list up to that time.[23]

Whatever her coursework, whoever her professors, and however much revolutionary rhetoric she was exposed to at her university, the situation was not independent of her personal agency, as Power herself acknowledged:

> KP: I looked for that searching analysis, I intuited that radical position before I had intellectual stuff to make it make sense . . . . I certainly read the accounts of the third-world liberation movements all over the world—their armed struggle.

Power did not imbibe dissident rhetoric passively and act it out reflexively. She chose to major in sociology, a discipline known for taking critical positions toward society and its institutions. She sought out knowledge that fueled her own proclivities. Not for the first or the last time, Power's personal leanings and external environment appear to have reinforced each other.

Even 25 years later when she was speaking in prison, I heard the caustic scorn of a young revolutionary for the "radical professors, quasi-radical professors," as she described them, "who were scathing in their condemnation of the social order they lived in, but nonetheless took their place in it very comfortably." Much as she had vilified "all these male stars" as egotistical "jet-set radicals," she vilified these professors as "comfortable radicals." In the eyes of Katherine Power, college student, these professors were anti-models:

> KP: I think this is where having the Catholic background and having taken it in seriously—"You *have* to do this" is, is what my conscience said to me . . .

> JL: "Have to do this," meaning?

> KP: You have to *do* something. You have to *do* something; you cannot just ignore evil and live a comfortable life. If you know that it's there, you must act.

No more beating around the bush: this time Katherine Power, adult, directly attributed her wrongdoing to her Catholic background. According to her Catholic conscience, the "comfortable radicals" were guilty of sins of omission. They could talk the talk but didn't walk the walk. When I asked Power what exactly her Catholic conscience had been telling her to do, she answered with empty abstractions: "You have to *do* this is, is what my conscience said to me"; and "You have to do *something*"; and "You must *act*." Must do *what*, must act how, she left vague.

***

What follows is a chronological summary of what I know of what was happening in Katherine Power's world in the 1970 run-up to the September bank robbery—most of it based on material other than my interviews with her, as she didn't discuss this period with me in detail.

As mentioned in the previous chapter, the Weathermen often sought to forge connections with the Black Panthers. Documents held in the Brandeis University Archives show campus attention to the Panthers in the spring of Katherine Power's junior year. For instance, in early April, 1970, two flyers announced campus events in support of the Panthers. One leaflet headed "How Much Do You Really Know about the Black

Panthers?" invited students to attend an informational session featuring films and discussion. Another flyer, connected with the same event, carried the heading in all caps, "WHAT DO THE BLACK PANTHERS DO? SERVE THE PEOPLE!" Apparently intended to de-demonize the image of Panthers sporting their famous firearms, this notice detailed benevolent ways the Panthers were serving their people, such as the highly successful program offering free breakfasts for children. This flyer also included a call to action: "Come to Boston on April 14 to protest the repression of the Black Panthers and the trial of Bobby Seale."

It notified readers that some unnamed "we" would be soliciting monetary support for the Panther legal defense fund, naming "Bobby Seale and 13 others on trial in New Haven" among those in need of financial help.

Katherine Power's name does not appear on any of these documents. Several facts, however, suggest that she would have at least been aware of these efforts, if not had a hand in them.* For one thing, a stated goal of Power's criminal activities five months later, we know, was to fund and arm the Panthers. In addition, Brandeis was such a small community, with a student body of fewer than 3000 in 1968, that surely a student who "was looking," would have known about these events. Finally, we know that two weeks after the Boston demonstration publicized in the campus flyer, Katherine Power traveled to New Haven for the very purpose of protesting the upcoming trial of Seale and other Panthers.

Tom Hayden, who spoke at the New Haven rally, writes in his memoir, *Reunion*, that large crowds, in the ten-thousand range, were expected to show up in New Haven.[24] Jacob Cohen writes that "some thirty Brandeis radicals, including Katherine Power, Susan Saxe, and two professors" went.[25] By sheer coincidence, the first day of the New Haven

---

* After our project concluded in 2012, the time for me to ask follow-up questions had elapsed. For this reason, this analysis includes rare instances of speculation, each of which I clearly flag and support with available evidence or logic.

demonstrations, which had long before been scheduled for that May Day weekend, occurred the day after Nixon announced his escalation of the Vietnam War into Cambodia. In Hayden's account, by Sunday, May 2, "the crowd had swollen to twenty thousand, and the Cambodian crisis was overshadowing the Panther trial."

While he was addressing the crowd, Hayden writes, a fellow member of the Chicago Seven, John Froines, handed him a note to read out loud. Hayden explains that the note "said that a group of student-government leaders, meeting in a nearby building, had just called for a national student strike. As I came to the closing words, the crowd began to chant 'strike, strike, strike' for what seemed like five minutes."[26] Just when everyone was getting tired of yet another futile demonstration, here was something new, dramatic, and sweeping—a national strike!

Cohen describes the same incident. In his account, it was "one of the Brandeis group" who handed Hayden the message, which "announced that there was to be a national student strike demanding the immediate release of all imprisoned Black Panthers and immediate withdrawal from Vietnam. For further information, the announcement concluded, contact the 'Brandeis University Strike Information Center.'"[27]

In their essence, Hayden's and Cohen's accounts are identical: a group of students proposed a national student strike and had Tom Hayden announce it. Only Cohen reports that the announcement brought up the Panthers and named Brandeis as the strike's central contact center. Of course, this latter fact would have had much more salience to Cohen than to Hayden (for whom it could have detracted from his climactic narrative).

The Brandeis University Archives hold a third description of the events, one closer to home than Hayden's or Cohen's. The single typewritten, unsigned page appears to have been composed almost immediately after the New Haven weekend, for the purpose of explaining the Brandeis National Strike Information Center (NSIC) to Brandeis students who weren't there. It opens: "As thousands of people gathered in New Haven on May Day weekend to protest the trial of Bobby Seale, and knew that they were not going to free him that way . . . ." Only someone who had been there could have testified so convincingly to the inner state of the demonstrators, or at least to that of the writer, who conveys an almost poignant sense of despair regarding the efficacy of demonstrations as instruments of change. The missive continues: "[A] group of about a thousand of the New Haven demonstrators met to discuss the possibility of a whole new kind of tactic—a national student strike. . . . [and] some people from Brandeis were mandated to establish the National Strike Information Center."

This statement needs some unpacking. Of all the many universities represented by a thousand student leaders, why Brandeis? That we are not told. Which "people from Brandeis were mandated" and who did the mandating? We are not told. One would have to assume, however, that only someone from Brandeis could have volunteered Brandeis for this role.

What is not a matter of speculation is that Katherine Power was in New Haven that weekend, that she helped found the NSIC, that the NSIC was set up in the lounge of the Brandeis sociology department, and that Katherine Power was a sociology major. Moreover, as we will see later, she was known on campus for taking the leadership role in political meetings. Therefore, it is speculation, but not out of the realm of possibility, that she helped run that meeting in New Haven, *or* pressed the case for a national student strike, *or* insisted on the reference to the Panthers, *or* volunteered Brandeis as the contact center, or all of these.

"Strike! Strike! Strike! Strike!" rose the chant in New Haven. Three days later, less than one week after the announcement of the American "incursion" into Cambodia, and exactly one day after the Kent State killings, two to four million students[28] at some five hundred campuses went on strike or completely closed down their campuses.[29] The national student strike was on. The media (and probably countless strikers) understood the strike to have one goal: to end the war. That interpretation is turned on its head by the following facts.

First, the national strike was born at the New Haven demonstrations (something on which Hayden, Cohen, and the unknown writer of the Brandeis document all agree), and the original purpose of those demonstrations was to protest the impending trials of Bobby Seale and other Panthers. In addition, of the three demands issued by the strikers, the second and third focus on ending the Vietnam War but not the first. The #1 demand (which is actually two) reads thus: "That the U.S. Government end its systematic repression of political dissidents and release all political prisoners, such as Bobby Seale and other members of the Black Panther Party." The national student strike, at least in the minds of those who initiated it, was at least as concerned with freeing Seale and other Panthers as with ending the war. Be that as it may, in early May of 1970, well over two million students at some 500 U.S. campuses went on strike.[30]

How this pregnant moment of massive student strikes played out at Brandeis is revealed through other documents from the Brandeis University Archives. In an open letter transmitted on May 5 to the Brandeis community, Charles Schottland, then-president of the university, voiced agreement with the antiwar protests (as did many of his peers, notably Kingman Brewster, Yale's president[31]). But the question of the moment was how Schottland was going to handle the strike about to hit his campus. He had recently been visited, he wrote, by two sets of students with opposing appeals: to shut down the university and to keep it open. "The requests of both groups of students will be granted," announced the president.

It would seem that either school is in session or it isn't. How could both requests possibly be honored? Here's how. To accommodate non-striking students, Schottland asked the faculty to continue teaching their classes as usual; to accommodate striking students, he "urged" faculty members "when possible, to take steps to enable those students who wish to join in the protest to continue their studies through [alternative] assignments, self-study, and other appropriate arrangements."

Katherine Power went on strike. In fact, she helped set up and run the National Strike Information Center (NSIC). And, according to someone active in the NSIC, she functioned as a leader there: "during the strike, she often ran student meetings and had a hand in most of the major decisions."[32] The natural authority I had noticed upon meeting her two decades later was clearly a longstanding trait.

The purpose of the National Strike Information Center, as spelled out in its inaugural newsletter of May 4th, 1970 (sent out mere hours before anyone knew about the students shot dead in Ohio), was to serve "as a central clearing house for all information regarding strike activity at high schools, colleges and universities across the country. We are prepared to receive and disseminate strike information."* One of the benefits of disseminating this information would be to shore up the spirits of strikers during the fallow summer months.

Some might assume that the National Strike Information Center at Brandeis was a rinky-dink organization of interest only to those overheated students who ran it. The FBI didn't see it that way. The Brandeis University Archives groan with boxes containing almost daily FBI reports on the Center. Following is a letter sent to J. Edgar Hoover by an FBI informant (a justice of the Superior Court of Boston, no less) on May 6, 1970, regarding the Strike Information Center. It is revealing enough to warrant quoting in full:

---

* The age of the personal computer not yet having arrived, students gathered information about the daily strikes by telephone and ham radio, and disseminated it via mimeographed and mailed newsletters.

My dear Mr. Hoover:

I have enjoyed corresponding with you over the years in connection with your splendid administration of the FBI, which has done so much to protect our country.

I enclose a 15-page document captioned "NATIONAL STRIKE INFORMATION COMMITTEE," Newsletter #3, May 5, 1970, which emanates from Brandeis University and is self-explanatory. Apparently, Brandeis has turned over to this subversive group its facilities, including telephones and office space. Additionally, it appears to be using the national communications network (developed by the Lemburg Center on the Study of Violence [at Brandeis]) to cause violence rather than prevent it. This center is supported by nontaxable foundation monies. I direct your attention particularly to page 8, giving the Communist version of the Kent State riot, and to page 10, urging that The White House phones be tied up by calling our President person-to-person.

I am shocked that this or any institution would make its facilities available to what is obviously the command post of the nationwide student strikes called for the purpose of destroying our country.

[The writer closes with a paragraph inveighing against the TV networks for, in his words, "bombard[ing]" viewers with "propaganda which must delight Hanoi and Moscow."]

My very best regards.

Cordially,
[name withheld by me]

It is true that Brandeis student activists, among whom was numbered Katherine Power, were "urging that The White House phones be tied up by calling our President person-to-person." I suppose one could call this prankish proposal "subversive." Hard to imagine, though, how it could be conceived as "caus[ing] violence." The informant's assertion that Brandeis University had in any official way "turned over . . . its facilities" to this group is not accurate. The Brandeis administration in fact ordered the Strike Information Center off campus. The allusions to "Hanoi and Moscow," as well as the characterization of the NSIC's write-up of what happened at Kent State as a "Communist version," illustrate of course the centrality of defeating Communism to supporters of the Vietnam War.

Days after the bank robbery and killing of Officer Walter Schroeder, a writer for the *Harvard Crimson* described Power as a leader in the Strike Center:

> Katherine Power worked very hard in the strike center, as did almost everyone on campus. Susan Saxe worked there, and Stanley Bond. But Katherine was one of the leaders. . . . During the strike, she often ran student meetings and had a hand in most of the major decisions. . . . [Someone identified as a friend was quoted as saying:] "In Brandeis there are about 50 people who are realy [*sic*] hard core. It's a bad word, I know, but ever since sophomore year she was one of the hard core at Brandeis. She really wanted to make her name a reality—you know, to have power; she liked to control."[33]

If Power, who had taken a leadership role in groups virtually all her life, "had a hand in most of the major decisions" being made at the NSIC, then she may well have had a hand in drafting its newsletters. Listed at the top of every newsletter sent out by the National Strike Information Center that summer were the demands purportedly being made by the nationwide strike, always the same three, from the first newsletter, dated May 4, to the last, dated July 22, 1970. The demands, which are identical to those reported in the post-May Day-weekend explanation of the NSIC written by someone at Brandeis to the rest of the Brandeis community, read as follows:

The strike has been called in support of the following three demands:

1) That the United States Government end its systematic oppression of political dissidents and release all political prisoners, such as Bobby Seale and other members of the Black Panther Party.

2) That the U.S. Government cease its expansion of the Vietnam War into Laos and Cambodia; that it unilaterally and immediately withdraw all forces from Southeast Asia.

3) That the universities end their complicity with the U.S. War Machine by an immediate end to defense research, ROTC, counterinsurgency research, and all other such programs.

In these demands, we again see top billing given to government oppression of the Black Panthers. The NSIC took this demand very seriously. They complained bitterly, Cohen writes, "that the press insisted on treating the strike solely as a liberal antiwar protest, neglecting the demands for the release of black political prisoners."[34] The May 11 issue of the NSIC newsletter, its second, was already railing against this situation:

> [T]he establishment press has willfully but subtly distorted the very nature of this unprecedented strike. Of the three national strike demands only one ever appears in print–one that corporate liberalism finds readily acceptable: withdrawal from Cambodia.... The Panthers are virtually unmentioned.... [T]he press tries to entomb us in the charnal [sic] house of "*peace*" rhetoric .... We are saying much, much more! [my italics]

The writers of that same issue of the newsletter spelled out what they meant by "much, much more." The purpose of the national student strike, as they saw it, was to change—or, failing that, to "smash"—"corporate liberalism," "technofascism," "global imperialism," and "advanced capitalist society." In a word: revolution. Interestingly enough, the word "smash" appears repeatedly in Mao Tse Tung's writings. During the Cultural Revolution of 1966 to 1976, he commanded his youthful revolutionaries to "smash the Four Olds," for instance, referring to old customs, habits, culture, and thinking. It appears that the writers of this newsletter may have been taking cues from Mao's playbook.

The press was not alone in its ignorance. The FBI portrayed the strike as an antiwar protest. So did Gitlin in his scholarly book on the Sixties.[35] The vast majority of strikers undoubtedly understood it that way, as well. When Power surrendered two decades later, this longstanding error, I would argue, helped maintain a misunderstanding of what was motivating her in mid-1970—which was not only, perhaps by then not even mainly, peace in Vietnam.

On May 19, Power participated in a debate about the war held at a high school in a town near Boston. Power argued the anti-war side, and

Edward King, a member of the Republican State Committee, the pro-war side. Later that year—and immediately after Power was linked with the bank robbery/murder—Mr. King was quoted in a Boston newspaper declaring:

> I do this a lot. I've been to lots of schools . . . . But I remember being shocked by her . . . . A clenched fist was stenciled on [her] sweat shirt. I remember she said, "Someday the police will eventually get their answer from students, black people, and workers." She made that statement several times.[36]

Katherine Power probably had in her wardrobe shirts emblazoned with slogans opposing the war, the topic of the debate. Her sartorial selection, with its Black Power fist, was likely *intended* to shock—as well as showcase her solidarity with the Panthers. Far more inflammatory than the Black Power fist, however, is what is insinuated by the word "police." It's not hard to imagine Power saying *something* that a member of the Republican State Committee would find shocking. However, more than a century of empirical research on memory affords grounds for misgivings about Edward King's memory of that particular word.

Mr. King was retrieving Power's words from long-term memory, four months after the debate. But human memory is no tape-recording. Memory drastically erodes with the passage of time, with 50 percent to 80 percent of it, on average, being lost in just the first 24 hours.[37] Furthermore, memory for exact details is much more fragile than memory for the gist.[38] She might have used any number of words other than "police"—"authorities," "oppressors," "establishment," "system," "the Man," "government," "State," for example.

Human memory is also highly susceptible to distortion based on context—to the point that what one originally hears not infrequently gets overwritten by something else, something matching the current context.[39] Mr. King was retrieving Power's words in a highly charged context—one day, or at most two, after he had learned she was involved in an armed robbery in which a police officer was murdered.

King appears very confident about what Power said, asserting that Power "made that statement several times." Shouldn't his confidence bolster ours? Definitely not. Research on memory has decisively established that one's degree of confidence in one's recollection is unrelated to its accuracy.*

Absent an audio-recording, we simply cannot know for sure what Power said in that debate. She might well have driven to the debate in a state of high dudgeon, as it took place fifteen days after Kent State and only four days after Jackson State. These killings, perpetrated by National Guard troops and by Mississippi state and local police respectively, had poured fuel on the rage of the young against law enforcement already enflamed by the 1968 police riot in Chicago and the murder of Panther leader Fred Hampton in his bed by police on December 4, 1969, for instance.

So let's imagine she did say "police." Even then, it is anything but obvious what she might have meant by stating that "the police will eventually get their answer." What immediately follows the word "answer"—"from students, black people, and workers"—strongly suggests that she was referring to the fond fantasy of an uprising of the oppressed. Come the revolution, the system would be replaced with new structures. Come the revolution, law enforcement and the military would not be wielding mortal violence at home and abroad. One can be a devoted revolutionary without, however, intending to kill police officers, or anyone for that matter. In light of what I know about human memory and about Power, the arguments against accepting Edward King's specific word recall, and its insinuation, outstrip those supporting them.

Be that as it may, by mid-summer the rhetoric of revolution was being openly voiced on the Brandeis campus. A flyer printed on shocking-pink

---

* We now know, for instance, that many innocent people have been erroneously convicted of crimes they never committed—because a jury used the confidence of eyewitnesses as a barometer of their accuracy.

paper stock cried: "Celebrate <u>Our</u> revolution—not theirs!"—referring to Independence Day. The flyer proposed alternative ways to celebrate the 4th of July, such as spray-painting slogans on buildings and monuments all over Boston. Among the four slogans suggested, "FREE BOBBY" came first, followed by "Power to the People," "Viva Che," and, sickeningly, "Off the Pig." On the reverse side someone had drawn an androgynous human figure bearing an assault rifle.[40]

Around the same time, Jacob Cohen chanced to have direct and dramatic interactions with one of the gang of five. Cohen was teaching a Brandeis summer course for older adults when Susan Saxe would repeatedly burst into the classroom to harangue his students about "the evils of American imperialism" and Brandeis University.[41] Hoping to persuade her to stop it, Cohen agreed to a debate with Saxe in that classroom. Among other things, he asked her what she and her radical companions wanted from Brandeis. An urban studies program, she said. But, he pointed out, the faculty had recently created an urban studies program. "'Yes, but that's not the program we wanted,' snapped Saxe. "It's your program.'"[42] To which Cohen retorted: "Well, if your idea of freedom is always getting every last thing that you want, then I agree that you are not free." (Twenty-three years later, he confessed he had been playing to his adult audience with that rejoinder.) In reaction, Saxe shouted: "Why don't you just kill us now and get it over with?"[43] At the time, this eruption seemed to him such a bizarre non-sequitur that Cohen did not respond. The debate ended with Saxe's words reverberating in the classroom.

Though the allusion undoubtedly comes across as hysterical now, in the summer of 1970, after six students had been shot dead on the orders of their parents' generation, it felt as if Kronos had returned to devour his own children. Only in retrospect did Cohen understand: Saxe was speaking the logic of apocalypse. He regrets to this day, Cohen writes, not having tried to say everything he possibly could "a thousand times in a thousand precise, literal, ways" to convince Saxe that—notwithstanding the delusional pronouncements being made by a few revolutionaries—the establishment was *not* planning a holocaust upon the oppressed and their defenders.

Meanwhile, the Brandeis administration had ordered the NSIC out of the sociology lounge and off campus. The writers of the July 22 issue of the NSIC newsletter were having none of it. They declared that the center was going to stay right where it was, and the administration would "have to throw us off. We will not go." The students had hired lawyers and were in the process of suing Brandeis, the newsletter reported, in order to exert the "legal and moral" right of the NSIC to remain on campus. Katherine Power and others brought a lawsuit in federal court against Brandeis.[44] In August, the students lost the lawsuit.[45]

The gang of five committed its string of bank robberies in August and September. They robbed banks in Los Angeles, Evanston, and Philadelphia, netting $45,000 from those holdups. The Sunday before the fatal bank robbery, they stole guns and ammunition from an armory north of Boston and set fire to the rifle range and the supply room storing military uniforms. Power "says she did not participate in most of these actions and is certain that she never went inside a bank."[46] She did steal cars, guns, and ammunition. She practiced shooting the firearms. And on September 23, 1970, she drove the getaway switch car at the bank robbery in Boston where Walter Schroeder was murdered. Again: why?

So far, we have focused on the external factors that Power brought to our first interview, including those familial, religious, educational, and historical contexts. Though she didn't mention them, social processes like interpersonal influence and group dynamics ought to share the explanatory spotlight.

***

When in late September of 1970 Power's parents had to face the fact that their daughter had been involved in the bank robbery and killing of Walter Schroeder, her mother could make sense of it only by recourse to the belief that Katherine had been manipulated: "I think someone has used her."[47] Power's mother had a name to attach to that someone: Stanley Bond. Mrs. Power asserted that Bond was "a con artist who could talk anybody into anything"[48] and had talked her daughter into becoming an armed radical. Reportedly, "detectives who worked on the case agreed."[49] At the time of her surrender Power's attorneys were also highlighting the malignant influence of Stanley Bond. Of course her lawyers had a stake in playing up Bond's influence to support their arguments for a more lenient sentence. The media too played up this juicy tale of the strikingly good-looking Stanley Bond preying on a wide-eyed college girl. Moreover, something Power said in the *New Yorker* article that appeared seven months after her surrender gives the impression that not only was she influenced by Bond but that she was in love with him:

> We were soulmates. There was this intense trust, this vision-sharing, life-sharing bond. I will never forget his story of not cutting his wrists—of being in prison and saying either I die now or I make meaning out of my life. At last, I thought—here, at last, in the universe is another person like me. There was a very deep part of me that was alienated and lonely, that I kept hidden at Brandeis, and Stan found that part.[50]

Unfortunately, sociopaths are virtuosos at making sad, lonely, lost people feel deeply known, the better to exploit them.

With me Power has always maintained that she was not "in love with" Bond in the conventional sense of the term. Oh, she had a crush all right, she told me—on a graduate student who was already taken.

But there was Stanley, working day in and day out, as she was, at the National Strike Information Center, avidly collecting funds for the antiwar movement, vehemently talking about making revolution. What she loved was what she perceived as Bond's passionately revolutionary vision and his alienation from conventional society. As she put it: "He wasn't about pretending to be radical. The very things that made other people so uncomfortable about him—his intensity, his passion, his commitment, his not-straightness—were what made me aware of him as a possible comrade."[51]

Clearly, Bond *was* pretending. He knew exactly how to insinuate himself into the NSIC and exactly how to feign comradeship with Power's ideology—for purposes that had nothing to do with the Vietnam War and everything to do with wads of ready cash.

But Katherine Power didn't see that. She saw "a possible comrade." And she was definitely looking for comrades.

She has fiercely insisted that she and Bond came together through a reciprocal process, comrade meeting comrade. For this reason, she took exception to Lucinda Franks's portrayal of her relationship with Bond, telling me that "Lucinda . . . kind of wrote off my personal responsibility for my own historical being by suggesting that I was under the sway of a charismatic man." "I was like a jihadi, and I wanted to be met that way," she told me.[52] With Bond, she felt she was being met that way.

A longstanding friend of hers who had witnessed Power's interactions with Bond agreed with Power's assertion that the Power-Bond link was mutual and equal:

> KP: I talked to other people who were around me at the time since then. I asked one person in particular who knew both Stanley and me, and who was angry over my closeness with Stanley and who was the kind of good friend who is just relentlessly honest and has real good insight. And she wrote about how she thought the connection was . . . and she . . . she resonated with my sense of it in every case. She said, "He was an outsider; people were prejudiced against him. He automatically had your sympathies because of those things. And he was serious, and you were serious" . . . . And so her sense was that we encountered each other and decided to act together, which is very much my sense of it . . . very much.

Via this friend's observations, Power was substantiating for me her narrative of Bond as political comrade on a par with her: "[W]e encountered each other," she said, "and decided to act together." There are others who give us reason to take Power at her word when she insists she was no pawn in the hands of Stanley Bond. In Jacob Cohen's view, Katherine Power's radical turn began at least "a year before she ever met Bond."[53]

So, who recruited whom? This is how Power elaborated on this vexed question with me:

> I was looking for someone to do clandestine actions with as early as June of 1970. I had met with one Vietnam vet who was willing to stay in Massachusetts and join me instead of going to heal himself on a farm in British Columbia.... I didn't want to use him that way; I wanted him to be able to go and recover from the war. Stanley Bond heard . . . that I was looking for some way to take more serious direct action and asked if I wanted to join with him in what he was doing.[54]

Having considered other alternatives, she decided to go in with Bond's "revolutionary action group." "I agreed," she said. "It seemed like what I was looking for." What she was looking for was revolution. Ready and willing to make revolution, with Bond's "skills" she felt able. Journalist H. Peter Metzger has phrased the reciprocity with a punishing parallelism:

> The formerly non-political ex-con Bond . . . learned how to be a student radical from the girls, while the girls in their turn . . . learned how to be stick-up thugs from Bond.[55]

When I wrapped up our first discussion of this issue by asking once again whether there was any truth in the idea that she had been "mesmerized by" Bond, she retorted: "You know, the irony is: the idea that any man can get me to do anything just cracks me up."* The bottom line is that, in conversations with me, Power has always stressed her agency.

---

* The instant Power uttered this sentence, the thought flashed into my head: if not a man, then maybe a woman. What about Susan Saxe? Over the years of our exchanges, Power has unswervingly declined to talk about Saxe. When I pressed her years later, she told me that she hadn't known Saxe personally until Bond recruited the two of them. Before that, she only "knew of" Saxe as another radical on campus. In any case, Saxe, she averred, "was not key" in her decision to take up violence.

At the same time, she has acknowledged that, once she decided to join up with Bond, she handed over a great deal of her agency to him: "That's the only time in my life I've ever let somebody else be the leader."[56] She has drawn on military terms to explain this aspect of her "holy war":

> I did surrender tactical autonomy, very much in the way that military recruits typically do, especially as the mission I committed to required me to perform actions that were contradictory to my core personality and general rule-following tendency. (Stanley Bond used to try to get me to litter, just to do something antisocial; I wouldn't).[57]

Of course, we know that one of the worst "tactical" calls she surrendered to Bond was the decision to use armed robbery as the group's method of waging jihad.

The above comments by her friend also bear out my assessment of Katherine Power as someone who deeply identified with the non-legits, the marginalized, the subjugated, and the outcasts of the world. This trait of hers inclines me to concur with those who suspect that Bond might have had a certain appeal for her beyond the purely political (and outside of the romantic). Margaret Spillane, who was an antiwar activist while a student at nearby Boston University, acidly attests to the allure of the dangerous for some radicals living in the same time and place as Power:

> I knew plenty of people like her [Katherine Power]: . . . kids who talked only to working-class people who could offer them the thrill of a window to the dangerous and forbidden. For them, the only true proletarians had gunshot scars and criminal records. At a lot of student parties that year, the dance cards of career felons were always filled.[58]

Reading between the lines, Spillane's censure could be read as diagnosing Katherine Power's attraction to Stanley Bond as a case of "radical chic." Remarkably enough, Tom Wolfe coined the term the very same year Power went criminal. In Wolfe's essay, it was the Black Panthers whose "dance cards were full" at the Park Avenue party at Lenny Bernstein's home. In Spillane's critique, it was career criminals at campus parties.

Katherine Power's attraction to Stanley Bond—and the Panthers—may have included an element of radical chic—although not at all for the social caché.[59] With her it had a lot to do, I believe, with itching to jettison a "bourgeois" background by dancing with danger, also with her private furies; but mainly it had to do with her identification with the oppressed. Power encountered Bond on the fault line between sympathy for the underdog and sympathy for the devil.

Bond invited; but she agreed. She was looking for a comrade in revolution; he heard and offered himself. No man could get her to do anything; but she let him be the leader. Why all the conflicting statements?

My sense of it is that Bond did play a significant (but not all-powerful role) in Power's ethical ruin, and that this evokes a great deal of shame for her. And why not? After all, how painful it must be for a natural-born leader and a passionate feminist to admit, even to herself, that she handed over to this man too much of her personal agency. She simply will not agree that Svengali made her do it. And, in the final analysis, he didn't.

***

One can admire Power's refusal, through all the complexities and all the years, to blame anyone else in the group. However, I don't buy the idea that she was not influenced by them.

No social psychologist would. In a recent book, *The Righteous Mind: Why Good People Are Divided by Politics and Religion,* Jonathan Haidt writes: "Many of us believe that we follow an inner moral compass, but the history of social psychology richly demonstrates that other people exert a powerful force, able to make [even] cruelty seem acceptable."[60] Haidt, who has played a groundbreaking role in recently establishing a new sub-discipline of psychology called moral psychology, explains how social processes can shape morality: "We can believe almost anything that supports our team."[61] In the beginning, antiwar activists were Power's team. Later, she took up with a different team.

I like Haidt's word *team*, because it helps illuminate something important about groups that can be all but invisible. It might seem logical that groups are simply the sum of the individuals in them. But when we think of groups as teams, we're more likely to understand that all groups becomes organisms unto themselves. Think of orchestras, theatre troups, choirs, successful sports teams, platoons, mobs, gangs. The gang of five. There is no doubt in my mind that Katherine Power came to participate in activities like armed robbery in part as a result of normal everyday **interpersonal influence** and **group dynamics.**

Once Power joined the insurrectionist group, she deferred too much to Bond: "I knew what to do, I knew how to act, and I gave it away. That's the only time in my life I've ever let somebody else be the leader."[62] Power is telling us here, I believe, something important about *when* exactly she crossed the line from revolutionary action to flat-out criminal action.

Power and Bond had been working together at the NSIC for months. Then Power and Bond became fellow revolutionaries, fellow jihadists.* But at some point Valeri and Gilday came aboard. Only Bond knew Valeri and Gilday (from Walpole prison), so he would have been the one who suggested adding them to the original Power-Saxe-Bond trio. Katherine Power had grave doubts about Valeri and Gilday. Despite her misgivings, she deferred to Bond; she "agreed to use them anyway," she told me. What exactly would she be "using" Valeri and Gilday *for*? That would be bank robberies. Together, the three ex-cons had a wealth of experience in pulling off armed robbery.

Early on, I had assumed (along with others) that Power had crossed the line into violence the day she joined up with Bond's revolutionary action group. After much reconsideration, I think the pivotal moment was when she went along with Bond's idea to add Valeri and Gilday to the group—and despite her misgivings, stayed. Then again, at this point,

---

* I am leaving Saxe out of this because Power supplied no information about Saxe's role (which lay outside the purview of my project).

neither Valeri nor Gilday had murder on their rap sheet.

I suspect that moving to the apartment off campus represented another pivotal point in Power's slide from antiwar action to criminal action. As we will see in a later chapter, Power has admitted that she rented the apartment, which served as a "base of operation" for the group. Maybe she volunteered herself as the one to rent that apartment. But bear with me while I spin out a slightly different, admittedly speculative, scenario.

As we know, Power had second thoughts about whether to stay with the group when Bond let Valeri and Gilday in. Let's imagine that those qualms cropped up sometime *before* the group decided they needed an off-campus space. Now let's imagine that someone in the group suggested that, because she looked so ordinary and wholesome, Katherine might be the best person to find them a place. What is not a matter of speculation is that she did it. She's the one who boarded the commuter rail at the Brandeis/Roberts stop and bought a ticket into Boston. She's the one who pored over newspaper ads for apartment rentals and located what seemed to be a suitable place. She's the one who spoke with the real estate agent about the basement apartment at 163 Beacon Street in Boston, and she put down the required security deposit and first and last month's rent. I imagine her paying in cash with money from the fund that Bond had been "managing," purportedly to support the operation of the National Strike Information Center and the Panthers.

Now about those qualms. Social psychology has established that we human beings very much want our outside to match our inside, our actions to match our internal states (our attitudes, for instance). If they don't match, we suffer the uncomfortable state of inner tension known as cognitive dissonance. The definition and origin of cognitive dissonance are well known. Far less understood is the crucial punch line of the research on cognitive dissonance—namely, what happens next. Once we experience cognitive dissonance, more often than not we unconsciously change (or intensify) our attitudes to line up with our action. Attitude change is *especially* likely to happen when the action is not coerced. This research would predict that if Power had doubts about the group prior to her securing an apartment for them, that act would likely have shored up her faith in the group—especially if she was not coerced, and we can assume she was not.

Of course, it is quite possible that it worked the other way around—that her already strong belief in the group sent Power apartment hunting. My analysis doesn't hinge on these particular acts. The point is that the workings of cognitive dissonance would have helped her justify *whatever* actions she took with a group about which she had misgivings. No manipulation or pressure needed at all.

When Power did what it took to rent the apartment, she was also making a concrete commitment to the group, and research finds that making an overt commitment to something tends to solidify one's belief in it. Then too, living off campus would likely have narrowed the circle of her social contacts, perhaps to the point of creating a closed circle, thereby narrowing the range of opinions she was hearing. Finally, the apartment gave the five what every revolutionary cell needs: a secret space to gather, to hash out the details of their missions, to stockpile weapons, to divide the labor, and in general to coalesce and bond as a group.

At this point in the life of the gang of five, another powerful group phenomenon might have kicked in. When like-minded individuals discuss their shared views with one another, group dynamics tend to move the initial attitudes of each individual to the more extreme end of the scale. It's called in social psychology the "extremity shift," and it works the same for leftist and rightist (and other) attitudes. If during discussions, someone in the group puts forward a more-extreme idea than the rest had previously entertained, individuals unconsciously try to go the others one better, and the group ends up with more extreme positions than they started with. This normal tendency would be drastically amplified in the Maoist-style "criticism" and "self-criticism" sessions common in revolutionary cells of the Weather Underground and its offshoots. The extremity shift might help explain how things went from "Let's collect money to fund Bobby Seale's legal defense" to "Let's sue Brandeis to keep the NSIC open" to "Let's do bank robberies to incite revolution."

Research conclusively shows that all of us, even people who, like Power, insist that they are the captains of their soul and the masters of their fate, are emphatically not immune to social influence. Our moral and political thinking is so susceptible to social influence that we will violate our own deeply instilled moral values in order to support our team, or to have the approval and acceptance of our team.[63] Interpersonal influence and group processes would go a long way to explain *how*, as Power said, "it all emerged." *How* she crossed the line into violent criminality. How it spiraled out of control.

Thus it was that, days after the bank robbery and murder, a police search of Power's apartment turned up, as reported by the *Washington Post,* an arsenal. They found Katherine Power's passport recently stamped Cuba,[64] "a shooter's manual, a telescopic sight, shotgun shells, gunpowder, and assorted ammunition for handguns. . . . [as well as] Army equipment, including .30-caliber and .45-caliber ammunition, radio transmitters, a field switchboard, explosive detonators, and two rifles."[65] Four hundred rounds of ammunition were stolen from the Newburyport armory alone.[66] The Boston apartment, geographically only some nine miles from her dorm room at Brandeis, was worlds away morally.

***

Twenty-five years later, and two years into her prison sentence, I asked Power *the* fatal question, the one we all want to ask—that is, why exactly on that September morning in 1970 she was participating, even in a "support" function, in a violent bank robbery.* My question immediately followed her assertion that all she "really wanted to do was clandestine actions that were effective sabotage against the process of the war-making."

JL: What was the link between the bank robberies and that [goal]?

KP: You need cohorts**.... I think, I think it's also another piece of really important historical information is the apocalyptic sense that a revolutionary change in the American power structure, culture, was building.... The country was on the edge of revolutionary, violent upheaval and that an action like that could have provoked that.... So that it isn't insane, it isn't... cognitively out of the logical to say "guerrilla warfare." ... So I felt like I was going to war on the right side ... and that meant, what does, what does war mean? You know, guerrilla war? Well, you know, I certainly read the accounts of the third-world liberation movements all over the world, their armed struggle. We believed in war.

[She pauses]

JL: War to stop the war?

KP: Yeah.

As for how logical or sane it was to rob banks at gunpoint as a way to sabotage the Vietnam War, according to a retrospective narrative prominent among radicals of the era: "the war made us crazy."

---

* Steven Black, her lawyer, told *Newsweek* that when Power was given the job of lookout during the robbery and torching of the armory, "she was so nervous she was physically ill. After that, she was relegated to 'support' functions, like driving the getaway car."

** In response to a later fact-check question of mine, Power explained that by "cohorts" she had meant the three ex-convicts: Bond, Gilday, and Valeri. Power viewed them as "professionals"—people who had the skills she could use to accomplish her goals.

Decades removed from the apocalyptic era of 1970, it does seem crazy to think that robbing banks "could have provoked" revolution. How would that work? In Katherine Power's mind, bank robbery might have represented but one of a blizzard of tactics of domestic terrorism (the "armed conflict" and "looting" promised by the Weather Underground) designed to destabilize the government and ignite a massive uprising on the part of students, blacks, and workers—who together would bring down the U.S. government.[67] If so, it's shades of John Brown's armed attack on Harper's Ferry all over again. The same John Brown whom Frederick Douglass had tried to talk out of the attack, telling Brown he was delusional to expect slaves to rise up in response. But, after all, John Brown* was a Weatherman hero.

On the other hand, she could have been robbing banks against her better judgment but in keeping with Bond's worse judgment. Cohen leans toward this explanation, writing: "This is speculation: but as I imagine the situation, it was at this point [late summer of 1970, when the national strike had petered out] that Stanley Bond came to the fore. What about a bank robbery, perhaps a series of them? I've got some friends who will help."[68] Power has admitted that, even while part of her recognized Bond's "lack of sense and attention to other people's safety," she had acceded to Bond's leadership, normally her role.

To return now to the rest of Power's answer to my question about the link between robbing banks and the goal of sabotaging the war: she may have been taken aback by the real or imagined accusation in that question—as this question was for me unusually direct and pointed. Feeling accused could have thrown her off balance enough that she could emit such uncharacteristically disjointed formulations and mutilated syntax as: "it isn't . . . cognitively out of the logical to say . . . ." and "I think, I

---

* And the same man who hacked to death in their beds five people in Kansas he thought were pro-slavery.

think it's also another piece of really important historical information in the apocalyptic sense . . . ."

Feeling accused might also explain her smokescreen language: her displacements ("third-world liberation movements"; "the *country* was on the edge of revolutionary, violent upheaval") and her abstractions ("power structure," "struggle," "going to war"). Much of this language amounts to ideological cant. But to a college sophomore or junior, it could have felt like fresh and thrilling ways of thinking about what she should do next.

This woman in prison, though, was now middle-aged, and she wasn't talking about the country or some third-world liberation movement. She was talking about herself, how sabotaging the war and violent bank robberies were connected in her mind. At this point in her ethical evolution, she seems to have found it impossible to come right out and say that she had, in Metzger's merciless words, allowed herself to become a "stick-up thug" in support of a delusion.

The full sentence in which she identifies where she went wrong—"going to war"—shows a similarly limited ability to state the unvarnished truth about her worst acts: "It was the going to war against the war of my time that made my attempt at doing a very good act turn out in a very harmful way." My writer's ear hears an admission, yes, but one framed in a form so abstract and aesthetically pleasing (the twin parallelisms of "going to war // against war" and "a very good act // a very harmful way") as to dress up a brutal reality—perhaps obscuring it even in the mind of the speaker. At least equally important is that second parallelism: "very harmful" being a decidedly understated way to describe the cold-blooded murder of an innocent man.

In this sentence the impersonal "it" also distanced her from her criminal acts. "*It* was the going to war . . . ." Admitting full personal agency would have required language more like: "it was my decision to go violent" or "when *I* decided to use ex-cons with assault weapons to help me make revolution . . . ." Power employed the first-person pronoun only once in this sentence—"*my* attempt at doing a very good act"—where it functioned to put a virtuous face on her crimes. And, what very good act is she alluding to here? Once again we hear Power at this early stage in her conscience work conflating her antiwar dissent (her attempt to do something good) with her violent crimes. The unattractive reality is that by the late summer of 1970 Katherine Power was no longer an antiwar activist but an armed revolutionary and common criminal.

My next question for her, although almost purely rhetorical, turned out to elicit better insight into her state of mind when she turned herself into an armed revolutionary:

JL: Did you believe in killing to stop killing?

KP: Does anybody who signs up for war say I'm going to kill? Of course not. They wouldn't go if they said that. They wouldn't go. No decent human being would sign on the paper and say, Let me go kill people. War *turns* you into someone who doesn't care about your own or somebody else's death. What I *never* imagined is someone else being hurt. I knew that the, the group of people that were acting together in this posed a danger. But . . . I only imagined that the danger was to myself . . . I was conscious, exclusively conscious that Gilday and Valeri were dangerous, and I . . . agreed to use them anyway. That's part of what happens when you go to war, you know. [emphases are Power's]

Instead of responding to my question about whether she believed in "killing to stop killing" with a clear answer, she tossed me a defanged non-answer about some abstract and third-person "anybody." My question may have thrust her too close to the raw subject she still desperately wanted to avoid, the specific killing that her war had caused: the killing of Walter Schroeder. Someone real. Someone's husband. Someone's father.

If she was thrown off balance by my line of questioning, that interviewer-implicating "you know" at the end of this passage might have been an unconscious feint to pull me back on "her side." It might also explain her ostensible self-contradictions. "War turns you into someone who doesn't care about . . . somebody else's death," professed Power, and in the adjacent breath, "What I never imagined is someone else being hurt." In fact, both statements were true of the 21-year-old Katherine Power. I believe that the complex truth of it is that she had no intention of killing, but neither was she allowing the right hand to know what the left was doing. What she was thinking about was making revolution.

Still, the parallels Power drew between *her* act of "going to war" and that of people who fight governmentally approved wars help fill in her non-answer. When Power says that no good person signs up for war planning to kill, perhaps she was projecting, imagining that every "decent human being" goes into war the way she did—with no notion of killing anyone.

It's true, of course, that generally only the rare sicko comes right out and says (or thinks) odious things like "Let me enlist. I wanna kill." At the same time, the unpleasant fact is that when people, decent people, sign up for war, they *are* in effect signing up to potentially kill people.

Likewise, when Katherine Power enlisted herself in what she romanticized as "guerrilla war," she was putting herself in a position where someone could get hurt or even killed. How could this good person have done things that so violated her own moral values? As already discussed, we tend to shape our political beliefs to support "our team," or what Power referred to here as her "cohort." Similarly, Tage Rai and Alan Fiske present research in *Virtuous Violence* showing that most people will not intentionally harm or kill others—unless two conditions converge: namely, they "believe that it is the *right* thing to do"—*and* "their primary social groups" support this belief.[69] In other words, Katherine Power's decision to engage in violent armed robberies could be explained in terms of the convergence of (a) her belief in 1970 that violent revolution was morally required *and* (b) her having narrowed her primary social group down to this five-member guerrilla squad, three of whom were ex-cons keen to pull off armed robberies. Like most enlistees, when she signed up for her war, she was in effect agreeing to harm people, possibly fatally.

***

This section of the interview shows a woman, two and a half decades after the fact, still for the most part armored against fully acknowledging what she was doing during the summer of 1970—elevating it as part of her original good intentions to stop an immoral war and normalizing it as going to war on the right side.

Even so, this armored woman is the same woman who could say and mean: "Part of the shame that I carried for 23 years was how could I think that up and go do it? What kind of horrible person am I that I could think that up and go do it?"

And this horrified woman is the same woman who immediately followed those words with these: "Well, I didn't think it up on my own." But these are not her final words on the subject either.

These are: "Even if you didn't think it up, [even if] you learned it from your elders, you need to be responsible for your acts."

CHAPTER 5

What It Was about Her That Could Help Explain Her Crimes

KATHERINE POWER WAS ONE OF A mere "handful of the most militant," as Todd Gitlin pointed out in an op-ed piece written at her surrender—militant extremists who acted out wild "fantasies in which they would form revolutionary commando squads that could short-circuit . . . the democratic process by—to use the repellent terms of the time—'picking up the gun' for 'armed struggle.'"[1] Logically then, a full explanation has to have more of her in it than we've seen so far.

When Katherine Power asked herself for this investigation how she had become an accessory to murder, the personal characteristics she singled out at our first meeting were: **empathy, depression, thoughtlessness,** and **attraction to a noble death.** I have added: **her youth, self-radicalization, and malformed conscience.**

***

This was how Power explained to me how **empathy** had motivated her:

KP: The mandate was to try to make it stop, and . . .

JL: The war stop?

KP: The war, and . . . I am blessed . . . and cursed . . . with empathy.

[At this point, tears are streaming down her face.]

JL: You had empathy for . . . ?

KP: For . . . God, for all of it. For the land, literally. For the vegetation. For the insects. For the human beings, and not only for Vietnamese human beings. I knew the people who were returning from that war. I was consumed with a need to make that suffering stop.

In my experience, Katherine Power is indeed an unusually empathic individual. Still, there are at least two problems with this explanation. First, if Power's antiwar convictions did stem in part from empathy, feeling others' suffering as if it were her own—and I believe they did—it was a fatally limited empathy. It failed to embrace, for example, the terror of bank tellers and customers confronted by armed, shouting, shooting robbers. Which brings up the second problem: once again she is conflating her violent crimes with antiwar activism. And yet—recent research shows that, when people are exposed to the suffering of strangers, more empathic individuals act more aggressively toward the perpetrators of the suffering (compared with the less empathic).[2] In Power's mind, the perpetrators of suffering were the U.S. government and the military. So the connection between empathy and revolutionary violence may not be so farfetched. On the other hand, the bank robberies actually aggressed on private citizens.

Serious **depression** was another personal factor to which Power attributed her crimes. A common conception of depression—as physically and psychologically immobilizing—might seem at odds with what we know of Power's activity level in the summer of 1970. However, depression is often not at all immobilizing. Irritable, ill-tempered, angry, on-the-warpath behaviors frequently accompany depression. Power's father, who was both seriously depressed and extremely angry, appears to be a case in point. In any event, what could depression have to do with her crimes? Here is how she explained it:

> KP: I was . . . I was certainly suicidal at the time, or as careless of my ongoing life as, as has to, has to be construed as suicidal . . . . I . . . I am quite sure now that for most of the time that I was at Brandeis, I was . . . in a severe depression. Other people who knew me at the time who have since become physicians have made that observation.

I've again retained her pauses, hesitations, and repetitions because I think they suggest discomfort with what she was saying. Some discomfort may have stemmed from her memory of the derisive rebuff she had gotten from her sentencing judge when she tried to explain away why she had stayed a fugitive for so long by pointing to depression, and perhaps some from her knowing that I knew that.

Nonetheless, it is a fact that Power has had a lifelong struggle with depression, which may have a genetic component to it, as the paternal side of her family had a history of depression. She felt like an outsider at Brandeis, she told me, overweight and the wrong social class—which could have contributed to depression. Probably another part of Power's spiral down into depression at Brandeis derived from the typical experience of the gifted high-school student who in college finds herself but one among a throng of the gifted. Having followed the advice of her high school guidance counselor, she might have found the big pond less easily navigable than she had anticipated. All in all, anger being so much less painful than depression, perhaps Power occupied herself in outrage against the war and its perpetrators in some measure as a reason to get up in the morning.

Days after the bank robbery and murder, someone identified as a "friend" told the *Harvard Crimson* that "Katherine was a very hard person to get along with."[3] If she was ill-tempered or difficult, that could have been an effect of depression. If she was hard to get along with, that would also render it unsurprising that she lost when she ran for student council president as a junior.[4] To complete the vicious circle, a public failure like that could certainly trigger severe and angry depression in a depressive.

That defeat in her bid for student council president shows at minimum that she was less than universally accepted at Brandeis. Thus her decision to join that revolutionary action group may have stemmed in part from the all-but-universal desire for acceptance and belonging. Another violent radical and fugitive of the Sixties, Jane Alpert, retrospectively recognized the place of this motive in her own crimes: "I still don't understand all the forces that drew me into the conspiracy or the underground . . . . [But I] know that my motivations stemmed as much from a longing for acceptance as from . . . my outrage at the United States government."[5] But for both young women, it had to be far more palatable at the time to think of themselves as acting out of moral outrage than out of a need for acceptance.

Then there is the Brandeis campus itself, placed atop those steep hills, located in a suburb of Boston, but a half hour train trip into the city, and not to the heart of it. Where can carless and friendless students go and what can they do, especially of a New England winter, to escape their beautiful campus and themselves? Even so, the connection between depression and armed robberies remains elusive.

Her above statement on the topic offers some elucidation. She was, she said, "certainly suicidal at the time." Recall that Power had come to realize that two of the ex-cons in her group posed a danger—to herself. Depression, working hand in hand with the revolutionary's expectation of dying a martyr's death for her cause, could help account for Power's catastrophically bad decision to stay with these men. Alternatively, or additionally, running around with dangerous men could have operated like a fast-acting adrenaline-laced antidepressant, generating a sense of risk, excitement, purpose, even hope.

The notion of risk raises another possibility altogether. Power qualified her claim of having been suicidal in 1970 with this phrase: "or as careless of my ongoing life as has to be construed as suicidal." It strikes me that this description could fit any number of people, especially *young* people. It is not unusual for adolescents and late adolescents who are not in the least suicidal to engage in behavior that appears to adults so patently life-threatening as to be "construed as suicidal." I think of gravely foolhardy behavior like drinking too much, driving too fast, having unprotected sex, hooking up with strangers—even perhaps sticking with a "revolutionary action group," the majority of whom are ex-cons.

In her surrender statement, Power wrote that her "illegal acts" in 1970 were well-meaning and at the time she thought right, but looking back on it, she saw that her acts had been "naive and unthinking." Given the deadly nature of the acts she was referring to, as well as the degree of calculation necessary to pull off the bank robberies, this language amounts to Power damning herself with faint censure. That said, many, if not most, 21-year-olds are guilty of naiveté and thoughtlessness. Although she never brought it up, her **youth** had to be a factor.

James Baldwin beautifully captures the difficulties of being young and making pivotal decisions in what he calls "the adolescent dark":

> And they always seem to be wrestling, in a private chamber to which no grownup has access, with monumental decisions. Everyone laughs at himself once he has come through this storm, but it is borne in on me, suddenly, that it *is* a storm, a storm, moreover, that not everyone survives and through which no one comes unscathed. Decisions made at this time always seem and, in fact, nearly always turn out to be decisions that determine the course and quality of a life.[6]

Baldwin was writing about students who were working to desegregate southern schools in the early- to mid-Sixties. Given the ethical disparities, the parallel may seem offensive. Still, Katherine Power was making decisions in the dark, monumental decisions that determined the course and quality of her life—and most importantly, the life of Walter Schroeder, his wife, and nine children. None of them came out unscathed.

Knowing that she had spent her high-school years at an all-girls' Catholic school, I asked Power whether she might have arrived at college even more naive than others her age. She said she had thought so three years earlier when she wrote the surrender statement, but no, she didn't think so anymore. I can't say I accept this denial. The following exchange shows how youthful naiveté and thoughtlessness might have figured in her turn to violence:

KP: My own experience led me to know . . . war is not okay. My experience . . . . it's the experience of it.

JL: So guerrilla war against, in order to stop, State war is not okay.

KP: It's not okay. Now, I could not know until I saw the consequences.

"I could not know until I saw the consequences." Is this a blatant rationalization begging for a "Whaddya mean, you *could* not know"?

Not at all. She was emphasizing the "I" not the "could." She was saying that for *her* it took the actual experience of seeing the consequences of her violence to fully understand how wrong it was. This interpretation squares with the characterization in her surrender statement of her crimes as naive and unthinking, as well as with her later explanation to me of why she had pleaded guilty to manslaughter: "I didn't know better than to run around with people with guns . . . . I didn't think it through . . . . I didn't be careful."

When Power talked about how she hadn't thought it through, didn't know better, and wasn't careful, I got the impression that she was confessing a personal failing. After all, she had learned early in Catholic school that seven is "the age of reason"—the age when we are old enough to tell right from wrong, hence able to sin.

According to discoveries in brain research, however, seven is far too young for rational ethical judgment, Baldwin's insight about young people making decisions "in the adolescent dark" is spot on, and Katherine

Power's failure to think things through wasn't a defect peculiar to her. Research in cognitive neuroscience has found that well into the twenties the brain is still developing the structures and circuitry of the prefrontal cortex needed to think like an adult. Due to the resultant taste for risk-taking and poor impulse control, young people tend to make some breathtakingly bad decisions. Temple University neuropsychologist Laurence Steinberg writes that into the twenties the brain has not yet fully developed the higher-order abilities to "plan ahead, weigh risks and rewards, and make complex decisions."[7] He argues that until the mid- to late twenties we are functioning with the brain of an adolescent. And, Steinberg asserts, "an adolescent is an adolescent, whether he is making fun of his teachers, *committing armed robbery*, or building a bomb. No matter how 'adult-like' the crime is, it doesn't change the fact that brain systems are still developing."[8] [emphasis is mine]

If Power was ashamed of her youthful stupidity, an even worse failing in her eyes was what she called the "grandiosity" that had fed her fantasies of heroic action and heroic self-sacrifice. Developmental psychologists David Elkind and Dan McAdams offer a less pejorative account of such fantasies, or as Elkind calls them, "personal fables."[9] McAdams writes: "The personal fable may look like a delusion of grandeur, but in its proper developmental place it is normal."[10] Adolescence is the proper developmental place. Indeed, young people, writes McAdams, *typically* weave grand ambitions that "celebrate the self's greatness, as when the young person spins fantasies about becoming the greatest scientist the world has ever known, writing the great American novel, or *changing the world in one glorious sweep*."[11] [emphases are mine] Those who do change the world in one glorious sweep are later of course called revolutionaries.

Revolutions and would-be revolutions have often been headed by the young. Arguably the most pertinent of the many examples is the Chinese Cultural Revolution, in which Mao Tse Tung shrewdly made use of young people, teenagers, to advance his own political purposes. Understanding and exploiting the yearnings of young people to dream big dreams of changing the world, Mao unleashed youth to literally smash up places, things, and human beings deemed counterrevolutionary. And smash they did. In the name of revolution, they ran amok. The youth-wilding early years of the Cultural Revolution, 1966 to 1969, overlapped almost perfectly with Power's undergraduate years. Members of the Weather Underground were fond of quoting from Mao's *Little Red Book,* with one of his most well-known maxims a favorite of theirs: "Political power grows out of the barrel of a gun."[12] The title of the Weather Underground's first manifesto, *Prairie Fire,* was directly inspired by Mao's aphorism: "A single spark can set a prairie fire."

Youth also renders individuals ripe for creating their fledgling identities in light of their historical situations.[13] Many of the other circumstances outlined in Chapter 3 (e.g., the escalation of the Vietnam War, its expansion into Cambodia, the killing of student protesters by the authorities) occurred during Power's late high-school years and her first three years of college. Being young, socially conscious, and (selectively) empathic in these historical circumstances undoubtedly contributed to her decision to define herself as a revolutionary.

Power's age—with youth's grand dreams, propensity for risk-taking, desire for meaningful action in the world, urges to smash things, and underdeveloped ability to think things through—definitely helps explain her crimes. But not completely. As hard a sell as moderation is for the young, and even more so in the overheated zeitgeist in which Katherine Power came of age, the fact is that the vast majority of disaffected youth in America at the time did not team up with ex-convicts committing bank robberies with loaded submachine guns.

***

In my initial letter I had specifically asked Power to consider both internal and external factors that she thought had contributed to her crimes: "What is/was it about *you* that contributed to these experiences? [and]

What is/was it about your life *circumstances and other people* that contributed?" I was taken aback at how conscientiously in our first interview she addressed my guiding questions—and taken aback too at her lopsided emphasis on external circumstances.

While reflecting out loud on the role that external forces might have played in her crimes, Power also acknowledged that none of this negated her personal agency. She said it: "Even if you didn't think it up . . . you need to be responsible for your acts." At this point in her dark pilgrimage, she was able to admit her responsibility for her worst acts—even as another part of her flinched, frozen in a defensive position. One of the sorriest examples of defensiveness was her response to my request to address what it was about *her* that might have contributed to her crimes. She turned that query (at first) into an opportunity to trot out a list of what amount to virtues and excuses—empathy, thoughtlessness, naiveté, and depression. Not a promising start.

It is worth bearing in mind, though, that when Power surrendered, people who had known her or the circumstances in 1970 were coming forward to write or visit her. They were harking back to external factors they thought relevant, including the revolutionary zeitgeist, the radical rhetoric of some adults in her milieu, and the absence of forceful leaders of nonviolent dissent—factors considered in Chapter 4 because she brought them up. Such information would have moderated the unbearable shame—"What kind of horrible *person* am I?"—accompanying her self-interrogations. And so for a while she embraced external explanations too readily.

When Power did bring herself into the picture at this stage, she did it most often by invoking **conscience**. Conscience permeates Power's narrative, as it permeates her life. If there remains any doubt, consider the following assertions she made to me: "In the end, in this moment, in every moment . . . I am responsible to be a good person" and:

KP: I actually had a, a psychologist say to me, don't you recognize that the stories of the saints are propaganda?

JL: Not when you're eight years old, you don't.

KP: I'm not sure I do even now. I am *not* sure that I can say as an honest statement that it's not very sensible to try to live as a saint . . . . I don't know any other way to live except by trying to be as good as you can. Well, if that's not an aspiration of saintliness, I don't know what is. I mean to me it's still very sensible. [Power's emphasis.]

It wasn't enough for her to try to be a good person most of the time, but *every moment*. Not enough for her to *strive* to be a good person; instead she felt *responsible* to be a good person—every moment. These aspirations to saintly perfection may perhaps reveal an aspect of what she called her "grandiosity," a wish to be anything but ordinary. They also reveal a dictatorial conscience.

In the ubiquitous metaphor, conscience is that white-robed angel telling us in that still, small voice the right thing to do. This metaphor, though vivid and highly memorable (hence its usefulness in instructing small children), is fundamentally unhelpful. Truer and more helpful is the definition supplied by scholar of conscience Louisa Thomas: conscience is our strong beliefs.[14] Strong beliefs, however, are anything but still or quiet. They are among the loudest and most importunate of all our thoughts and emotions.

Katherine Power was not the first person in history to wreak ruin by hanging out with a bad crowd, or the first unable to find the wherewithal to leave when she realized her mistake. Thomas's analysis, however, provides three important pieces of the complicated puzzle that explains how Power's conscience took her so far off course.

First, as Thomas reminds us, conscience is *us*, and if, as Thomas has it, conscience consists of our strong beliefs, just as our thoughts and beliefs are not always virtuous, conscience is not always a force for good. Katherine Power became a revolutionary in the name of conscience: her outraged belief that the system was wholly evil and had to be destroyed. When good people do bad things, it's *often* because they are convinced that conscience demands it. As scholar of violence Tage Rai has put it, almost always "violence is motivated by moral sentiments":

> Across practices, across cultures, and throughout historical periods, when people support and engage in violence, their primary motivations are *moral*. By "moral", I mean that people are violent because they feel they must be; because they feel that their violence is obligatory.[15]

Or as Power told me: "And there I was [at age 21 in 1970] feeling morally compelled to break the rules . . . . I was violating something, but I was feeling that I had to do it; I had to do this to be an OK person."[16]

Second, if we can make something a matter of conscience, we can justify anything, even heinous crimes.[17] Power did not intend to abet the heinous crime of murder. However, when she chose to commit violent crimes that carried a nontrivial potential for spinning out of control and harming others, she did it in the name of conscience. Her very phrase for it, "holy war," is immersed in conscience, as is the language she chose to explain what she meant by holy war: "I felt like I was going to war on *the right side*." In the name of conscience, she convinced herself that taking up arms for the right side was justified by the transgressions of the wrong side.

Most paradoxically of all, conscience can lead people to do wrong, Thomas writes, in order to "protect [their] purity at the cost of harming other people."[18] As we have seen, Power chose to go violent, at least in part, to protect her own moral purity. She had to do it "to be an OK person." Immediately after telling me how and why she had repudiated the opportunity to take on a role as a national spokesperson against the war, Power summed up her motivations: "I was being my most ascetically, disciplinedly moral self . . . . All I really wanted to do was clandestine actions that were effective sabotage against the process of the war-making."

The truth is this was not "all" she really wanted to do. She had multiple and mixed motives, some of them far from disciplined or moral or even centered on the war. She also wanted to make revolution and, like the Weathermen, to do it violently and clandestinely. And as late as age forty-five, two years into her prison sentence, she was still misrepresenting her terrorism and crimes as something good, as conscience-based antiwar activism.

***

The media has always understood the end of Power's junior year, the summer of 1970, as the time when suddenly and inexplicably Katherine Power went off the rails. In fact, it appears that she was building up to it for nearly two years before the Boston bank robbery and murder. Starting in the middle of her sophomore year, December 1968, she was stoking the converging fires of antiwar outrage, Weatherman fantasies, Panther sympathies, and private furies into a revolutionary conflagration. She was radicalizing herself.

She didn't tell me about her **self-radicalization**—me, or anyone else I am aware of. So only she knows all that went into her deterioration from antiwar activist to armed, clandestine revolutionary. I pieced together some of the when and how of it from information in the Brandeis University Archives, from other historical documents, and from the first-hand reflections of former Brandeis professor Jacob Cohen. From his position as a close observer of the radicals on campus, Cohen states that "Katherine Power's initiation into radical [thought] came in December 1968, the middle of her sophomore year."[19] This assertion concurs with the independent report by a friend of Power's who, as I mentioned in the previous chapter, told the *Harvard Crimson* after the bank robbery and murder that "ever since sophomore year she was one of the hard core at Brandeis."[20]

What happened to initiate Power into a radical worldview? In December 1968 a group of Brandeis students took over a campus building to offer "sanctuary" to a deserting soldier, in their minds "daring" the U.S. Army to invade campus to arrest him. Some of these students, Katherine Power among them, writes Cohen, set up a commune inside the occupied building.[21] For most of the students, the commune was just a commune. But, in Cohen's view, a few, including Katherine Power, took it as a literal auxiliary of the revolution. Intense, heated, and interminable discussions went on inside the commune, and the usual group dynamics and peer pressure would have gone on, too. Students would have gotten categorized as cool or uncool. The coolest were the hard-core "true radicals," who would have derided the others as "liberal elitists."[22]

Cohen describes a dramatic meeting where a group of black students accused the white "Sanctuarists" of being oh so good at talking but of, in so many words, lacking the *cojones* to take action when it was called for. Cohen writes that a few—"just a few"—took this indictment "as a rebuke to be pondered, a further challenge not only to talk the talk but, somehow, to walk the walk."[23] Whether or not Power attended that meeting, she was one of the Sanctuarists—and she intended those weapons stashed in her apartment and the money bagged in the bank robberies to go to the Panthers.[24]

By May 1970, Katherine Power was recognized outside of Brandeis as a spokesperson for political dissidence. The *Christian Science Monitor* interviewed her and quoted her as cautioning: "If the political tactics people use now don't work, either they will become apolitical and not work at all, or they will find other tactics."[25] I would like to think that young Katherine Power was speaking in a constructive spirit, but, at least retrospectively, what she said to the *Monitor* has the whiff of a threat. I suspect that the voices of machismo, whether arising from the Panthers, the Weather Underground, separatist feminism, or all of it—the whole impassioned zeitgeist—had by that time drowned out for her the deeply unromantic voices of moderation. Just four months later, Power had found other tactics. Having rejected the path of the "jet-set radical" as a near occasion of the sin of pride, the path of the "comfortable radical" as a sin of omission, and the path of activist-working-within-the-system as futile and namby-pamby, she deployed herself far outside of the political system.

***

Katherine Power chose to try to bring about change at the barrel of a gun. The bad decisions and bad behaviors were her own.

Then, there is *outcome*. Although certainly related, outcome is distinct from decisions and deeds. Even when the bad behavior is robbing banks at gunpoint and therefore *some* such outcome would seem predictable, at least for people with an adult understanding of things—even then outcome is a separate matter. Even such a horrific outcome as the death of Walter Schroeder is separate from those things.

To think comprehensively about outcome, we need to circle back to the topic of Chapter 4, factors extrinsic to the individual. I am talking about luck, randomness, blind chance. Unfortunately, when it comes to the role of luck in people's lives, we in the West find it hard to think straight. I'm as surprised as anyone by the research that has uncovered a strong tendency in the West to hold individuals "more responsible (and 'chance' or 'luck' less responsible) for acts that have *serious* consequences than for acts with trivial consequences."[26] Which is illogical. Illogical or not, it can feel profoundly wrong to point out the error of this thinking—when the consequence is the death of an innocent husband and father of nine. This feeling of wrongness, insensitivity, even indecency, I would argue, is itself a testament to the power of the bias. Regardless of how indecent it might feel to insist on it, luck cannot be less responsible for grave outcomes than inconsequential ones (holding everything else constant). Thinking it can is a cognitive error, not logical, not rational— and therefore not just.

Keeping this in mind, let us now consider two 1970s-era female radicals. The first woman plants pipe bombs underneath two patrol cars, intending to kill at least two police officers;[27] the bombs fail to detonate, are successfully defused, and no one dies.[28] The second woman participates in armed robbery, not intending to kill anyone; a rogue accomplice shoots a responding police officer, who dies. Both women flee and live as fugitives for more than 20 years. These are not hypothetical scenarios. The birth name of the first woman is Kathleen Soliah; her fugitive name is Sara Jane Olson. The birth name of the second is Katherine Ann Power; her fugitive name is Alice Metzinger.

Neither of these women is an innocent. Both voluntarily took up violent criminal activities. But intent matters. Soliah intended to kill, and Power did not.

How a fugitive comes forward to pay her debt also matters. Power turned herself in, confessed her identity, and pleaded guilty to her crimes. Soliah did things differently. Having lived the life of a "soccer mom" for more than two decades in Minnesota, she was arrested in 1999 based on a tip following an *America's Most Wanted* program. First she denied who she was and inexplicably had her name legally changed to her fugitive name, Sara J. Olson. Three years later, in 2002, Soliah pleaded "guilty to possessing bombs with intent to murder police officers"[29] and to involvement in a bank robbery in which a mother of four was murdered.[30] Then, almost instantly after her sentencing, she announced to reporters that she was *not* guilty. Soliah's guilty pleas stood,[31] she was sentenced to 14 years to life, and she served seven years.[32]

Differences in intent and in manner of finally reckoning with their crimes divide these two young women. But at issue here are the differing outcomes of their terrorist acts. It could be said that, in part, the outcome of Soliah's botched bombings—no police officers died—exhibits the working of good luck, and the outcome of Power's botched bank robbery—a police officer died—bad luck.

They say that people make their own luck, one of those bromides steeped in the fundamental attribution worldview, and valid for some of the people some of the time and only up to a point. In staying with the ex-cons after she realized they could be dangerous and in failing to care sufficiently to think it through enough to foresee the potential for some such awful outcome, Power made herself responsible for the consequences of what they did as a group. Still, Soliah's good luck does not render her any *less* responsible for her terrorist acts than Power.

To be clear. Katherine Power has never broached the subject of luck with me. This analysis is all mine. No matter how strongly we resist bringing circumstances extrinsic to the person into a conversation about bad conduct, they need to be included. And no matter how strongly we resist bringing chance into the conversation when bad conduct ends with grim consequences, a full analysis has to include it.

***

Even if chance played a role in the consequences of her acts, in the end, Power freely chose to do what she did—radicalizing herself, joining a revolutionary action group, staying with it after it became a criminal action group, stealing ammunition and weapons, practicing firing them, stocking her apartment with munitions, firebombing an armory, partic bank robberies—and installing herself in the driver's seat of a getaway car for the violent bank robbery that ended Walter Schroeder's life.

CHAPTER 6

"I WALKED AWAY AND I KEPT ON": THE FUGITIVE

POWER TOLD ME VIRTUALLY NOTHING about the logistics of her fugitive period and I didn't ask, because that was "her story," not mine. This project did not concern external events per se but inner significances.* Another reason for Power's reserve stemmed, I believe, from protectiveness toward those who had helped her hide.

Wanted Poster

---

* I have relied on published accounts, especially the *New Yorker* article, for the nuts and bolts of the external events.

At least two different accounts exist of Power's actions right after the armed robbery and killing. In one, Bond gave Power money to buy a used car, and he and Power drove it to Philadelphia and then Atlanta, where they separated, planning to meet later.[1] In another, Power, Bond, and Saxe flew out of Logan airport, with their final destination being California.[2] When I asked Power about these conflicting chronicles, she said that the confusion accurately reflects her shell-shocked state of mind at the time: she can't remember much of what she did immediately after the crime.[3]

What happened in the St. Louis airport, however, Power does remember. Vividly. At some early point, she flew to St. Louis with a suitcase that Bond told her to take. "She claims she did not know a fully cocked shotgun was inside"—not until the gun went off at the luggage carousel at the St. Louis airport, injuring two workers.[4] Power was waiting at the gate for a standby flight to Detroit when she heard an "obvious code" over the P.A. system.[5] She saw men running towards her, flipping through a pile of tickets. They scrutinized a particular ticket once, twice, and then they took it out of the stack. At this point, Power said: "Very slowly, I walked away, and I kept on until I reached the airport door. That's when I heard my alias being paged."[6] She took a taxi to a department store, where she bought a matronly wig, a polyester dress, and a suitcase. Thus camouflaged, she waited in the bus station for four hours for the bus to Detroit. Police drifted through, but they did not recognize her.[7]

Power met up with Saxe in Detroit, and the two of them kept on the move. The first eighteen months the pair lived on the east coast, picking up and moving whenever they thought they were in danger of getting caught. The FBI had finally figured out that women's groups were often hiding them, and the agency started coercing those who were lesbians to betray the fugitives by threatening to "out" them to their families and employers—and actually doing it. Three women chose jail (one for seven months and two for over a year) rather than reveal the whereabouts of Saxe and Power.[8] This could have stemmed from devotion to the admired women. It also bears the hallmark of the Weather Underground's ethos of proving one's commitment to revolution either by going underground or, at the very least, aiding those who had.

During her 23 years as a fugitive, Power moved from state to state to state. She lived in Connecticut, Kentucky, Maryland, Michigan, New Jersey, New York, and Oregon, among other places. In 1974 Saxe and Power split up, and the following year Saxe was captured. In 1977 Power got hold of a birth certificate and took over the identity of Alice Metzinger, a baby who had lived and died a year before Power's birth. Using this birth certificate, she obtained a Social Security number and a Maryland driver's license. Her life of serial identities was over. Outfitted with this relatively solid identity, she moved to Portland, Oregon and started a new life. Though she was living in a lesbian relationship, she was thirty and longed to have a baby. In January 1979, she gave birth to a son, Jaime Lee Metzinger.[9]

In 1980 Power met Ron Duncan at a poverty agency in Portland, where he worked as an accountant and she as a nutrition coordinator. They fell in love, and because she felt he was someone who shared her values and who could be trusted, almost immediately she told him who she was.[10] He left his wife and daughter to be with Power.[11]

Whenever Power got antsy, which was often, her little family packed up and moved. In 1984 she worked as a cook and instructor at a community college near Corvallis, Oregon.[12] They bought a house nearby. In 1989 she and another cooking instructor opened a restaurant, which they operated in keeping with an egalitarian philosophy in which employers and employees had equal say.[13] In her first 18 years as a fugitive, Power graduated from every variety of safe house: from dumpy single room to cheap apartment to home of her own, and from every variety of work: from menial job to passable job to full-time career.

In 1991 she left the restaurant to paint and repair their house. In the winter of 1991-92 she worked manically—"managing one Corvallis restaurant, consulting at three others, and leading a consortium of friends to buy yet another."[14] In the spring of 1992, it all stopped dead.[15] Power was paralyzed by despair.

Her breakdown, I believe, was the cumulative effect of over two decades of trying to walk away from or fight down a confusion of distresses—regret,* remorse, guilt, shame, denial, alienation, anguish, anxiety, and perhaps secret wishes to be caught. Although Power had evaded legal punishment for 23 years, she could not evade interior punishment. With Emily Dickinson, she could have said, and must have in those 3 a.m. moments, that she "felt a Funeral, in [her] Brain."

A fugitive cannot take her despair to a therapist, for she cannot risk being known. So Power did the next best thing: in May of 1992 she went to a class on depression offered by a therapist, Linda Carroll. The press of her pain forced the door ajar so that after the lecture she found herself approaching Carroll. "She was in the most intense psychic pain of anyone I've ever seen," Carroll recalls. "She couldn't speak without crying."[16] In Carroll's office Power's story came tumbling out. In response, Carroll did two things: she saw to it that Power was put on antidepressants, and she suggested that Power look into the charges against her. She recommended a Corvallis attorney known as something of a maverick, Steven Black.[17] Power told Black who she was, and he looked into the charges against her.

Black contacted a prominent lawyer in Boston, Rikki Klieman, to work with them. Power and Black had hoped for leniency. They soon found that the Boston authorities were not at all inclined in that direction. For a year, tense and secret negotiations flew back and forth between her lawyers and the authorities in Boston. Later that summer, she had finalized the terms of her surrender.

---

* Strictly defined, regret is feeling sorry about one's acts or failures to act. Guilt is regret over a specifically ethical and/or legal wrong. Remorse includes all of this plus a firm resolution never to repeat the regretted matter.

Some 12 years after meeting Ron Duncan, she married him, and he adopted fourteen-year-old Jaime.[18] A week or so before her surrender, she told her son who she was. She had already sold her share of her restaurant to protect her co-owner in case the government were to seize her assets upon her surrender. In September of 1993, she turned herself in, pleaded guilty to manslaughter and armed robbery, and began serving her prison sentence in MCI-Framingham.

The central question I explore in this chapter is why it took her over two decades to come clean. I have no simple and no single answer to that essentially ethical question. The reasons were complex and multiple, a tangled jumble of the proverbial good, bad, and ugly.

***

There is no question that Power regretted the killing, as shown in her stricken reaction upon learning that Gilday had shot someone:

> I couldn't believe it . . . I was saying "What? What? How could this have happened?" It was a sharp, intense pain . . . There was this overwhelming sense of wrongness. This wasn't supposed to be about taking lives—this was about stopping the taking of lives. I have memorized that moment, replayed it again and again—so many times. I will never in my life ever forget it.[19]

When she talked about the killing of Walter Schroeder, she wept with interviewer Lucinda Franks soon after her surrender, and she wept with me two years into her prison sentence. Some may doubt the authenticity of Power's tears. What I saw looked and felt like the real thing. Neither the intervening years nor my many re-readings over those years has changed my assessment that her **sorrow** over the murder is deep, genuine, and unremitting.

I also have no question about her **regret**, the cognitive and emotional state of feeling sorry about one's mistakes—whether acts or failures to act—as in her disastrous decision to go along with Bond's leadership and her failure to leave the group when she began to have her doubts. In recounting how Bond had sent her off with the suitcase packed with a loaded shotgun, Power made this admission:

> Somewhere I had known all along about Bond's narcissism, his patriarchal arrogance, his lack of sense and attention to other people's safety, but I had only paid attention to his astonishing noble qualities. I knew what to do, I knew how to act, and I gave it away. That's the only time in my life I've ever let somebody else be the leader.[20]

I can testify to the leader part; she has a natural, effortless authority about her. And I have no doubt she knew how to act ethically. What tragic folly that she gave it away—to a treacherous sociopath. But this is an old story about how decent people come to do things they regret—by ignoring misgivings, gut feelings, and warning signs, and by letting someone else make calls that go against their own better judgment.

Soon after she surrendered, Power sat for the *New Yorker* interview with Lucinda Franks.[21] There she explained how she could have lived with herself so long as a fugitive. "I vowed that I would make my life an act of contrition for my wrong to the Schroeder family," she said. In her mind, she was atoning in private.

While the lowercase phrase "act of contrition" is understandable in and of itself, the uppercase "Act of Contrition" has a specific meaning and a specific place in the Roman Catholic liturgy familiar to Power. It is recited during the sacrament of Penance (formerly known as Confession), after the individual admits her *guilt*, expresses her *sorrow* for having sinned, and conveys *remorse* by promising not to repeat the sin. Following are the exact words of the Act of Contrition, as found in the *Baltimore Catechism*:

> O my God, I am heartily sorry for having offended Thee, and I detest all my sins because of Thy just punishments, but most of all because they offend Thee, my God, Who art all-good and deserving of all my love. I firmly resolve, with the help of Thy grace, to sin no more and to avoid the near occasions of sin.

Like anyone in her age cohort who attended Catholic schools, Power knew the Act of Contrition by heart. She had said those words every time she went to Confession in her youth, which was regularly. "I remember folding one of my mother's scarves into a triangle and tying it under my chin for Saturday afternoon Confession, perhaps every two weeks," she told me.[22] Through the sacrament, she was granted forgiveness of those sins—but only after confessing the sins to God through the person of the priest, after reciting the Act of Contrition aloud, and after performing the penance assigned by the priest.

At one point in our first interview, I asked Power how and when she repudiated the use of violence. In other words, I asked specifically about **remorse**, a resolve to commit that sin no more. She responded: "I can say that it [her repudiation of violence] began to happen at the *moment* when I was confronted with the reality that because of my decision to go to war, somebody had died." [Power's emphasis] "From that moment," she said, she "became committed to nonviolence."

We have learned that, for this 21-year-old, it took the personal experience of actually seeing the horrific consequences of her violent acts to make her reject violence. Unlike some Sixties' revolutionaries, Power did not continue to perpetrate violent acts while underground. She was living the remorse expressed in the Act of Contrition: she had firmly resolved to commit that sin no more.

What other specifics went into living her life as an act of contrition? It appears that she tried to do good by, among other things, more than once organizing her fellow workers to demand better working conditions and/or pay. Once, when she helped three women clerks join a union, she was fired. In sticking her neck out like this, she was putting herself at risk of being noticed by the wrong people. Possibly, at that moment she didn't care if she were caught. Her labor organizing, however, is best explained in terms of a longstanding social conscience. The principal of her high school attested to this trait of Katherine Power's. She was by nature an idealist and an activist.

Years later, although Power had worked herself up to the levels of chef and later co-owner of a flourishing restaurant, she and her husband, Ron, chose to live what he referred to as a life of "voluntary poverty."[23] Her *New Yorker* interviewer writes that Power had also "tried to atone for the damage she had done—for instance by giving part of her income away."[24] Among friends and neighbors she was known for giving things away. This former Oregon neighbor supplies some specifics: "Alice [Power's alias] got me to walk for my health. She gave my daughter her car, and she wouldn't take a penny. Whatever Alice had, you were welcome to it."[25] When Power sold her interest in the restaurant before her surrender, she gave a quarter of the proceeds to Oxfam, the international hunger-relief agency.[26]

Though social conscience, non-materialism, and generosity may have been integral facets of Power's pre-crime character, these traits may have developed a post-crime life of their own in the service of **atonement**. It appears that she thought—hoped—that she could "pay the price" for her crimes by living a life of private virtue, a not uncommon rationalization among fugitives from justice who are also decent human beings.*[27]

Compared with the moral emotions of regret, guilt, and remorse, **shame** has less straightforward origins and consequences. Psychologist Erik Erikson defines shame as a "sense of having exposed [one]self," and as accompanied by wishes to "destroy the eyes of the world," to make oneself invisible.[28] In a televised interview in February, 1994, soon after Power's incarceration, Barbara Walters asked Power what her reaction had been upon hearing about the shooting of Walter Schroeder. Power expressed this wish to make herself invisible, saying: "The depth of shame is unimaginable and my response was, of course, to flee."[29] How she wanted, among other things, to hide herself from the eyes of the world.

Shame does provide another part of an answer to the question of why, if her regret, guilt, and remorse were so real and so intense, she took so

---

* When fugitive Frank Dryman was found in 2010, after 40 years of hiding out, he was quoted as saying he'd "tried to make up for it [a murder] by being an honor citizen."

long to surrender. Empirical comparisons of the moral emotions find that shame engenders far more pain than guilt (or remorse). Why? Because guilt (and remorse) implicate "merely" one's behavior, whereas shame implicates one's very self.[30] Power's previously quoted description of her shame evinces this emphasis on the self (even as it includes behavior): "What kind of *horrible person* am I that I could think that up and go do it?" An attack on one's very character, whether the attack comes from outside or from within, generally provokes defensive measures.

Treating memory as her enemy, Power went about her business only semi-aware of what she had done that September morning in 1970. So strong were her defenses against shame that she fended off the truth apartment after apartment, season after season, year after year, until 23 years had passed. **Denial** was arguably the shabbiest and the most common of the psychological contortions Power employed while a fugitive. She worked too much and drank too much, time-honored means of anesthetizing unwanted thoughts and feelings. Like Dostoevsky's fictional fugitive, Raskolnikov, she attempted to "flee from any clear and complete understanding of [her] position."[31] She acknowledged in 1994 that she had spent much of her fugitive life "living only in the present, wiping out any memories of the past."[32] She didn't in 1994 remark on how her denial directly clashed with her stated intention to live her life as an act of contrition.

In choosing denial in its various forms to tamp down disturbing thoughts and emotions, Power was choosing morally specious (and ineffective) strategies. As Freud put it, when psychological afflictions are denied overt or sublimated expression, they grow wild and "ramify like a fungus...in the dark."[33] Cognitive science has come to similar conclusions via empirical research.[34] Attempts like Power's to suppress, deny, or otherwise circumvent unwanted thoughts, feelings, motives, or impulses simply do not work. Not for long. And not unless you are a sociopath— which she isn't. The fact that she had abetted a murder ramified within her like a fungus, and this fungus would continue to proliferate unless it got exposed to the light of day.

Living as a fugitive requires practicing deception and detachment like a vocation, and living this way inevitably produces an intense sense of **alienation** from family, friends, and community. When in 1974 Power and Saxe went their separate ways, Power's continuing flight cut her off from everyone she had known and loved before September 23, 1970. Franks registers the loneliness attending this period of Power's life underground:

> [W]hen the war ended [in April 1975] and her fellow-radicals dispersed and slipped back into the establishment, Power was left alone with the myth, a revolutionary without comrades or a revolution.[35]

Such estrangement from the human community is precisely what Albert Camus predicts for the violent. In *The Rebel*, Camus writes that anyone who murders for a cause

> . . . is no longer justified in using the term *community of men* . . . . [I]t suffices for a man to remove one single human being from the society of the living to automatically exclude himself from it. When Cain kills Abel, he flees to the desert.[36]

So it was with Power. Having involved herself in murder, she fled to the desert of self-imposed alienation and exile. Act of contrition or no, this desert was never going to bloom.

What did bloom, in the dank subterranean world of her unconscious, were several types of poison fungi. **Despair** was one, despair so toxic that at times it became life threatening. Periods of paralyzed depression alternated with periods of frantic motion. When I asked Power whether she thought the perpetual busyness had both reflected and maintained a condition of moral stagnation, she agreed: "That's exactly the way I would express it," she said. And: "From a very young age I learned to use activity against my depression." What is more, she has said that she believed that nonstop doing was a matter of life and death for her, to the point that what she most feared about prison was its constraint on activity: "The central reason I didn't give myself up before is that I was so afraid that my frenetic activity was my only weapon against suicide."[37]

I believe that Power suffered periods of suicidal depression while a fugitive (and before), but I don't think that this was "the *central* reason" she waited so long to surrender. It is reasonable to assume (though I have never heard her say it) that the main reason she remained a fugitive is quite simply that she did not want to go to prison. That said, my guess is that her most salient reason for remaining a fugitive morphed over time—with fear of suicide perhaps rising to the top of her motives when she first became a mother, or a bit later when she watched over that beloved boy who (as expressed in her poem) thought "they had all the years / Of their lives to buy pizza and cold / Drinks for his friends."

Still, she must have had flickering thoughts of ending her self-exile in the desert. Eerily akin to Dostoevsky's Raskolnikov, Power seems to have **courted capture** at times.[38] In 1977, seven years into her fugitive life, she used to frequent a bar in Portland, Oregon, called, of all things, "The Slammer":

> Then, one night, I looked up from the long-neck Bud I was drinking to stare right into my own picture on a "Wanted" poster on the wall. The place was plastered with "Wanted" posters and jail bars. The customer next to me was a Portland police officer. I had let my hair grow long and it had gone back to its natural color, so I didn't even look that different from my poster. Now, did I stop going to The Slammer after that? No. Sometimes, in your despair, you invite change.[39]

If Power had secret wishes to be caught, and I think she did, the prolonged timespan of her fugitive life has to imply even stronger wishes not to be caught. Power's occasional impulses to risk capture probably stemmed from some barely conscious mix of honorable and dishonorable motives expressed by the vagueness in her words about inviting "change." What exactly did she mean by "change"?

Change typically brings both anxiety and exhilaration, chills and thrills. Could she have continued to go back to a bar plastered with her own Wanted poster in part for the thrill of putting one over on the authorities—yet again?

It appears that Power was saying that at times the pain of her despair made any change at all—even prison—preferable. Any fugitive must have moments of wishing for relief from the state of constant anxiety and vigilance, hyper-vigilance at times, rising to the point of panic and paranoia. After her surrender, she described experiencing such relief, saying she had "felt buoyantly light, disentangled at last from the heavy net of lies, aliases, and invented selves."[40] Risking capture mainly to invite relief from the anxiety of always having to look over one's shoulder wouldn't especially pass ethical muster. The same applies to a wish for relief from a life of constantly building and then fleeing her series of cells in the desert, relief from all those aliases. Insofar as she was (ambivalently) wishing to undo all the lies, however, she would have been inviting the honorable change of publicly telling the truth of who she was and what she had done.

***

In this chapter we have gotten a glimpse of how Power careened between trying to atone for the wrongs she had done and trying to suppress full knowledge of those wrongs in her own mind. No amount of denial, suppression, or thought-stopping was ever going to relieve her anguish about the murder of Walter Schroeder. To her credit, Power ultimately "failed" the self-help directives so often urged upon us Americans—to put the past behind us, to move on, not to waste energy on "negative" emotions.

The ethical transformation of Katherine Power was going to have to take place beyond the "secret grotto"[41] of her individual heart and mind. Her crimes made purely private rehabilitation—even a vow to live her life as an act of contrition—a contradiction in terms.

CHAPTER 7

Showing Up: The Surrender

On September 15, 1993, Katherine Ann Power surrendered. It was national front-page news. She was commended, as mentioned earlier, by no less than her prosecutor, Ralph Martin, who said: "She certainly deserves credit for coming forward, because we probably never would have caught her."[1] Everyone, it seemed, wanted to know all about this woman. She was the cover photograph and cover story of the September 27, 1993, issue of *Newsweek*. Her photo appeared on the front pages of the *New York Times* (see photo above), the *Washington Post*, the *Los Angeles Times*, and other newspapers.[2] Editorials ran in the *New York Times*, the *Washington Post*, and the *Christian Science Monitor*—and commentary and articles in the *New Yorker*, the *Nation*, the *Wall Street*

Journal, Time, National Review, and other venues. Barbara Walters interviewed her. Rikki Klieman, Power's high-profile attorney who negotiated her surrender from the Boston side of the country, appeared not only on the *Donahue Show,* but also on the *Today* show and *Good Morning America* on the same morning.[3] Katherine Power was all over the news. She was swimming in eye-poppingly huge offers for book and movie rights to her story.

The *New York Times* editorial closed with these judiciously forbearing sentiments:

> Her crime must not be made light of, but she can be understood. Not all the casualties of the 60's served in Vietnam. Some, like Officer Walter Schroeder, were victims of the era's lunatic "revolutionaries." Others walk among us, still trying to make sense of the past, or to pay for it.[4]

Newsweek was less judicious and far more forbearing than the *Times,* stating: "After all these years, it's hard to know whom to feel the most sympathy for: the children who lost a father . . . [or] the young woman who lost her way in the tumult of the '60s."

The day after her surrender, the *New York Times* printed a written statement Power released to the media. Here it is in its entirety:

> I am surrendering to authorities today to answer charges that arise from a series of acts 23 years ago. I am here to plead guilty to these charges, and I am prepared to accept whatever consequences the legal system will impose.
>
> Those who know me now and those who reflect on my two decades of life as an apparently exemplary citizen will wonder how someone such as myself could commit such outrageously illegal acts. The answer lies in the deep and violent crisis that the Vietnam War created in our land. At that time, the law was being broken everywhere: at the very top, where an intransigent President defied international law as well as the express intentions of Congress; in Government services, where Daniel Ellsberg leaked the Pentagon Papers in the hope that citizen scrutiny could hasten an end to the war; among the clergy, where priests and nuns destroyed draft records; in neighborhoods, where young men defied the draft.
>
> The illegal acts that I committed arose, not from any desire for personal gain, but from a deep philosophical and spiritual commitment that if a wrong

exists, one must take active steps to stop it, regardless of the consequences to oneself in comfort or security. Although at the time those actions seemed the correct course, they were in fact naïve and unthinking.

My intention was never to damage any human life by my acts, and there is no accusation that I was directly responsible for the death of Walter Schroeder. His death was shocking to me, and I have had to examine my conscience and accept any responsibility I have for events that led to it.

In response, I have lived my life as something of a penitent, ever seeking to grow as a person of peace. I have much company on this path, including many Vietnam veterans who have reflected on their actions in the war and on the lives that were damaged as a result.

Leaving my son, my husband, and my friends to enter prison is not easy. But I know that I must answer this accusation from the past, in order to live with full authenticity in the present. A lifelong, untreated condition of endogenous clinical depression has prevented my taking this step before. Experiencing life without that distorting lens, I am now learning to live with openness and truth, rather than shame and hiddenness.

I have deeply regretted the repeated separations caused by my status as fugitive. I invite past friends and associates to forgive my absence, and to renew their acquaintance with me. I will accept with grace the ordeal ahead, and I will return to my community prepared to continue a life of connection, service, and joy.[5]

In this statement, Power admitted guilt and addressed questions she anticipated people would have: why she had turned herself in, why she had committed her crimes, why she had stayed a fugitive so long, who she was now, and what she hoped for from the future.

Everyone, it seemed, had their opinions about why Power had turned herself in. The last line of the *New York Times* editorial portrayed her as trying to pay for her crimes. No doubt, the media, some of them, took their cue from her language in the surrender statement—those exalted phrases about examining her conscience, about living her fugitive life as a penitent, and about her philosophical and spiritual beliefs in taking action against evil—therefore explaining her surrender as an act of conscience. I too took my cues from that language at first. The *New York Times* titled its editorial "The Prodigal Daughter," a biblical reference, of course, to the sinner who after many years repents and comes home to a forgiving parent. (Her mother liked that phrasing, Power told me.) "A Conscience Haunted by a Radical's Crime" ran the title of a *New York Times* article; in the *Christian Science Monitor* it was "Conscience Calls a 1970s Radical to Face Her Past" and in *Macleans* "The Guilt behind a Tragic Deed."[6] She was a "special fugitive—pursued by her conscience," wrote Todd Gitlin in a *Washington Post* commentary.[7] I think the phrase was meant to be taken straight, not ironically, although I'm not absolutely sure. (Gitlin did not respond to my query about this.) I do know that in the same piece he strongly condemned her crimes. For my part, Gitlin's phrase "pursued by her conscience" conveyed exactly my first take on the surrender of Katherine Power. It took years for me to attain a more complex, truer perspective.

In actuality, certain language in Power's surrender statement supported less elevated reasons than conscience for her surrender. The *Wall Street Journal* editorial denounced her statement as a "'New Age' apologia" about a journey to "'authenticity' and 'healing.'"[8] Expanding on this theme, Charles Krauthammer blasted her for the reason she presented in her surrender statement for turning herself in—"to live with full authenticity"—writing: "What a pathetic trajectory . . . from revolutionary slogans to New Age psychobabble." He accused Power of surrendering not out of "repentance but . . . personal growth."[9] In an otherwise fairly sympathetic article, two *Wall Street Journal* reporters noted that some thought Power's surrender amounted to a "wallow in self-absorption."[10] Besides condemning her reasons for surrendering, some noted with distaste the media frenzy that greeted her surrender and the media's largely glowing stance subsequent to the surrender.

Jacob Cohen witheringly panned the *New York Times* editorial as "avuncular."[11] As for *Newsweek's* extraordinary statement that it was "hard to know whom to feel the most sympathy for: the children who lost a father . . . [or] the young woman who lost her way in the tumult of the '60s," Charles Krauthammer shot back incredulously: "That's a hard one?"[12] Within a week after Power's surrender, the Schroeders' hometown paper, or one of them, the *Boston Globe,* asked its readers to call in their opinions of Power's sentence.

One of the many readers who considered Power's punishment too lenient deplored the impact on Schroeder's widow of all the media attention being lavished on Power: "It is unfortunate that this poor woman, with nine children to raise on her own, . . . now has to see Power just about made a hero. I find this treatment absolutely disgusting."[13]

At Power's sentencing, Clare Schroeder delivered the Schroeder family's victim statement. Clare expressed their own disgust with the media's extravagant attention to Power and singled out that statement in *Newsweek*:

> When Katherine Power and her friends robbed the State Street Bank in Brighton with semiautomatic weapons, my father responded to the call. One of her friends shot my father in the back and left him to die in a pool of his own blood. Katherine Power was waiting in the getaway car, and she drove the trigger man* and her other friends away to safety.
>
> Twenty-three years later, Katherine Power stands before you as a media celebrity. Her smiling photograph has appeared on the cover of Newsweek. She has been portrayed as a hero from coast to coast. Her attorney had appeared on the Phil Donahue show. [She] is receiving book and movie offers worth millions of dollars on a daily basis.
>
> For reasons that I will never comprehend, the press and public seem far more interested in the difficulties that Katherine Power has inflicted upon herself than in the very real and horrible suffering she inflicted upon my family. Her crimes, her flight from justice and her decision to turn herself in have been romanticized utterly beyond belief.
>
> One of the news articles about this case described it as a double tragedy—a tragedy for Katherine Power and a tragedy for my father and my family. I will never comprehend, as long as I live, how anyone can equate the struggle and pain forced upon my family by my father's murder with the difficulty of the life Katherine Power chose to live as a fugitive.
>
> The tragedy in this case is not that Katherine Power lived for 23 years

---

*In Power's account, Gilday was not in the car she drove, and she never saw him again after the bank robbery.

while looking over her shoulder. The tragedy is that my father's life was cut short for no reason, shot in the back with a bullet of a coward while Ms. Power waited to drive that coward to safety.[14]

Clare's *cri de coeur* conveys with unpretentious eloquence what a world of hurt the media celebration of Power caused the Schroeder family. How hideous to have this woman painted as a hero. How excruciating to read news accounts equating the Schroeder family's suffering with Katherine Power's, as in the sentence from *Newsweek* carved into Clare's heart. Having the media idealize this woman, who had for 23 years hidden in a maze of false identities, tore open and poured salt on wounds that had scabbed over. All this comes clear.

Why Clare remarked so bitterly on Power's smile—"her smiling photograph"—is perhaps not so self-evident. Not unless you see what Clare saw. The photo Clare is referring to shows Power wearing a white suit, handcuffs—and a smile. Not a small, pensive, rueful smile. A huge, buoyant, radiant smile. What could such a smile have meant? To the Schroeders it was the smile of a "media celebrity" basking in the warmth of all those flashbulbs.

The smile might have reflected a less abhorrent kind of basking, however: soaking up the wide-open daylight shining on her now that she had emerged from her underground life of deceit and despair. Basking in the relief of finally telling the truth about who she was. That smile might have been directed to the sunlight at least as much as the spotlight.

Or: Power's smile might have arisen from an ethically better place than any of these: from a long-unfamiliar sense of self-respect earned by facing the consequences of her crimes. (Although as I imagine it, her gladness to be facing justice, 23 years late, would have shaped itself into one of those small, pensive, rueful smiles.)

Rikki Klieman, in her role as Power's defense attorney, recognized that the photo "was a public relations disaster," in that the "ear-to-ear smile" made it appear that "Katherine was dancing unrepentant on

Walter Schroeder's grave."[15] Klieman, however, provides a different explanation than any of those considered above. This photograph, she states, was taken just as Power first entered the Boston courtroom for her arraignment: "When Katherine left her holding cell and entered the courtroom, she saw her entire family, old and new, sitting in the front row. Her passive face broke into a beatific grin." If Klieman's account is accurate—and she was there, then that smile was neither contemptible nor virtuous, but simply human.

I want to accept Klieman's explanation. However, this wasn't Power's very first glimpse of her family; she had had a celebratory reunion with her parents and at least one sibling the night before.[16] Still, it is true that she was actually seeing all of her family, some for the first time in decades, when she entered the courtroom. Further supporting Klieman's explanation is an AP photograph taken seconds before she entered the courtroom showing her smiling, though less broadly than seconds later when she laid eyes on her entire family.[17]

This is what I think. First of all, it must be said that Katherine Power is someone who smiles readily and broadly. Based on her surrender statement and what she told me later about why she surrendered, I think she was doing some basking of all the kinds mentioned above, I think Rikkie Klieman is right, that she was ecstatic to be reuniting with her family and with friends from her past. And, as the Schroeders intuited, I think that at that moment she wasn't thinking about Walter Schroeder.

Possibly, astonishingly enough, at that particular moment her crimes were not at the forefront of her thoughts. An empirically based analysis of offenders' accounts of their crimes provides a valuable lens through which to examine precisely how Power was viewing her crimes in her surrender statement.

This research finds that offenders' explanations of their crimes typically fall into four categories: refusal/denial, justification, excuse, and admission.[18] Through denials, or refusals, offenders reject personal responsibility for an offense. This may entail direct "denial of an offense or the actor's role in it, denial of the right of witnesses to issue reproaches, or ascription of blame to others." Justifications, or rationalizations, entail redefining the crimes or their consequences as "less blameworthy than they might at first appear." Excuses entail denying full responsibility due to "mitigating factors," such as "lack of intent, unforeseeability, or uncontrollable circumstances." Concessions, or admissions, acknowledge full responsibility for the offense; in their admissions, offenders may also express remorse and offer restitution.

In effect, every one of the 8,395 days of Power's fugitive life represented a denial: a **refusal** of the right of society, the criminal justice system, and her victims to reproach her by holding her responsible for her crimes. Then when she did surrender, she wrote a statement that was greater parts denial, excuse, and rationalization.

Power's surrender statement opens with what at first appears to be a straightforward **admission** of guilt: "I am here to plead guilty." But the words immediately following "guilty" show virtually no admission at all: "to charges that arise from a series of acts 23 years ago." Power doesn't name what it was she was pleading guilty *to*. Nothing about armed robbery. Nothing about manslaughter. She speaks in euphemism ("a series of acts") and other forms of elusiveness ("charges"), where it would seem that integrity calls for admitting to specifically named crimes.

But wait. As Steven Black explained to me, this elusiveness was attorney-talk. While the statement was put together collaboratively by Power and her attorneys, he said, that first part was very carefully edited "by attorneys, with an eye toward protecting" Power's legal interests. At the time of Power's surrender, Black said, it appeared that she might be subjected to civil suit. In addition, the surrender statement preceded her arraignment and her sentencing, and at either of these points she still could have decided *not* to waive her right to trial. If she admitted to specific criminal charges up front and later decided to go to trial or was later brought to civil trial, she would have already incriminated herself. So that vagueness does not necessarily represent blameworthy evasiveness on Power's part, but routine legal practice.[19]

Setting aside its first paragraph then, still the surrender statement clanks with three forms of *excuses*, or "mitigating factors." When Power invokes a "lifelong, untreated condition of endogenous clinical depression" to explain her fugitive years, it comes across as an excuse-by-uncontrollable-biology. Power's sentencing judge, Robert Banks, appears to have taken it that way: "In a voice thick with distaste, he told Power . . . that he was unimpressed by her claims of being clinically depressed."[20]

Furthermore, Power edges toward claiming lack of intent in characterizing her "illegal acts" as "naive and thoughtless." Krauthammer repudiated Power's explanation this way: "One does not ordinarily think of a bank robbery . . . as an act of naiveté." And: "Let's remember who Katherine Power was and what she did. This was not a flower child caught up some wild afternoon in a robbery."[21] He makes a valid point. Recall that it is known that as a member of the gang of five she committed a number of bank robberies during the summer of 1970—in Los Angeles, Evanston, and Philadelphia, for instance. And days before the fatal bank robbery, they stole guns and ammunition from the armory north of Boston before setting fire to it. This crime spree took more than a little thought on the part of Katherine Power.

In fact, though, she does more than edge toward lack of intent; she directly asserts it: "My intention was never to damage any human life by my acts"; and she exempts herself from full responsibility for the murder: "[T]here is no accusation that I was directly responsible for the death of Walter Schroeder." Inasmuch as these two statements are factually true, they are technically not excuses. But when read in the context of the depression excuse, the plea of naiveté, and the several rationalizations and justifications to be addressed next, they contribute to a global impression of self-exoneration.

The single longest paragraph in the surrender statement, the second, sets forth two kinds of justification for her crimes. First, she acted out of pure motives, she says: "The illegal acts that I committed arose from a deep philosophical and spiritual commitment that if a wrong exists, one must take active steps to stop it, regardless of the consequences to oneself in comfort or security." With these words, Power makes a virtue of her crimes—the virtue of taking action to right a wrong, the virtue of relinquishing personal tranquility and safety to do the right thing, and the implied virtue of practicing civil disobedience against an unjust war.

At least as appropriate as the words "philosophical" and "spiritual" would have been something like "ideological" and "political." But to come out and admit the ideological or political nature of her motives would have opened her to censure—the kind of censure she got from some in the media, the Schroeder family, her sentencing judge, and others. Clare Schroeder repudiated Power's assertion that her "illegal acts" had anything to do with trying to stop the Vietnam War: "Murdering a police officer in Boston to bring peace to Southeast Asia was utterly senseless then and it is just as senseless now."[22] Judge Banks, too, rebuffed this rationalization of Power's, curtly informing her: "I reject the proposition that your criminal acts were justified, excusable or even mitigated as acts of a political or social nature."[23]

Second, in that long second paragraph, Power presents an "everyone-was-doing-it" **rationalization**, casting her crimes as less blameworthy than they might otherwise appear. She lists others—ranging from the U.S. president to priests and nuns—who at the time Power committed her crimes were also, according to her, committing "outrageously illegal acts."

Leaving aside that U. S. president (Nixon), those clergy members were committing acts of *nonviolent* civil disobedience to protest the Vietnam War. Furthermore, they were willing to—and did—accept the consequences of their acts: namely, exile, criminal trial, and incarceration.

Jacob Cohen took indignant exception to Power's equating her crimes with acts of civil disobedience *or* even with antiwar protest, telling the *Boston Globe*:

> I was very frankly sickened by [Power's] statement, which kind of draped her in the civil disobedience, in the antiwar feeling of the time, because nothing of that adds up to going into a bank with a machine gun, and she must have known that the guys she was with had machine guns, even if she wasn't there pulling the trigger.[24]

He's right, of course. Armed robbery is not civil disobedience. Participating in violent bank robbery bears no resemblance to acts of destroying draft records or leaking government secrets about the execution of the war. These were not acts of civil disobedience against the war. They were, at least in Power's mind, acts of insurrection intended to trigger overthrow of the government.

She knew about the machine guns. She had been stashing them in her apartment, converting it into a secret arms depot. She slept in that virtual armory the night before that September morning when the gang of five loaded the assault weapons and carried them out to their cars. Bullets from one of those weapons took the life of a good man. In the *Wall Street Journal* Dorothy Rabinowitz countered the idea put forth by Barbara Walters and the *New York Times*—that Walter Schroder was a victim of the Vietnam War and the Sixties, respectively. He was "in fact, a victim of robbers and murderers whom Ms. Power chauffeured from the crime scene," wrote Rabinowitz.[25]

But at the time of her surrender, the media, Clare Schroeder, and Judge Banks had no way of knowing that Katherine Power's antiwar motives had morphed into the conflagration of revolution-by-any-means-necessary. She had omitted this information from her written statement. Even two years later, when I asked her about her crimes and she did admit to having been a revolutionary, she kept these vexing aspects of the storyline and timeline vague. So it was that the media picked up and sustained the false narrative of Katherine Power as an antiwar activist.

Those who had been antiwar activists knew better. In a piece that appeared, perhaps surprisingly, in *The Nation*, former antiwar activist Margaret Spillane wrote: "Every radical I knew was outraged by the vanity, flippant cruelty and political irresponsibility of the Power-Bond-Gilday bank robbery, and their shot-in-the-back murder of Officer Walter Schroeder."[26] Todd Gitlin agreed, stating that "the overwhelming majority of the movement hated the violent crimes and was demoralized by them."[27] For Power or the media to locate her crimes as "part of the 'antiwar movement,'" Cohen told the *Boston Globe*, "is to conduct an exercise in Orwellian double-talk."[28] To phrase it less vividly, at her surrender, Power was conducting a disingenuous exercise in self-justification. In my judgment, at that time it wasn't that she was trying to deceive others; rather, she was still deceiving herself.

***

The surrender statement and the media reactions to it do not, however, represent the last word regarding the reasons for or the timing of her surrender.* She spoke at greater length about these matters later, with me and others.

She had surrendered, she stated in the *New Yorker* interview, to "quit living this sick-making life."[29] "Sick" perhaps as in the AA slogan sick: "You're only as sick as your secrets." After two decades of secrecy in which her shame, alienation, dread, despair and other toxicities were building in intensity, Power decided that she had to live with "full authenticity," starting with showing up and answering to her true name. Her references to a "sick-making life" versus a life of "authenticity" handed ammunition to those critics who accused her of surrendering out of self-centered "New Age" motives, only to feel better about herself. And they have a point. However, Power's reasons for surrendering did not center completely on

---

*Nor do they represent the last word about her crimes, which we revisit in Chapter 11.

herself. What she wanted most was **to make well her relationships with those she loved**.

Power identified her son, Jaime, as "my first step in attachment to the world of humanity—a relationship that was permanent, that I couldn't walk away from."[30] Having this baby in 1979 must have afforded Power, for the first time in nearly a decade on the run, a sense of possibility, of a future, of settling into a normal life. But her efforts to wall off her fugitive status from her role as a mother could not be sustained. Eventually, being a mother helped impel her decision to give herself up—in at least four different ways.

For one thing, Power had come to feel that she had no right to continue to deprive her son of a whole set of grandparents, aunts, uncles, and cousins (and vice versa).* Second, given the kind of person Power is, it was important to her to teach her son public political engagement by example. This piece of the puzzle came to the fore through a phone conversation I had with Steven Black:

> She told me a couple stories about where she lived in Lebanon [Oregon], about activities involving her school where, the school where her son went, and that she did not feel capable of speaking out at public sessions in which various positions were taken on social issues, including the [1991] Iraq War, because of her fugitive status. So she could talk about these things privately in her home, but it wasn't good enough. I mean, she needed to show her son that there was a public side, that you have to stand up for what you believe in public, not just in private . . . . And in the end she decided . . . in favor of showing her son the right thing to do.

The triangulation of information here shines an altered light on the same story Power had told me about the town meeting in which she had wanted to speak up publicly against the Iraq War. The moral of the

---

*The wish to give a son his extended family was also one of the reasons for the Power-inspired surrender of Richard Lunderman in 1994. Mr. Lunderman "wanted his son to be able to enroll in his Sioux tribe, but didn't think the tribe would allow it with an alias." (Pacheco, "Fugitive Gives Up 16 Years Later," C1)

story as Black tells it here is both more sympathetic and more convincing than the moral of the same story as she had related it to me, which was about a priest's voice (retroactively) telling her she "must become an outlaw." There is undoubtedly some truth in both tellings. However, the way she told me the story, shoehorning it into the Catholicism-made-me-do-it narrative, is logically and chronologically deficient. I sense more truth in Black's account, which not only came from the time she was in the throes of deciding to surrender but also requires no contortions of logic: she decided "in favor of showing her son the right thing to do."

Once, when Jaime wasn't doing so well in school, Power was having a talk with him about making better use of his potential. He looked at her and in so many words used her own deeds against her: Oh yeah? You were a straight-A student, and *you* dropped out of college. She couldn't answer his challenge, because he didn't know why she had dropped out. At that moment she realized that to parent her son well, she'd have to let him know the whole of who she was.

Finally, after living in their small town for several years, in 1991 Power began again to panic, and she talked with the family about moving. That time Power's urge to run collided with her teenaged son's determination to stay, as described in the *New Yorker* piece:

> [I]t was Jaime's self-protective instincts that stopped her. "He was just so deeply attached to his friends—fierce, really fierce," Power told [Franks]. "He said, 'If you move away from here, you will have to leave me behind, because this is my home town and I'm going to stay here.' And, through some wonderful grace, we were able to hear him."[31]

Predictably, having a child complicated life considerably for Katherine Power, fugitive—to the point that mothering her son well became one of her most compelling motives to surrender.

People were quick to assume that surrendering must have damaged her son. And of course Jaime was not unscathed. When Katherine Power informed him that she was not Alice Metzinger, she was jarring the foundations of his own identity, since all his life he had been Jaime *Metzinger.* She "could see something pass over his face, like a small earthquake inside him . . . . And then the alarm was gone, as though he had shaken it out of his head."[32] This mix of alarm and resilience on Jaime's part is evident in both the preceding and the following. When Jaime was asked at age 15 (less than a year after Power's incarceration) how he felt about his mother's absence, this was his response:

> "It's hard not having her here, but I'm just glad she did it now instead of five years from now, when I'll really need her," he says. He pushes away a newspaper article someone had sent him about Power. "The way I like to remember her is when she took me and my friends swimming. She was great with my friends, and she would sit on the edge of the river in her little straw hat, smiling at us, smiling at all of us while we swam."[33]

Not surprisingly, Jaime held fast to his memories of the good mother he had known and avoided information about the woman with the unfamiliar name now in prison for manslaughter and armed robbery. In the main, though, it is the deep and reciprocal quality of his attachment to his mother that shines through in this response of his. Its poetic loveliness echoes, even more movingly, lines from "Sestina for Jaime." Again: "He dreams it is summer; / That he still has a mother holding back from the cold, /And watching, watching him."

Jaime's statement that he was "just glad she did it now" also suggests why these were relatively unproblematic years for his mother's leave of absence. The developmental tasks normative for 14-to-20-year-olds in this culture are separation and individuation from one's parents. Which means that not too many kids that age are pining to spend more time with their mothers. As Power's poem put it, he and his friends were by then swimming "too well to need her at the river."

Power's statement that Jaime's birth represented her "first step in attachment to the world of humanity" rings entirely true. That attachment, that love, became one of the primary reasons, if not *the* primary reason, that Power surrendered. In the end, as Power expresses it in "Sestina for Jaime," "he alone could coax her from the house / Where she hid out."

***

Power's surrender was also driven by her own longings for reunion with her birth family. What had her parents and siblings been thinking about her, her crimes, and her self-chosen long separation from them? She didn't know, but she thought they might be judging her harshly. Just before her surrender, her lawyers delivered to her a letter from them, welcoming her back home. Their reaction brought her tremendous relief, which she described in the 1994 interview: "In an instant, I was lifted of so much deep psychic shame. I thought they had written me off, condemned me."[34]

***

Then too, Power wanted to **reconnect with a larger human community**—friends and colleagues, whom she hadn't allowed to really know her. This theme came up when I asked her what she thought of Hume's writing that emotion, not reason, is the basis of morality:

> KP: Um hmm . . . . And it's also the cut-offness from community, that they'll be mad at me, they won't think I'm a nice person. It's a valuable test for whether your behavior is right, even though it's not an absolute test.

> JL: It's not always . . . accurate. It's not always valid, but it has some informational value.

> KP: It has extraordinarily important value. Only sociopaths are immune from fear of being cut off from connection. If there's something that's deeply wrong with our civilization, it's that we're so used to being disconnected that we think that this is human existence.

Again, Katherine Power, fugitive, had avoided deep and lasting attachments, because they would jeopardize her secrets. But she simply isn't made to live that way. Very much unlike Raskolnikov, Power has never sanctified individualistic isolation.* To the contrary, she goes so far as to insist on the vital importance of others' moral judgments of her and her conduct.

Power didn't say exactly who "they" meant, as in "*they*'ll be mad at me," and "*they* won't think I'm a nice person." I suspect she was thinking of her family, but also her friends, neighbors, and colleagues in Oregon. Plus, she had reasons to be carrying around vivid internal images of people being angry if they found out about her crimes, images derived from her personal involvement in an extraordinary event in her local community. This event (a story that would never fly were this fiction!) merits a digression.[35]

In May 1992, Power was conferring with her lawyer Steven Black two or three times a week about her legal situation. One day that summer Black, a Vietnam veteran, confessed to her some appalling things he had done in Vietnam. He had taken it upon himself to fly around in his little plane in his off-hours, shooting and killing Vietnamese who were posing no threat. Power told me that by the time she met him, Black was "horrified at himself," and, she added, "One of my marks of a moral person is that they're horrified at themselves." She joshed with him that "he was the one who should be put on trial."[36] Black's response? "What a good idea!"[37] Immediately he made the idea a reality—putting himself through a public mock trial.

The trial of Steven Black for war crimes took place in the fall of 1992 in the county courthouse in Corvallis where he himself practiced law. The jury consisted of over thirty of Black's friends and colleagues, many of them "prominent citizens" of Corvallis.[38] The judge was a local

---

*Raskolnikov commits murder to prove to himself that he is a "superior" individual, which he defines as someone able to live in isolation from society and its mores.

physician. The prosecutor was the Deputy District Attorney. At Black's request, Katherine Power (then Alice Metzinger) acted as his defense attorney. The State charged Black with having perpetrated the gratuitous "'extracurricular killing' of a hundred or more people in the free-fire zone he had patrolled in the Mekong Delta."* [39]

Black testified: "I would take my plane, the Iron Butterfly, out 'hunting.' I would look for people. I would shoot at anything that moved."[40] When the prosecutor asked him how he had felt on his "hunting" expeditions, Black answered: "I enjoyed it . . . . It was a game. I killed a lot of people, I probably killed extra people."[41]

In her role as his defense lawyer, Power came down fairly hard on him when questioning him about his personal responsibility for his acts. Conversely, she called as an expert witness a cultural anthropologist who argued that Black's crimes should be judged in their military and historical contexts.

The experience upset two jurors so deeply that they excused themselves. Moreover, Black told me, the jury "could not reach a consensus opinion, so they each decided to give their own verdict," filling out separate verdict forms.

The majority judgment? Not guilty by Vietnam-War standards; guilty by customary standards. The sentence? Fifty hours of community service (which he performed in the emergency room of the local hospital). Power wept when she heard the verdict.

Black described to Lucinda Franks how he felt after the trial: "I went home almost beatific . . . . I have never felt such a sensation of lightness,

---

*I asked Black to explain to me precisely what a "free-fire zone" was, and he told me this: "The rules of engagement govern when you fire ordnance at something or somebody. You basically have to get permission to do it, and they had free-fire zones—places where you could go and if you found somebody there, you'd call up to get permission to shoot these people and since the laws of that land said nobody's supposed to be there, nobody legitimate was supposed to be there, and if there was somebody there, then it was assumed that they were not legitimate. And I was never refused the opportunity to shoot."

of relief. The absolute worst things I had ever done, the worst part of me, was finally out there, and my friends, most of them, could forgive me."[42]

It came as little surprise to me to learn, when I spoke with him, that Steven Black was also raised Roman Catholic. I asked him whether he thought his eagerness to put himself on trial had any connection with his Catholic background. "Makes sense to me," he said. "I mean I like the idea of being forgiven for your sins. That's a terrific concept. But you also have to do penance for your sins."

Black explained why he had asked Power to participate: "What I was thinking was that if I could show her that something positive would come out of a trial, . . . maybe it would allay her suspicions and fears . . . . She so mistrusted the system." In the end, his trial didn't live up to the kumbaya experience he had hoped Power would have. Franks explains: "[N]ot all the jurors could forgive Black, or understand his actions. 'Nobody would get me in a position where I'd kill like that,'" stated a friend of Black's, himself a Vietnam veteran.[43]

So Power had reason to fear how people she loved and cared about would react to finding out who she was and what she had done—that they might no longer consider her a good person. At the same time, she respected others' judgments of her, and she didn't want to be cut off from people anymore.

∗∗∗

Ironically enough, Power's opposition to another U.S. war contributed to her decision to surrender and to its timing, as she told me:

> KP: The beginning of the end of the sustainability of my fugitive life was the [1991] Iraq war . . . . I don't know . . . what . . . was or is demanded of me individually and *us* collectively, meaning everyone who knows the wrongness of war. I don't know what was, would have been, demanded of me if I could have acted in a full range of actions, but I know that I couldn't because I was a fugitive. I was the employer and friend of a number of people

who looked to me to be one of the elders . . . about that event, and I couldn't do it.

People who knew Alice Metzinger recognized her as someone with a strong, articulate, and persuasive voice, and they wanted her to speak out for them against this war. What they did not know was why she refused to speak, how unbearably her self-imposed silence weighed on her, how she ached to **reclaim her voice as a citizen.**

* * *

When her birth family welcomed her home at her surrender, she took immense solace in their forgiveness. She singled out only one family member by name: "Even my uncle Ted, the priest, forgave me."[44] For Roman Catholics, of course, only the priest has the power to bestow **God's forgiveness** of sin. It appears that—at least by two years into her prison sentence—Power was hoping that her surrender would succeed in re-uniting her not only with her family and friends, and not only with the larger human community, but also perhaps with God.

* * *

Power decided to surrender for many reasons, but personal and relational concerns took the lead. More than anything else, she wanted to make an honest ("authentic") woman of herself in order to repair her personal relationships.

Not yet discussed was an enormously important set of relationships badly in need of repair. Twenty-three years earlier back in Boston, Power's crime had locked the family of Walter Schroeder into an entirely unwelcome relationship with her. And yet her surrender statement made no mention of the Schroeders or their abiding catastrophe. Not a word about the family who had had their husband and father torn from them at the armed robbery she had abetted.

This omission is especially puzzling in light of the fact that before her surrender she had wanted the Schroeders to join her in a mediation process. Through her lawyer, she asked them to enter with her into mediation to be conducted by an experienced Boston-area victim/perpetrator mediator who was also a priest. They refused. When I asked Power what she had hoped for from mediation, she said: "My wish was, broadly, that I would acknowledge my responsibility for the Schroeders' loss and that I would do whatever community-repairing acts were mandated by a reconciliation process." Confession, community service, reconciliation. Nothing specific about alleviating their terrible pain. One has to wonder whether, at the time, she was hoping to alleviate her own pain (caused by the Schroeders' open antipathy toward her) at least as much as theirs. This might explain how she could have left them out of her surrender statement.

***

At that first interview I did not get what I had expected: a report on many years of fruitful ethical work accomplished by Power while a fugitive. Instead, I learned that she had spent most of the time during those years trying to outrun herself. She had studiously refrained from turning around to look back on her past. A solid body of empirical evidence, however, has established that trying to forget things simply doesn't work.[45] In the case of the moral sentiments, it is ethically hazardous to try. There are things in life worth caring about and misconduct worth being horrified at oneself about—and what more than a killing?

Festering underground, the moral emotions, above all shame, mutated into a dark mass of despair. It was the despair that first drove Power to excavations that raised the tentative insight that perhaps, just perhaps, it was time to give herself up. Once she could think clearly, other things drove her to actually do it: first and foremost, her desire to make right her relationships with those she loved, but also her wishes to reconnect with the larger human community and to regain her public voice as a citizen. All in all, Power's surrender was an inelegant lurch out of the darkness of guilt and despair into the daylight of owning up.

CHAPTER 8

OWNING UP:
THE GUILTY PLEA

EVEN HER PROSECUTOR acknowledged that Power might well have been acquitted had she gone to trial, stating afterwards: "We had zippo . . . . No admissible evidence, no credible witnesses. Basically, no case."[1] Steven Black told me that, knowing the weaknesses of the legal case against her, he had advised her to opt for a trial: "I wanted her to go to trial, and I think that she would have won and come out not guilty, but she refused to do that." At the time of Power's surrender what had impressed me more than anything else was the fact that she had voluntarily given up what she was entitled to, a right to a trial in which she might have been acquitted. Why, I wondered?

I have never doubted that Power was genuinely remorseful about the murder of Walter Schroeder. At the beginning I assumed that she had waived trial because she wanted to get on with the last big ethical tasks remaining to her, confession and expiation. As stated early on, I wasn't sure whether she was a genuine penitent, period—or a genuine penitent tangled up in "Catholic guilt." I didn't credit her most aggressive critic, Charles Krauthammer, who charged that Power's "New Age psychobabble" about "authenticity" showed that she was a phony penitent, not seeking repentance but merely "personal growth." The New Age language, however, did bother me enough that I went to our first interview session with that question near the top of my agenda. After quoting to her what Krauthammer had written, I commented, "but when you speak of authenticity, that's a personal growth kind of word. I . . . I don't see that it's *necessarily* a put-down." Actually, I did see it as a put-down, and a legitimate one. Personal growth by itself would be an ethically insufficient goal for someone who had done what she had. In responding to my probe she didn't deny wanting personal growth. But she rejected Krauthammer's contemptuous definition of it:

> KP: "Personal growth" can encompass everything from being conscientious to worrying about your percent of body fat—in the same way that people can use the word "political correctness" to dismiss everything from real sensitivity to the blind bludgeonedness of the European-derived culture to a slavish-to-fashion way of speaking . . . . The work of soul, . . . the work of therapy, . . .these are not indulgences. These are not feel-good things . . . .

To Power, personal growth wasn't a shallow, self-indulgent matter of trying to feel good about herself through, say, facile affirmations. It demanded work, hard work, work that didn't feel good at all. That reference to "soul work" dispatched for me the personal-growth slur, and simultaneously encouraged the more pervasive assumptions—mine and others'—about so-called "**Catholic guilt.**"*

Given the attention I've already given to the possible role of Catholicism in Power's crimes, it might feel as if I'm about to beat a dead horse. To clarify: at this point I am exploring whether "Catholic guilt" might have pressed her to plead guilty to armed robbery and manslaughter.

A reader of an early version of this manuscript felt strongly that it was irrational for Power to have pleaded guilty to manslaughter. His reasoning was that she had had no intention of killing anyone, she did not shoot Walter Schroeder, and, unlike the others in the group, she was not in the bank with a gun. In his opinion, she should have pleaded guilty only to

---

*As explained earlier, I use this term to refer to a reflexive, excessive, masochistic, or otherwise neurotic state of mind.

armed robbery. He felt that she had chosen punishment that exceeded her crimes,[2] thus evincing an appetite for extreme suffering, which he attributed to her socialization in what he referred to as an "extreme" religion.[3]

In the view of this reader, himself raised a Roman Catholic, Catholicism exacts from its adherents doctrinal and moral extremes not found in other faiths. In Catholicism the words (certain of them) of its leader are regarded as not only wise, but infallible; the Eucharist is not merely a symbol but literally blood and literally body; its clergy are enjoined not only to live an ethical sexual life, but a life of celibacy; not only abortion but even artificial birth control is forbidden; divorce is not merely discouraged but is punished by excommunication. I do not share the assessment of Power's guilty plea as extreme. But I did think it possible that some version of "Catholic guilt" might have played a part in it.

Two different "Catholic-guilt" hypotheses seemed to me potentially relevant to Power's guilty plea: what I thought of as the "Five-Our-Fathers" and the "purgatorial suffering" hypotheses, respectively. These notions came from my reading of Power's emphasis on the formative role of Catholicism in her life and my own formative experiences. These hunches are, however, more doctrinally unsophisticated than anything she had said, particularly the first. My "Five-Our-Fathers" theory was based on the idea that in the Sacrament of Penance sinners must earn forgiveness by performing a tangible penance in the form of prayers (e.g., reciting 5 Our Fathers and 10 Hail Marys). The "purgatorial suffering" theory* proposed that Power might have been impelled to seek an extended period of purifying suffering in a "penitentiary" before her conscience could rest.

In that first interview, I asked Power directly about the "Five-Our-Fathers" hypothesis—whether her guilty plea had had anything to do

---

*Of course, Catholicism posits hell as another possible outcome for sinners. But since Power had confessed and undertaken the penance associated with a prison sentence, I consider this a moot point.

with "the Sacrament of Penance, in which you do a tangible form of rep-aration like 5 Our Fathers and 10 Hail Marys?" She said, "You know, my friend Sandy from college . . . she said: 'Look at . . . you and your little Catholic conscience, you *wanted* to do this jail time.'" Sandy's allegation suggests that my "Catholic-guilt" hypotheses hadn't completely come from out in left field. At no time, however, did she, her friend, her husband, her lawyer, or anyone else come even close to a "Five-Our-Fathers" account of her guilty plea. Some years later, I asked her one more time whether any experience with the tangible penance assigned during the Sacrament of Penance might have entered in to her decision to plead guilty. She said it hadn't, and I believe her. I have no evidence whatso-ever that her guilty plea can be reduced to an act of earning absolution through a tangible penance.

According to Steven Black, at the time of her surrender Power was "obsessed with a desire to be punished, to seek expiation,"[4] an observa-tion that lends credibility more specifically to the purgatorial-suffering hypothesis, indeed to the extreme version posited by my early reader. In our first interview, I asked Power whether her guilty plea might have been influenced by a wish to be punished through suffering. This was her response: "No. I'll tell you something . . . If I pursued this really uncom-fortable course out of the sense that I deserved to be punished, I would say that that's a piece I've worked on in therapy since and have a healthier relationship with."

So, at least at the beginning and at least in part, something like a "Catholic-guilt"-driven need for suffering had factored into her guilty plea.* But she had come to view such thinking as neurotic.

Immediately after repeating to me Sandy's inference about her "little Catholic conscience," Power continued:

---

*She never used the word "purification" or any of their variants, so that specific aspect of the purgatorial hypothesis (suffering in order to be purified) was not substan-tiated.

KP: What I can tell you is this: I could have pleaded not guilty.

JL: Yes, you could have, and they might not have had a case.

KP: I know. In 1986, the *Boston Globe*—

JL: Why didn't you?

KP: —carried an interview with the . . . with Ralph Martin's predecessor in which he was quoted as saying he would not want to have to try this case.

JL: Yes, I've heard that a couple of times, that they said they knew they didn't have a case on you.

At this point, instead of answering my question, she kept interrupting to make sure I understood she had a good chance of acquittal had she gone to trial. And yet, in emphasizing the "out" she had waived, Power might have been answering my question. She might have been saying once again that a wish for extreme self-punishment *had* taken its place in a twisted tangle of motives. It's not so unusual, after all, for decent people, Catholic or not, to feel intuitively that suffering is required to rectify one's serious transgressions.

In any case, impatient to get on with it, I asked her point-blank: "So why *did* you plead guilty and choose to be put in prison?" Her answer:

KP: Because how could I . . . it was an act of redemption, not for the events of 23 years ago, . . God, I am just realizing at this moment as I answer this: it was an act of redemption for my dishonesty with the people I had to lie to in my fugitive life, the declaration in action that I understood the importance of authenticity, honesty, owning up, speaking, in order . . . in order to be, in order to be somebody that anybody could trust ever. I thought . . . that people would be very angry and very hurt that I was not what I seemed. What I didn't know is that they weren't confused, and I was exactly what I seemed; but I think part of that, part of why they know that is because I insisted on plead-ing guilty. How could they trust me [if I hadn't]? How could they not assume some sleazy level of inability to be honest and to act with integrity if I had said, "Oh, maybe I did it and maybe I didn't do it. What can you prove?"

There is a lot to attend to in this response. Clearly, she considered it a matter of integrity to admit her guilt. I was initially quite taken with her way of putting the alternative—"Oh, maybe I did it and maybe I didn't do it. What can you prove?"— and I quoted it many times.[5] Later it occurred to me how this riff also drove home how virtuous it was to forgo trial.

Choosing to explain her guilty plea using that "act of redemption" phrase, with repetition, might plausibly reflect Power's Catholic upbring-ing—except that what she said here isn't remotely Catholic, or even reli-gious. She said she pleaded guilty to set right her personal relationships (e.g., with her son, parents, friends, neighbors, and colleagues). She pleaded guilty to expunge the deceptions about who she was, her very identity, that had tainted her relationships with those she cared about— and to earn back their trust. The fact that this jibes with what appears to me to be her primary motive for surrendering adds to its credibility.

Now, for the part I did not see coming—that *not*-phrase. Her guilty plea, she said, was an "act of redemption, *not for the events of 23 years ago . . . .*" At first, I had skimmed over this phrase, thinking she had mis-spoken, that she must have meant to say "not *only* for the events of 23 years ago." Trouble is, Power typically expresses herself clearly and accu-rately. On two separate occasions in the first interview, she misspoke and immediately corrected herself.* Also here again she fell back on the fuzzy

---

*(1) She stopped midstream to revise the grammatical error of a misplaced modifi-er: "I try to use language that *both* affirms . . . affirms *both* the possibility and the require-ment of redemption." (2) She revised on the spot an instance of simple misspeaking (which will come up again later): "You know, the thing about suffering is . . . people who are addicted to suffering . . . no, to *comfort* . . . People who are addicted to comfort. . . ."

phrase for her crimes that had marred her surrender statement two years earlier: "the events of 23 years ago"—except this time there was no need for lawyer-speak to keep things vague. How else to take the *not*-phrase than that she had *not* pleaded guilty to redeem herself for her part in the murder of Walter Schroeder?

We can all admire Power's wish to redeem her relationships with those she loved by finally telling the truth about herself. But for her to state that she had not pleaded guilty to redeem herself for her crimes— that seemed to defy both logic and ethics. It seemed to directly conflict with her guilty plea and with what I knew about meritorious ethical development. And yet. This wasn't the first time I had heard this. Other statements in which she had rejected guilt as her reason for surrendering had appeared in the media, and I had come to the interview prepared to clear up what I was sure were mis-quotes. So I asked her directly about the issue of guilt, starting with this interchange (which takes up at a point when she was discussing what she felt she owed to young people):

> KP: To be transparent. It *is* their right. And it's not martyrdom and it's not masochism and it's not guilt . . . .

> JL: It's not guilt? That interests me, what you mean by that exactly . . . . What's wrong with a little guilt? But you say it's *not* guilt. And . . . Ron [her husband] was quoted . . . I don't know whether he was quoted accurately, but some places saying that you didn't turn yourself in out of guilt . . . . One question is what did Ron mean and what do you mean when you—*if* you—say that you didn't return out of guilt? And then, secondly, *is* this a journey of expiation of guilt? Are you seeking forgiveness . . . when you talk about redemption?

> KP: Let's talk about *whose* forgiveness. When Ron says this is not an act motivated by guilt, I think that's a way of saying what I have said in other contexts—that I have lived my *life* as a penitent. I didn't have to come to prison. I did not have to surrender.

But how could she think, after all these years, that she did not have to do prison time, that she could do all her expiating in private? How could she still think that she got to decide what her penance should be and how much was enough? Fortunately, she had much more to say on the subject of her guilt:

> KP: I will say—I'm too stupid to be afraid—I will say that I do not regard the justice system of this country as a legitimate authority. It is not [inaudible phrase due to loud singing in background] legitimate to judge me, because it would not judge Robert McNamara,* Westmoreland,** all of them. William Calley*** spent two years in house arrest. Steven Black has medals on the wall. I owe the criminal justice system nothing. I owe God, myself, and the human community, but I don't owe the criminal justice system. In that sense, you could say that I continue to be an outlaw. I think it's really an important thing to say, although it's frightening, and it's very much why Robert Banks imposed what was meant to be a lifelong gag order on me [the "special condition" forbidding Power from profiting from writing or telling her story, under penalty of life imprisonment].

I confess I was taken aback—and bewildered. She believed—strongly, judging by the repetition—that her crimes required no expiation of a legal nature: "I didn't have to come to prison." But wasn't this at odds with her having pleaded guilty two years earlier, knowing that doing so would put her in a prison cell for years?

Several years after that first interview, for the first time I "saw" Katherine Power in the courtroom where she had pleaded guilty. She,

---

*Robert McNamara was Secretary of Defense during the early period of peak escalation of the Vietnam War, from 1961 to 1967.

**General Westmoreland, the very hawkish Commander of U.S. forces in Vietnam from 1964 to 1967, kept demanding and getting more and more troops and more and more bombs.

***William Calley supervised and avidly participated in the My Lai massacre, the slaughter of over 500 Vietnamese women, infants, and old men.

her physical personage, appeared in filmed footage in the documentary film *Forgiveness: A Time to Love and a Time to Hate*. There she was in that Boston courtroom, defiance written in the forward jut of her jaw and all over her face, body, and carriage.[6] She looked for all the world like a still-angry revolutionary there to get this damn thing over with.* She looked bitter beyond words that prison was part of the package deal required for her to live an honest and authentic life. So bitter that two years into her prison sentence she was telling me that there was no positive reason for it. Notably, at that juncture she made no mention of the murdered man or his family.

At a different point in the same interview she repeated her denunciation of the justice system, elaborating on her view of her responsibility for the murder. She was describing her reaction upon learning of the death of Walter Schroeder:

KP: At that moment, I had to say, "How did I bring this damage? How . . . What responsibilities do I have to take for this damage that came from my hands?"

JL: *What* responsibilities?

KP: To become nonviolent, to be peace, to understand the origins of war-making, to . . .

JL: To take on an 8-to-12-year prison sentence?

KP: You know the difference between the temporal realm and the spiritual realm? The temporal realm says that I have to take that sentence on. It's about power. Robert McNamara doesn't have to take that sentence on and I do. The temporal power is fraudulent and immoral. I have to go along with it because it isn't right for me to live as an outlaw. It's what I have to do.

---

*Had I seen this footage before that interview, my overly favorable preconception of her surrender would have collapsed back then.

On one hand, Power was acknowledging her personal responsibility for "this damage that came from [her] hands." On the other, in that last sentence she was emphasizing that the reason she had submitted to the prison sentence was to do right by herself. What came across perfectly plainly that day was Power's reasoning for despising the criminal justice system. "It's about power," she said. This temporal-realm power had exempted the managers and slaughterers of the Vietnam War, but not her, from punishment for their war crimes. She came perilously close at this point to portraying herself as a political prisoner.

These statements also help clarify the question of why Power chose to forgo trial. That decision, it appears, represented, along with the other explanations I will set out in this chapter, a personal revolt against the criminal justice system. By pronouncing herself guilty, she pre-empted the opportunity for that system to sit in judgment of her.

One can agree with Power's objections to the fact that agents of the Vietnam War, especially those known to have committed atrocities, got off scot-free for the murders that came from their hands. In fact, when the International Criminal Tribunal was established in the Hague in 1993, Robert McNamara's name often came up as an example of an American who deserved to be tried there as a war criminal.* In his *Washington Post*[7] essay prompted by Power's surrender, Todd Gitlin made reference to, without coming right out and naming names, "high-level war criminals . . . still lionized in Washington."[8] Everyone knew who he meant.

I don't accept, however, Power's corollary about herself. In my view, Mr. McNamara, General Westmoreland, and the others should be held

---

*In the 2004 documentary film about McNamara, *The Fog of War,* McNamara spoke about his experiences as a soldier in World War II. He volunteered the idea that, had the U.S. been defeated by the Japanese, he and his commanding officer would have been—and "*should* have been"—"tried as war criminals" for their firebombing of Japanese cities. Mr. McNamara had to have been aware of all the war-criminal talk swirling around him in the 1990s. Therefore it is hard for me not to read McNamara's confession of his "war-criminal" role in World War II as a displaced and not-so-veiled admission of guilt for his role in the Vietnam War.

accountable for the deaths* they brought about in Vietnam without ever personally firing a gun or dropping a bomb—just as Power should be held accountable for a death she helped bring about without personally entering a bank or using a gun. Justice was not served when William Calley was sentenced to two years of house arrest—any more than justice would have been served had Power evaded prison altogether. One travesty of justice does not justify another.

Power handed herself over to a criminal justice system she considered fraudulent, immoral, and illegitimate, because, in her words, "it isn't right for me to live as an outlaw." "Right": as in the spiritual realm. "Me": as in mother, daughter, friend, citizen, member of the human community, and child of God. "Outlaw." Twice she chose that word—"it isn't right for me to live as an outlaw" and "you could say that I continue to be an outlaw." Why? Why not "fugitive from justice?" It may be that at that time Power was still attached to her self-concept as an outlaw. In declaring that the defiant heart of an outlaw continued to beat inside her, "in that sense" she got to keep that self-dramatizing sense of self—at least for the time being.

Examined from an ethical perspective, we see that, although Power had surrendered and pleaded guilty, two years later she still could not admit (could not understand?) that to have continued fleeing the charges of manslaughter and armed robbery would quite simply have been unjust.

***

Katherine Power has a fairly uncommon way of thinking about justice, and that thinking helps explain how she could surrender herself to a criminal justice system she so despised. It's called *restorative justice*, and it downplays the value of prison.

Power had heard about restorative justice before her surrender from a friend in Oregon who worked with a victim/offender reconciliation

---

*To reiterate: the estimates are that some 58,000 Americans and well over three million Vietnamese were killed.

program. "As soon as I heard the phrase from her mouth," Power told me, "I knew there was something there for me."[9] In Howard Zehr's book *Changing Lenses,* she found out what restorative justice offered her. It was tailor-made for her sensibilities and her needs. However, it stands in polar opposition to *retributive* justice, which holds sway in this culture.

In contrast to the punishment-centered tenets of retributive justice, the restorative justice approach centers on repair and reform. It tries to bring the "victim, the offender, and the community [together] in a search for solutions which promote repair, reconciliation, and reassurance."[10] Truth and Reconciliation Commissions (e.g., in South Africa and Rwanda) exemplify the restorative justice approach. Such commissions, though by now familiar, were unknown in 1993, as the first one was called in 1995 in South Africa.

In the U.S. retribution-centered criminal justice system, Power was accountable to submit to its punishment[11]—in her case, a prison sentence of over six years, 20 years' probation, and the "special condition" preventing her from profiting from telling her story. In the restorative justice approach, the offender is accountable to reform herself, and the purpose of prison is not punishment but rehabilitation.

Second, from the perspective of the criminal justice system, Power's crimes engendered a debt to an abstract entity, the State. As viewed by Power through the restorative justice lens, her crimes created highly concrete obligations.[12] "I owe God, myself, and the human community," she told me. She rejected the idea that she owed the State anything. Her priority was to try to repair the people and relationships she had harmed.[13] Here I am reminded of what E. M. Forster once wrote: "If I had to choose between betraying my country and betraying my friend, I hope I should have the guts to betray my country."[14]

Power's allegiance to restorative justice informs her thinking about guilt, as we see in the following discussion, which resumes my attempt to understand what she meant by saying she did not return out of guilt.

KP: Let me talk about guilt.

There's an important difference between guilt and responsibility that I'd like to draw. Guilt is emotion. Guilt is . . . I don't see guilt as transforming. Guilt seems to me that it implies irredeemability . . . and so I try to use language that both affirms . . . affirms both the possibility and the requirement of redemption. Guilt as it's commonly used in culture, "Oh . . . I'm horrible" . . . is—

JL: I thought you were going to say "mea culpa, mea culpa, through my fault. . ."

KP: "Through my fault" is a world of difference from "Oh, I'm terrible." "Through my fault" means that I have to do something. The purpose of feeling bad is to be moved to do the hard work of change . . . .

JL: But when you say guilt—and emotion—is worthless or can be worthless in the conscience work, I guess . . . I see regret—and guilt too—as motivators to change . . . . Nothing motivates often better than bad feelings.

KP: Exactly.

JL: So if you just . . . you need to linger with the bad feelings long enough to figure out: what do I change.

KP: Exactly. It's like . . . okay . . . all emotions . . . carry information to us; they make use of our body to carry important information to our consciousness . . . . The value of [guilt], like the value of all emotions, is to sit with them to get the information from them and to use that information as the fuel, the energy, to change . . . is not useless. Being *trapped* in guilt is useless. So, it becomes a shorthand then when we say, let's talk about *responsibility* rather than talking about guilt. It's to be *stuck* in guilt [that is useless]. . . .

Now what does it mean to be responsible? Does it mean that I'm going to be a person, a worthless person forever? Of course not. I'm not a worthless person now, and I never was.

Ah. When Power said she had not chosen prison out of guilt, she was not denying her responsibility. She was rejecting an emotion that she felt had sucked her down into a sinkhole of worthlessness, thereby impeding her felt responsibility to change herself. In addition, while in her mind it was guilt that had been telling her "I'm horrible," technically it was shame. Remember, the defining feature of shame is that it points the accusing finger at one's very self, as opposed to guilt, which focuses more on one's acts than on oneself.[15]

The rest of her statement shows that she very much took to heart a definition of guilt that stressed personal accountability to specific persons: "My mother says to me, leave guilt behind; you are forgiven. And I say, wait a minute. I say, I will *always* be answerable. I will *always* be answerable to a set of human beings who were hurt by the acts of my life."

When Power's mother, in motherly fashion, advised her to call off guilt, Power declined this counsel, and turned the conversation to the restorative justice concepts of responsibility and accountability. *This* sense of guilt Power embraces, going so far as to assert—accurately, I believe—that she can and should never exempt herself from her obligations to those she harmed. She did not repudiate guilt. She lived and breathed it, as she lived and breathed the air of restorative justice.

***

The *Portland Oregonian* carried Power's first public statement about why she had refused a trial; there she said that she "didn't want the divisiveness of a trial that was sure to be politicized."[16] I had initially understood her to be referring to the potential for a trial to stir up national passions about the Vietnam War—that war which had ended some 20 years earlier but was not over and done with.[17] Because I assumed I understood what she meant, I did not ask her about it when I interviewed her. As I got to know her, however, I came to believe that she would have pretty much shrugged off reproaches resulting from national debate over the Vietnam War. What she could not so easily have shrugged off were certain local, relational, and personal reproaches.

A trial would definitely have brought to the surface and intensified polarizations in local communities. The crowd amassed outside the Boston courtroom the day of Power's sentencing, for instance, was "passionately divided over the sentence, some pronouncing it too severe and others too lenient."[18] Squared off against those who considered her sentence too severe were representatives of the local law enforcement community, which when she surrendered included four of Walter Schroeder's children. This division overlapped with class differences—or perceived class differences—making for an especially caustic clash. I don't know whether the depth or intensity of these Boston-based tensions had registered with Power in 1992 when, sitting in the office of her defense lawyer some 3000 miles from Boston, she was making the decision to surrender. I do know that, as a result of doing her prison time in Massachusetts, she would have become aware of the local divisions by 1994 when she spoke to the *Oregonian*.

Besides these local threats, with her guilty plea she pre-empted certain personal and relational threats. Steven Black's hopes to reassure Power through his mock trial had backfired, sensitizing her to the possibility of getting beaten up in a trial. As he told me, she mistrusted the criminal justice system so much that he could not persuade her to go through with one. She had to have known in 1992 when she was making this decision that, under the floodlights of courtroom and media, a trial would have meant thorough interrogations of her 1970 motives and criminal acts. And she wasn't ready for this—not even in private. She would have wanted to spare her family and friends—and herself—these ordeals. Nor would she have wanted to be questioned under oath about those who had aided her in her underground life. I believe that in Power's mind a trial represented a plunge into unwanted exposure.

Some years after her surrender, an aha moment struck me when I first heard, really heard, the phrase "plea deal." Suddenly I saw it all very differently. It took, after all, more than a year of tough negotiating between her lawyers and Boston and federal authorities for both sides to agree on the terms of her plea. During that year, she had bargained for the best deal she could get (which included, for instance, the government's agreement to drop federal charges against her in connection with a Philadelphia bank robbery committed 22 days before the one in Boston).[19] Eventually I realized that, rather than "waiving a right," Power was waiving a danger, a many-headed danger.

***

One final question about Power's guilty plea. She pleaded guilty not to felony murder, which technically all five in the group were chargeable with, but manslaughter. Why?

Again, in those states, such as Massachusetts, with felony murder laws, anyone who was engaged in a felony (e.g., armed robbery) during which someone is killed is guilty of felony murder. Under the felony murder law, the person driving the getaway switch car is as guilty as the trigger man. Many laypeople and legal experts consider the felony murder rule fundamentally unjust. In fact, as a reliable legal website notes, it may be on its way out: "The future of the felony-murder rule is in doubt. Some jurisdictions have abolished the rule and others continue to limit its application."[20] When Susan Saxe was tried on felony murder, the jury deadlocked. According to the *Wall Street Journal*, "most jurors reportedly voted for acquittal."[21] This outcome testifies to how problematic people find the concept of felony murder. (In a second trial, this time on the charge of manslaughter, Saxe pleaded guilty.*) Only Gilday, the shooter, was convicted of murder.

If not felony murder, could Power have been charged as an accessory before or after the fact, an accomplice, or at least aiding and abetting? Under the law, Power's participation does not meet the defining criteria for any of these charges.

One of the readers who wrote the *Boston Globe* that her sentence was too harsh argued: "Katherine Power was an accessory . . . and not a participant in the murder. I think a shorter sentence is more appropriate . . . ."[22] However, Power's acts fail to correspond with the legal definition of *accessory* either before or after the crime, in that she did not "with knowledge" of Gilday's intent or [later] his guilt, do anything "to hinder the felon['s] detection, arrest, trial or punishment."[23]

Nor could she have legally been charged as an *accomplice* of Gilday in murder. She did not "knowingly, voluntarily, and with common interest, participate in the commission of [Gilday's] crime," and, absent the felony murder rule, could "not be charged with the same crime"—murder— which Gilday committed.[24]

She couldn't even be charged with *aiding and abetting*, in that "mere knowledge about the crime or presence at the scene will not suffice."[25]

Steven Black defined manslaughter for me thus:

Manslaughter is a kind of homicide—homicide being basically murder, taking someone's life. Manslaughter is inadvertent, unpremeditated, unintentional. . . . If you hit somebody with your car as part of an accident, and you did that by running a red light . ., then you're guilty of manslaughter because you clearly did not intend to kill that person. If you have a plan to kill a particular person, which you do, or a particular group of people, and you carry it out, then that's murder.

---

*Judge Nancy Gertner, who served as Saxe's defense attorney, details Saxe's trials in *In Defense of Women: Memoirs of an Unrepentant Advocate.*

The core commonality is that in both murder and manslaughter someone is killed. The core difference is that murder involves premeditation
or intent but manslaughter doesn't.

The commonwealth of Massachusetts does not draw a statutory dis-
tinction between voluntary and involuntary manslaughter. (The distinc-
tion is grounded only in "common law.") The punishment for the two
situations does not differ. Nor does the standard of proof, which is "that
the defendant knew, or *should have known* that his conduct created a high
degree of likelihood that substantial harm would result to another."[26] [my
emphasis]

When Power explained her manslaughter plea to me, she showed
that she had brought that legal language home and made it her own: "I
pleaded guilty to manslaughter because it's a literal description of the way
that my actions were wrong. *I should have known better*."

In sum, in pleading guilty to manslaughter, Power took the appropriate level of responsibility for her role in the killing of Walter Schroeder.
She should have known better than to engage in armed crimes with
known criminals. When she recognized the dangerousness of her comrades, she should have left.

Inasmuch as she had not put herself in the bank with a gun and
inasmuch as everyone in the group but Gilday was found guilty of manslaughter, for Power to have pleaded guilty to felony murder would have
amounted to excessive self-punishment. Her manslaughter plea affords
further evidence that Power's guilty plea should not be trivialized as a
masochistic infatuation with sackcloth and ashes. Nor, on the other
hand, should this plea, which required her to spend over six years in a
medium-security prison, be understood as giving herself a break. Justice
was served.

***

Power's decision not to contest but to plead guilty to her crimes did represent an ethically pivotal moment. At long last she publicly admitted

her crimes. With her guilty plea she asked—albeit with ambivalence— to expiate her crimes on *society's* terms, not hers. Her guilty plea cannot be reduced to "Catholic guilt." Instead, it enacted multiple goals—to act with honesty and integrity; to repair herself and her close personal relationships; to pre-empt the opportunity for the "fraudulent" criminal justice system to sit in judgment of her; to protect herself and others from unwanted exposure. Forgoing a trial represented, it appears, an act of self-interest more than the act of selfless penitence many of us had initially mistaken it for. She was no saint, but human. "Only" human, as we say—complete with the false starts, the wrong turns, the zigs and zags, the failings and falterings—that go into being human.

CHAPTER 9

REDEEMING TIME:
THE PRISON YEARS

You know, this . . . this is a place where the conscience work goes on . . . . You would not believe, prison is a very holy place—*despite* itself, despite the condemnation of the people that you are, you're irredeemably shit. This is an intensely moral cauldron where people take time out to pay attention to the effects their actions, their sicknesses, their addictions, their brokenness has had on other people—and affirm their intent to change. [emphasis is Power's]

THUS DID KATHERINE POWER DESCRIBE her experience of prison. Yes, this woman bristling with contempt for the criminal justice system is the very same woman who made of prison a holy place. She's a woman of many layers. She was neither passively doing the time nor defiantly crashing up against the prison walls at every turn. She chose to make use of the time, isolation, and break in routine of prison to do what she calls conscience work. The prison time she did, to loosely paraphrase T. S. Eliot,[1] was "redeeming time."

A skeptic might be forgiven for wondering whether Power's talk about intent to change and conscience work amounted to anything more than glittering generalities. Was this talk a fraternal twin to that vague and unconvincing pronouncement often made by transgressors—that they have found Jesus or are otherwise turning their lives around?

When I asked her about the accusations that she was only interested in "personal growth," she told me this: "I do think that the mandatory response to wrongdoing is transformation . . . . If you're bad, you have a responsibility to be good, to become good."

She was animated by a deep sense of responsibility to transform herself ethically. To become good. And that's just for starters. "In the end, in this moment, in every moment . . . I am responsible to be a good person," she said.

This sentence warrants a brief pause. To be a good person "in this moment, in every moment"? As discussed earlier, this would seem to be an exceptionally weighty, in fact an impossible, obligation. For now, I simply want to underscore this as something about Katherine Power worth keeping in mind.

Far from talking in generalities, she was laying out for herself a concrete and original catalog of ethical tasks for *how* to turn her life around. Here are some of the items on her list, some of the conscience work she was requiring of herself:

> KP: The purpose of feeling bad is to be moved to do the hard work of change . . . of breaking habits; of becoming conscious; of becoming aware; of understanding that your comforting myths have flaws, that the world is not as secure and sure as you need it to be. It's scary to do this work, and I'm going to say that the work of conscience *is* the fundamental work of personal growth; that all of the rest of the personal growth work that exists is trivial if it is not sitting on the work of conscience.

> . . . I think that "to be a good person" has to be expanded in a way that Buddhism teaches us, because Christianity and European-derived civilization does not. Christianity took on in its ideology, its worldview, an "Other"—brought it into its worldview. . . . [T]hat's what formed our civilization, and it carries in it the concept of holy war, whereas Buddhism . . . demands that we see suffering and respond to it. And so I say [Buddhism is] a better tool for understanding; it expands us; it takes us past a blind spot in our own culture. The essence of Buddhist nonviolence is that

there is no "Other." That suffering must be acknowledged and responded to in action.

So I think that, by looking outside of what our culture has taught us, we know something really important: if we have caused suffering, that's information to us; we must become sensitive to it. We must take it in, and we must say, what caused that suffering? . . . . Where can I act? Everywhere that I can act is my responsibility.

Sometime during her first two years in prison Power had mapped out a highly specific inventory of what exactly the "hard work of change" would mean for her. A tall, tall order this work. And an extraordinary gift to anyone, criminal or not, concerned with advancing ethical transformation.

The mind, or let's say the Power-Point-trained mind (pun not intended), loves bullet points.* Even though human life is always messier than this format can possibly capture, bullet points do help to disaggregate large or unmanageable sets of material, including the compilation of redemptive tasks discussed by Power:

- taking personal responsibility for her crimes

- becoming aware of and sensitive to the specific ways she had caused suffering to specific human beings

- analyzing how it was that she came to cause such suffering

- figuring out where and how she could take action to relieve that suffering or to make amends

- taking responsibility to reform herself

- abandoning comforting but fallacious myths

- refusing to turn any human beings into "Others"

---

*For greater clarity, I have converted to bullet points words and ideas that were expressed by Power in ordinary conversational language.

- breaking bad habits

- accepting that the world is not as sure a place as she'd like

In her first letter Power wrote me this: "I think that what you're asking about, *how* does the transformation come about . . . is *really* important." For her, this question was anything but academic and her answers anything but glittering generalities. In agreeing to meet with me, she had made herself a working partner in my exploration of the *how*: how a wrongdoer might convert regret, guilt, shame, and remorse into something good.

***

All this talk of sacred places, moral cauldrons, and conscience work sounds very serious—and very religious. And it raises one last "Catholic-guilt" question, a different one from those in the previous chapter and one that can be addressed briefly: that is, whether a need for purgatorial suffering might have applied to the *way* Power served her prison sentence.

At our first meeting, I asked Power whether she had received the draft of my "Crime and Punishment" essay in the mail. She had. I told her I wanted to know what she thought of the analysis—which, among other things, was exploring whether, like the murderer Raskolnikov whom Sonia had converted to an über-penitent, Power might have had an especially strong need for punishment. Laughing, she said that some people at MCI-Framingham had made the same connection. She told me a story about a painstaking painting job she once did as a prisoner:

> I was part of this painting crew, part of this stripping crew, and *I* took on myself the job of scrubbing on hands and knees the *entire* length of the hall, both sides, and oh, the perimeter of one dayroom and the kitchen and another dayroom, and I was on my hands and knees for three days, and it was cause for comment on the part of a couple of people I know. One was the unit counselor, who said: "It's more like Raskolnikov every day!" [Power's emphases]

This self-sketch does nothing to dispel the suspicion that she was seeking excess suffering in prison. Neither does a remark Power's husband, Ron, made about her. When she was first imprisoned, Ron said, his wife had "spent three or four hours a day making collect calls to . . . friends and colleagues."[2] Then some 20 months later, she refused to call anyone except her lawyers—"in protest against a new prison practice of tape-recording all personal calls made by inmates."[3] Ron ascribed Power's decision to an outsized need for punishment, stating in 1994: "'It's so like [her]—the degree of suffering she needs to experience in order to give her act of principle value."[4] It wasn't enough for her to have come forth, thought Ron, she needed to add to the suffering already inherent in prison.

Taken together, these anecdotes portray Power as the very figure of self-flagellation, suggesting the possible validity of the purgatorial suffering hypothesis. I asked her about this directly:

JL: What about the concept . . . the concept of purgatory, the purification of guilt through suffering, where the more suffering, the sooner purified?

KP: You know, the thing about suffering is . . . people who are addicted to suffering . . . no, to *comfort* . . . People who are addicted to comfort, and you must admit that's a theme of our culture, . . . people who are addicted to comfort think that people who experience suffering have sought it out for a purpose. They don't understand that suffering just *is* . . . that suffering is something you put up with because it's the price of something that's important. Discomfort, I mean . . . cold is discomfort. Would I give up playing in the snow? . . . . I have worked hard to recover that encounter with existence that people who are not afraid of discomfort have, and suffering is. I don't seek it, and I don't value it.

JL: Back to what we were just talking about. Something Ron was quoted as saying . . . he was quoted as saying, I think by Lucinda Franks, that you seek out *extra* suffering [here in prison] . . .

KP: It must seem that way. It must seem that way. The pain that I'm going to suffer, the awareness of suffering . . . You know, something hurts somebody that you care about, you [i.e., her husband, Ron] judge it and you want it to go away. It's hard to see why it could be valuable or important. You interpret it in a way that makes sense to you if you were doing it. I know that not everybody feels . . . at least seems to feel, this open to awareness of suffering. I think that comes too in the Catholic background . . . . And . . . you know what? And I still feel the pain, and I still say that it is a priestly function to be willing to sit with the pain.

The purgatorial-suffering hypothesis appears to receive more support here—in Power's "priestly function" phrasing and in her statement that the worldview inculcated in her religious upbringing might help explain the salience of suffering to her. Power, however, rejected the purgatorial-suffering idea that she *sought out* suffering in prison, let alone gratuitous suffering, as a path to redemption. I find her denials credible. For one thing, it is believable that Ron and others were projecting onto her something from within themselves when they imagined that she had a need for surplus suffering. In addition, the way she talked about suffering exhibited nothing excessive or neurotic. Finally, her thinking and language about suffering owed at least as much to Buddhism as to Catholicism.

Central to the Buddhist worldview is the understanding that "suffering just *is*," as Power put it. That is why, according to Buddhist principles, individuals are asked not only to expand their "awareness of suffering" (along with awareness of all life experiences, pleasant and unpleasant), but also to figuratively "sit with" suffering (at least those aspects that one cannot change). In Buddhist practice, often called "sitting practice," individuals *literally* "sit with" their experience—on the meditation cushion, for instance.

Power views suffering through a third lens, as well: a clear-eyed, rational, cost-benefit lens. "I don't seek it," she said, "And I don't value it"—for its own sake. Instead, she accepts suffering if it's the price of something important. She backed up this appraisal with an analogy—putting up with being cold for the pleasure of playing in the snow—a comparison whose very playfulness solidifies for me the sincerity of her stated beliefs. There's not a whiff of purgatory in this analogy.

Power draws on this same line of thinking to explain why she embraced the work of conscience as her responsibility. "In a comfort-addicted culture, the work of conscience is uncomfortable," she said. Nevertheless: "Discomfort is important . . . in the care of the soul . . . . [in] soul work." For Power the rationalist, suffering or "discomfort" (to use her understated choice of words)—the discomfort of prison, the discomfort of conscience work—was the purchase price attached to something she very much wanted: ethical transformation.

What then to make of that scouring on her hands and knees and denying herself those phone calls in prison? Acts alone do not reveal motives, and these acts of Power's could have stemmed from any number of motives other than wishes for purgatorial suffering.

The phone protest might have been stimulated by her longstanding passion for social justice, in this case by a desire to stand in sisterly solidarity with her fellow inmates against this injustice. Or simply to refuse to subject those she spoke with to taping.

The scrubbing could be explained by the love of physical activity and hard physical labor I heard in her happy conversations about lugging those heavy pails of water out to her prison garden and in the pride she took in having worked her way up to 100 push-ups a day. Or maybe she simply wanted to relieve some of the boredom entailed in prison life. In none of these motives would discomfort have been an end in itself.

In sum, a purgatorial-suffering account of either why or how Power chose to do prison time was not supported (except for the early and soon overruled reflex of hers), and the "Five Our Fathers" account of any of it was definitively disconfirmed. Power was not a penitent driven by "Catholic guilt." It was not self-abnegation but redemption she sought.

***

Having laid to rest the last remnant of the "Catholic-guilt" hypotheses, let us return to the matter at hand: that remarkable catalog of redemptive tasks. How did she come up with such a list? Her inspiration came from several of what she referred to as "redemption, [or] transformation, philosophies." Here she discusses three:

> KP: I think that three redemption, transformation, philosophies all say the same thing: . . . . the Christian [Sacrament of] Penance and forgiveness, ... [in which] to be forgiven, you have to . . . go make amends, ask forgiveness, repair the healing tear, intend to sin that sin no more; 12-Step responsibility for your actions and intention to transform your life, *commitment* to transform your life; and therapy's understanding "where does that come from in me?" [emphasis is Power's]

The only treatment program with a demonstrable track record of helping people actually free themselves from the moral ruin of addiction is Alcoholics Anonymous (and its variants), and the 12-Step Program is its transformative pathway. As Power recognized, the transformative value of the 12-Step Program extends beyond addiction to include other failings. As for psychotherapy, research, including some of my own, has clearly established its efficacy, as well.[5] Of course we have no data about how well the sacrament succeeds in producing moral transformation.

In her ruminations during her first two years in prison, Power had noticed how much these approaches overlap:

> KP: In all three, the demand on you is to become responsible, to become *aware* that it's not okay to hurt people, to become *aware* that your actions have hurt people, to transform yourself to prevent that recurring in the future. So all three of them are intensely positive. [emphases are Power's]

Both the Sacrament of Penance and the 12-Step Program are built on a foundation of awareness of and honesty about one's wrongdoings. And both oblige wrongdoers to admit those wrongdoings to someone else. In

Step 5 people must admit to "God, to [them]selves and another human being the exact nature of [their] wrongs." In the sacrament, too, one must confess to a human being, but in this case a certain kind of human being, a priest, who according to Church doctrine is functioning as God's representative on earth.

In several ways, however, the 12-Step Program seems to demand rather more of people. Telling one's sins to a priest, for instance, strikes me as far less daunting than confessing to an ordinary human being you have hurt. After all, hearing such revelations is part of the job description of priests. Plus, they are bound to secrecy. Similarly, where the 12-Step Program requires wrongdoers to specify the "exact nature" of their offenses, in my admittedly dated experience with the sacrament, wrongdoers get away with confessing sins that are more or less generic, as in: "I lied once, I took the Lord's name in vain about a dozen times, and I had impure thoughts about fifty times." At this still somewhat early stage of her ethical transformation, it appears that Power had acknowledged that her acts as a revolutionary and a fugitive had hurt a number of people. It could be said that in pleading guilty to armed robbery and manslaughter Power was admitting the exact nature of her wrongs. On the other hand, it could be said that these confessions are also somewhat generic, compared with acknowledging *each specific wrong move* that brought her to the driver's seat of the getaway switch car.

Perhaps most important of all, making "direct amends" to the people they have harmed, the onus of Step 9, has no built-in counterpart in the sacrament. It does correspond, though, to the piece of conscience work Power articulated for herself as *"figuring out where and how [she] could take action to relieve the suffering"* she had caused. It should be noted that Step 9's mandate to make direct amends comes with a remarkably wise and humane caveat: "*except* when to [make amends to those one has harmed] would injure them or others." The Schroeder family might have declined mediation with Power in part because they had suffered fatal harm from her acts and anticipated that personal contact would only cause them further harm. I didn't get the impression that Power saw it this way, at least not early in her prison sentence.

Therapy, the third transformative practice from which Power drew, is where she had first turned when she broke down in 1992. Later she actively participated (at times with her family of origin) in the psycho-therapy offered in prison, which she assessed as surprisingly high in qual-ity. But therapy is a two-way street. If asked, her therapist might have attributed the excellence of Power's therapy to her uncommon openness to doing the tough inner work. In addition, Power understood how *not* to use therapy. She was not there for warm and fuzzy reassurances, a piece of wisdom she expresses in this interchange:

> KP: Too often, the work of therapy is an *evasion* of the work of conscience. It's about self-comfort . . . [my emphasis]
>
> JL: Saying, "I'm okay."
>
> KP: That's right.

Therapy offered a safe place to do the work of making conscious the exact nature of her wrongdoings and the suffering they had caused—and to thoroughly scrutinize these issues in the company of another human being, this one a trained listener. It was the place to tackle the related and painful pieces of conscience work that she articulated as *"analyzing how it was that [I] came to cause such suffering,"* identifying the *threads that led* to her trans-gressions, and uncovering the sources of *the violence in her.* Working such questions so close to the bone is, as she well knew, anything but a feel-good matter. As we saw in Chapter 7, at her surrender and at the two-year point in her prison sentence, Power was still flinching from questions about the personal sources of her crimes. I suspect that part of the work of therapy entailed her quieting down the tyrannical conscience that would deter her from admitting that she was then or had ever been less than perfect.

Power didn't discuss with me this personal quality of carrying violence within herself beyond telling me about her violent father. I imagine, though, that she might have discussed this more extensively with her therapist. Perhaps at some point she reflected on the first time she felt the cold heft of a gun in her own hand and the first time she fired one. If so, she would have had to confront parts of herself that had come alive then—rage, defiance, and desires to prove herself as a badass outlaw, for instance.

There are other relevant transformative philosophies besides these identified by Power, including one developed by 20th-century British philosopher Joanna North.[6] In North's framework, genuine repentance requires a wrongdoer to live out a three-stage set of processes. In the first (two-part) phase, the wrongdoer "recognizes that he has done wrong . . . [and] recognizes the injured party's right to punish."[7] Next, the wrongdoer "experiences 'other-oriented' regret or remorse for the wrong."[8] The final tasks include: "resolv[ing] to reform, [and] undergo[ing] a process of reframing" herself.[9]

So closely does Power's thinking tally with North's, it is almost as if Power had read North's work. (She hadn't.) Conversely, North's model has the benefit of specifying cardinal elements of Power's conscience work that Power hadn't brought up—namely, experiencing regret that is primarily other-oriented and reframing one's self-conception.

There is no doubt that by her second year in prison Power had already taken the first step to self-reform specified by North (and by the 12-Step Program and the Sacrament of Penance): that is, she *recognized that she had done wrong:*

KP: My own experience led me to know nonviolence is mandated. War is not okay . . . .

JL: So guerrilla war against, in order to stop State war is not okay.

KP: It's not okay . . . . when I saw the consequences, it became my moral obligation to know that, and from that moment I became committed to nonviolence.

Too late, but immediately upon learning of Walter Schroeder's murder, she recognized how wrong she had been to participate in violent crime. She turned away from violence and committed herself to nonviolence. She has steadfastly kept faith with that commitment.

Conversely, Power's fugitive years testify to a two-decade long refusal to *acknowledge the right of the injured party to punish her.* This transformative task came with a couple of hitches for Power. For one thing, punishment is not something she values—in any realm, whether childrearing or criminology. Part of her attraction to the restorative justice philosophy lay in its rejection of her culture's emphasis on seeing wrongdoers punished. Besides, she had convinced herself she had been punished enough, having lived her whole life as a penitent. Finally, during her fugitive years, she had probably had dreadful punishments meted out to her, at least in private, by that whip-wielding superego of hers. Still, society and the Schroeder family had a right to have her punished in the socially sanctioned way.

Another stumbling block for her was the question of who the "injured party" is. From Power's perspective, as we have seen, it was definitely not the criminal justice system, and she angrily rejected its right to punish her. Although everyone, including Power, would agree that Officer Schroeder had suffered the worst injuries, his right to punish is sadly moot. But it was important to his family that Power undergo the punishment of time behind bars. Again, one would assume that her plea deal, negotiated before her surrender with the input of the Schroeder family, would have spelled out to Power in neon lights the Schroeders' right to see her punished. But it hadn't, at least not in a straightforward way. Not at her surrender. And not two years later when I first talked with her. For all these reasons, at this point in her ethical trajectory Power fell short on the transformation criterion of acknowledging the right of anyone (but herself) to punish her.

No surprise then, Power's other omission from her redemptive inventory: the rehabilitative element North calls *other-oriented regret*.[10] As I have said earlier, I have no doubt that she experienced genuine regret and remorse for Walter Schroeder's death. But I do have doubts how other-oriented were her pre-surrender attempts to effect mediation with the Schroeders. Otherwise, how to explain her failure in her surrender statement to say anything at all about the great damage perpetrated on the family left behind by the murder of Officer Schroeder? As we have seen, self-focus saturated her surrender statement. Because I talked with Power over the last four years of her prison sentence, however, I am able to track how her thinking about these issues evolved. And evolve it did.

In our first interview I asked Power what she had hoped for from the mediation process. Her response exemplifies the openness she had mentioned in her surrender statement as one of her ethical duties:

> KP: I would listen to that process and its outcome, whatever that was.

> JL: What kinds of things did you have in mind?

> KP: If the mediation process said, the really right way for you to make amends is to be quiet and humble . . . I'd say okay. I'd trust that process.

This last part of her response reflects an understanding I don't think she had at her surrender. By her second year in prison, Power had begun to understand how much her flashy surrender had compounded the suffering of the Schroeder family, and she would have loved to be able to undo that damage—by being "quiet and humble." Her sympathies were beginning to expand to include her living victims.

She was going to need all the openness she could muster to make good on the penultimate phase of moral reclamation outlined in North's model: *reforming oneself.** At her surrender Power had promised only a weak-tea version of reform: "to live with full authenticity." Two years later, however, she spoke explicitly and often about needing to transform herself, as in: "If you're bad, you have a responsibility to be good, to become good." The set of transformative tasks Power laid out for herself constituted her personal blueprint for how to reform herself.

Reframing, the final stage of transformation according to North's model, means changing how one thinks of oneself, changing one's self-conception.[11] She was going to have to undergo painfully honest self-interrogation to acknowledge and absorb hard truths regarding what in her character had made her think it was right to run around with criminals committing armed robberies and other violent crimes. As we have seen, when I asked her directly at our first interview what it was about *her* that had led to her crimes, her response was on the whole defensive. Worse, it appears that she was taking the defiant stance I will paraphrase as "I'm basically OK but this bogus legal system insists on its selective and barbaric form of punishment." Other parts of her, however, knew she was not OK. Otherwise, she could not have put this item in her compendium of redemptive tasks: *purging the violence that was in herself.* That she was able to admit, even obliquely, that her crimes had stemmed from violence within herself demonstrated progress in reframing two years into her prison sentence.

In the following interview passage, Power expands on the process of reframing as she understood it (without labeling it as such). These thoughts were informed by Senate hearings going on at the time concerning a controversial decision made by a Cabinet member, which resulted in unforeseen deaths. (The particulars are not relevant to her point— although it is notable that the incident being critiqued involved the use

---

*As with so many stage theories, the posited *sequence* of North's theory fails to match the real-life sequence shown by Power. As for me, I generally favor keeping babies whose bathwater gets thrown out.

of violence.) As Power recounted it, somebody involved in the hearings was dismissing the analysis as "nothing but hindsight," while someone else took it seriously. She was so struck by the latter's response that she quoted it to me:

> KP: Of *course* this is about hindsight. Hindsight is what decent people apply to events like that so that they will never happen again. That's the work of conscience. [Power's emphasis]

> JL: Kierkegaard said that life is lived forwards and understood backwards.

> KP: Exactly, and if you do not carry that, if you don't do the work of that understanding, carry it into your present, what you carry into your present, and therefore into your future, is callous, blind damaging of other people. *I will never put behind me what I've done. It shapes me.* The degree to which I have a conscience is the degree to which *it shapes me.* [my emphases]

By this time Power knew it would be wrong—and futile—to keep trying, as she had during her fugitive years, to put behind her the transgressions of her past. She knew that it was time, past time, to look back, that looking back was fundamental to her conscience work. By this time she was able to own up to the parts of her past in which she had been guilty of a lethal form of "callous, blind damaging of other people." Refusing to dismiss this as mere hindsight, she understood that she had to bring into her present the worst of her past, to the point that it would reshape who she saw when she looked in the mirror. Again, she had never read North, but allowing hindsight to shape her is synonymous with reframing.

On April 5, 1998, in a one-hour edition of a Boston-area cable TV program "Murphy's Law," attorney Bob Ahearn conducted a prison interview with Power. The program aired on the Community Television station in Milton, Massachusetts. In this interview, Power spoke again about the value of hindsight and of digesting the worst parts of herself:

"In a sense, you could say I tried to forget what I'd done in my life. I tried to put it away. But you know, we just *can't* forget. The real work is we have to incorporate it into who we are. We have to take it into the future of our lives." Here Power brought to life another defining feature of reframing. She had to incorporate her crimes and their horrific outcome into her sense of self. And she knew it.

Power appears ever so close to accomplishing this final task of moral rehabilitation posited by North's philosophical model. But, if measured only by what she said here to me and to Bob Ahearn, she hadn't quite arrived. Before anything can really be incorporated into who we know ourselves to be, we have to be able to call it by its name. Full reframing would require her to go beyond the vague "what I'd done in my life" or even "callous, blind damaging of other people." Full reframing would require the moral fortitude to *name the awful specifics of what she had done—and* more painfully, *the awful specifics of who she had been.*

In sum, two years into her prison sentence Power had made significant progress on certain aspects of North's philosophical model of moral reclamation: acknowledging that she had done wrong and resolving to reform herself. She had begun to develop other-oriented regret for her crimes and to reframe who she was in light of those crimes. Contrariwise, she had out-and-out rejected one of the two elements identified only by North and not by herself: that is, acknowledging the right of the State to punish her. Despite mixed scores on North's measures, without question she was taking seriously the ethical responsibility to transform herself.

∗∗∗

What Power meant by the redemptive task that she had called *relinquishing false but cherished myths* was at first a mystery to me. Upon reflection, I identified four such myths: those in which she had regarded moral self-righteousness, guerrilla warfare, martyrdom, and clandestine action as virtues.

She had embarked upon her series of "revolutionary actions" during the summer of 1970 in part out of moral outrage about the Vietnam War. Like so many of us back then, she steeped herself in moral outrage, she stewed and steamed herself in it. The myth of the unquestionable probity of moral outrage, I would argue, held pride of place in her ability to rationalize turning to violence.

In a 2001 letter, Power wrote that she had come to understand exactly why acting from moral outrage, or rather moral self-righteousness, is "wrong and dangerous": namely, because it means acting out of "blindness."[12] To indulge moral outrage is, among other things, to blind oneself to means-vs.-ends complexities. But refusing to attend to complexities like these corrupts the conscience. From the false heights of moral self-righteousness, it is all too easy to convince ourselves that, as paragons of morality, we cannot possibly do wrong. From this conviction, this myth, it is but a short plunge to perdition. Power's moral self-righteousness had permitted her to, of all things, take up arms as a holy way to protest war.

"My Journey to Nonviolence." This was Power's title for a 45-minute talk she gave (with no notes) on October 5, 1999, three days after completing her prison sentence. Delivered in the chapel at Babson College in Wellesley, Massachusetts, at my invitation, it was an educational talk for students, faculty, and staff, not open to the public. The chapel was packed, and she transfixed the audience. Among other things, she spoke about how in 1970 she had bought into the romance of violence and the belief that "going to war against war" was a sacred duty. The problem, Power said in that chapel, is that whenever we go to war, "someone's father dies." Too late, she had understood the concept of holy war for what it is: an oxymoron. That myth died with Walter Schroeder.

Third, and tied in with the previous myth, is the myth of noble martyrdom. We already know plenty about Power's lives-of-the-saints-based attraction to martyrdom.[13] Back in 1970, when she realized that she might be putting her life in danger through her criminal activities, she accepted that possibility, because in her mind she would be dying a noble death for a noble cause. Years later, in prison, Power critically assessed her willingness to die a martyr's death as a distortion stemming from early religious teachings and a concurrent suicidal level of depression.

The myth of the virtue of clandestine action is a fourth one Power wrestled down. As discussed earlier, rather than take on a role as spokesperson for the antiwar movement, she thought it would be, in her words, "morally superior" to choose action where she "had to stay hidden, where [she] could not be *known*."

By 2001 (if not before), Power had wholly repudiated the myth of the virtue of clandestine action. Far from morally superior, she wrote me, clandestine action is morally wrong, because "clandestinity creates a closed system where you remove yourself from accountability." And: "Civil disobedience includes a willingness to be held accountable by the whole society—law enforcement and citizenry."[14] We know how, even two years into her prison sentence, Power was condemning the law enforcement system as immoral and therefore illegitimate. Some six years later she had come to view this system as a legitimate societal authority to which dissenters must always hold themselves accountable. As Dr. King wrote in his Letter from Birmingham Jail: "One who breaks an unjust law must do it openly, lovingly, . . . and with a willingness to accept the penalty."[15] Power's rejection of this particular myth demonstrates her unequivocal rejection not only of her months as a clandestine domestic terrorist but also her years as a fugitive from justice.

Seeing through to the falsity of these myths represents hard-won ethical achievements. Perhaps it goes without saying, but I would like to say it just in case: none of these changes means that Power now advocates inaction in the presence of injustice. Rather, as she now understands, social action must always be responsible, nonviolent, open, and accountable.

***

Self-interrogation that ends in such thoroughgoing rebuilding, I would argue, is never merely a calm, cool, cognitive process. Moral transformation depends at least as much on emotional as on intellectual change. But how in the world are we to change our emotions? After all, in our subjective experience, emotion seizes us, commandeers us, and there is nothing much we can do about it.

Seventeenth-century Dutch philosopher Baruch Spinoza posited in *Ethics* that we *can* do something about it, and he suggested how. The very best way is to replace unwanted emotions with other, better, stronger emotions—particularly ones that transcend the self, such as love or wonder.[16] In four instances I observed Power *replacing lesser emotions* (shame, anger, despair, contempt) *with better ones* (remorse, gratitude, love, forgiveness, empathy).

Power's story contributes something often missed by both the retributive and the restorative justice perspectives, as well as by moral philosophy and psychology—the fact that a wrongdoer's shame can block her from even starting out on the path to self-reform.* As discussed earlier, shame is an emotion that makes one want to hide, and not only from the eyes of the world but even from one's own eyes.[17] While a fugitive, Power was evading, unsuccessfully, the shame of her crimes with an attitude she described as "can-I-please-just-not-look?"[18] Power explains certain consequences of her shame in this brief exchange from the televised interview with Bob Ahearn:

BA: You had to live with that [knowledge of her part in the

---

*Shaming is a technique often used in *both* systems of justice—although to different ends: in retributive justice to induce the pain of self-blame and guilt in a presumably unrepentant, shame-less perpetrator and in restorative justice as a step in the process of reintegrating the offender into the community (Braithwaite, *Crime, Shame, and Reintegration*). In either case, as discussed in Chapter 7, Power's experience bears out critiques suggesting that shaming tends to prove counterproductive (e.g., Cohen, Ron. "Provocations of Restorative Justice").

murder of Walter Schroeder] for 23 years . . . . It must've worn on you mentally.

KP: It did. It certainly did. The shame particularly was a source of certainly depression in my life and also a kind of self-punishment . . . . I felt really undeserving.

Though it does not excuse her vanishing for 23 years, Power accurately anticipated that the criminal justice system would rub her face in that shame. It started at her surrender, intensified at her sentencing, and continued through the 20 years of her probation. Power described the earliest public shaming in an essay she wrote six years later in prison:[19]

> *Murder* is a hard word to hear about yourself. At 6:30 in the morning on September 16, 1993, in the Boston College Law School parking lot, . . . Boston Police Department Lt. Tim Murray looked me in the eye and read me the charges on my 23-year-old arrest warrant. When he came to the word *murder*, it was as if he had punched me in the solar plexus, hard enough to knock the wind out of me. I turned my face, as if I could turn away the accusation.
>
> Three weeks later, robed in his official ceremonial black, Judge Robert Banks glared down from his high bench, his face twisted, spittle flying. He hurled that same word at me as he sentenced me to eight-to-twelve years in prison and a twenty-year probation that carried the threat of a life sentence. I could not turn away.[20]

But she could try. In fact, shame was still hampering her from facing her shame and moving forward ethically in prison.

According to Spinoza, somehow she had to temper the self-punishing aspect of shame, which convinced her that she was an "irremediably horrible" person, "irredeemably shit." She had to cultivate the better emotions of guilt, remorse, and regret until they grew large enough to overcome shame. What do I mean by "better"? Guilt, remorse, and regret (properly done) center on the harm done to others (where that is relevant), and that other-orientation represents an ethical improvement over shame, which is self-centered. Furthermore, these emotions have the constructive potential to flush one out of one's hiding places into the purifying light of the sun.

In an essay titled "In a Convict's Heart," which Power wrote five years after her surrender, she explicitly discussed the remorse and regret that she finally folded into the very fabric of her being:

> Remorse is a turning of the heart. It cannot be compelled. It is achieved only in a state of exquisite vulnerability. To feel terrible regret and sorrow, to face everything you are, have been, must be, is like cutting clean through your flesh, all the way to the bone . . . .*
>
> Yet remorse is a powerful transformative experience. It is an essential step in the process by which one who has done violence to the spirit or body of another redeems him- or herself from the self-hating isolation of shame ("I am my own worst acts"). Remorse hurts more than any suffering that can be imposed from the outside. Remorse is relational. It engages the formerly anti-social in a network of support for behavioral change.
>
> My own remorse was achieved in spite of, not because of, my experiences at the hands of the Department of Corrections [DOC]. Where the Department of Corrections projected onto me monstrousness, strangers as well as friends expressed their vision of me as a whole and mostly decent person who had erred badly, and in doing so, had hurt people terribly. Where the DOC promised lifelong condemnation as an outcast, my friends and former neighbors and business associates promised full social redemption. To protect myself from lacerating shame, a shame that made me feel as if I should die, a shame the DOC would have defined as my whole experience at its hands, I was closed.
>
> I was able to open thanks to the presence of genuinely confidential and non-invasive therapy and the Catholic chaplaincy. Together, they provided an unconditionally loving, forgiving, yet expectant-of-change cosmology and community. They preferred the invitation to turn toward wholeness as a sacred obligation to myself. Through them, I found the courage to face the people whose pain I had caused and express my sorrow for it.[21]

Whereas Power's expression of guilt at the time of her surrender left room for doubt about its genuineness, these words leave little doubt that by her fifth year in prison her guilt and remorse are the real thing. She had sat vigil with these emotions until they grew strong enough to override the defensive ingredients in shame. How? Well, with a little help from

---

*The painful nature of remorse is revealed in its etymology: the root meaning of the word is "to bite again"—to be bitten repeatedly by one's conscience.

her friends—and family, therapists, clergy, even strangers. It appears that their forgiveness* permitted her to open a heart that she had kept tightly closed against the self-punishment, as well as the societal and criminal-justice-based punishment, of shame.

Shame that made Power feel that she should die pitched her into the slough of despair. Early in prison, she struggled with desolation so intense that at one point she began to make specific plans to end her life. But instead of going through with these plans, she made a very Spinozian promise—that *love* for her family would prevail over her suicidal despair, which, if enacted, could do irreparable harm to them:

> My strongest weapon against suicide is my contract with God and my family. This time, I am going to come back—not like the other times, where I've walked away from my family and everyone that I knew in my life. Now I have said I will not leave anymore. I will not hurt anyone anymore.[22]**

When I asked Power in 1995 what the worst part of prison was, she named the separation from her son, Jaime, who was at that time sixteen. In the second stanza of her poem "Sestina for Jaime," Power had penned these autobiographical words: that, although "she" (Jaime's mother) is "now . . . walled behind an official sort of rock/ . . . . she plans to return in some years." She resolved to live in order to return to her much-loved son and everyone else she cared about.

In the years I knew her as a prison inmate, I observed a third, even more compelling example in which Power allowed finer emotions—in

---

*Power points out that the forgiveness she received from the Catholic chaplaincy came with expectations that she had already transformed herself—or was in the process of doing so. In making this linkage, she implicitly concurs with the position of those moral philosophers who argue that the only *moral* basis for forgiving a wrongdoer is the wrongdoer's repentance (e.g., Haber, *Forgiveness*; Murphy, "Moral Epistemology, the Retributive Emotions").

**This aspiration is of course admirable. However her last line gives me pause. No matter how hard they want it and how hard they try, it is of course not possible for human beings never to hurt anyone. That Power thought it is reveals once again the impossible burden of perfection she was carrying.

this case, gratitude and empathy—to override a lesser one—in this case, anger. According to Power, her pre-surrender negotiations had stipulated that she would serve her prison term on the west coast, where her husband and son lived and could visit frequently. After her surrender, she was told she would serve her sentence in Massachusetts, where the crimes were committed, but where her husband and son could afford to visit only rarely. She was seething about this, bitterly raising the topic both in the *New Yorker* interview published in 1994[23] and in my first interview with her more than a year later.

I was stunned, therefore, when, during a 1997 prison visit, Power told me how profoundly important it was that she had been incarcerated in Massachusetts. Why? Because there she had been confronted up close with the specifics of the harm she had brought to Walter Schroeder and his family.

For one thing, although she didn't say this, had she been imprisoned near her home on the west coast, it seems likely that family and friends would have been assuring her at every visit how unfair it was for this good woman they knew to be incarcerated. Furthermore, as she did say, the geographic distance from her crimes would have kept at bay knowledge of the suffering of the Schroeder family and the resentment and anger many other residents of Massachusetts felt toward her. In prison in the Commonwealth, she had to face the full sting of that fury. Watching the local news and reading Boston media, especially the *Boston Herald* (which never missed an opportunity to vent its disgust for her), she learned the details surrounding Officer Schroeder's death and the resulting suffering of his family. It took about four years in the refiner's fire of prison, but finally, as required in North's philosophical model, her regret fully oriented itself to the Schroeders. Where her 1993 surrender statement was all about *her,* by 1997 she had turned her concern to *them.* What she learned in prison in Massachusetts about the immeasurable sorrow she had brought the Schroeders supplanted her hard self-focused dudgeon with softer, other-focused *empathy*. This empathic other-focus is revealed in the next chapter, in her remarkable parole statement. And in accord with Spinoza's insight, her rage about being incarcerated in Massachusetts turned into something better—gratitude—for what she had found out about the Schroeders and herself.

Power had listed in her redemptive portfolio a piece of conscience work that she referred to as *ceasing to paint someone else as Other*. This element had turned up when she first discussed with me how, immediately upon learning of the killing of Walter Schroeder, she had committed herself to nonviolence:

> KP: . . . to nonviolence in the larger aspects of it, to recognizing that to act from anger is violence, to be polarized so that somebody else can be seen as Other is violence.

> JL: The enemy?

> KP: The enemy.

As mentioned earlier, I didn't quite understand at the time what she was getting at with this broad view of violence. A last Spinozian example explains it.

Into her second year in prison, as we know, Power was invidiously contrasting the criminal justice system's insistence on putting her behind bars for an unintended and indirect killing versus that same system's complete lack of interest in the crimes committed by those who had managed the war or had committed massacres in the war. *They* got away with murder, the intended killing of millions. If I am not misreading the subtext, she was also tacitly and invidiously contrasting her own attention to the demands of conscience—she had "lived [her] *life* as a penitent" (her emphasis)—with their presumed failures of contrition. Rage, "moral outrage," roiled beneath these comparisons—and righteous *contempt* for Robert McNamara, to many opponents of the war Satan incarnate and a stand-in for all war criminals. Power's rage and contempt, buttressed as they were by the intersecting steel beams of the political and the personal, were virtually impregnable.

The day before my interview with Robert McNamara discussed earlier, I visited Power. According to my prison notes, sitting with her at the Formica table in MCI-Framingham's visiting room the evening of January 12, 1999, I told her how apprehensive I was, especially given Mr. McNamara's reputation as a brutal interviewee. She responded that she hoped that in our conversation McNamara and I would perhaps "touch each other's souls." Excuse me? Touch each other's *souls*? Up to that point, I had the distinct impression that in her mind Robert McNamara had not come equipped with anything she would dignify with the word "soul."

There was more. She suggested that I forget about Mr. McNamara's prominence and reputation when I talked with him and instead, she said, "remember that he is just a flawed and suffering human being—like myself."*

That winter evening, three years after her righteous rantings about him, here was Katherine Power expressing genuine empathy with Robert McNamara. Here she was seating him in the same boat as herself. She had stopped demonizing Robert McNamara as Other. Where contempt had smoldered, fellow-feeling now shimmered.

Nowhere does Spinoza imply that replacing lesser emotions with better ones is easy. It does not happen by fiat, and, as Power wrote, it cannot be forced or rushed. How then did she get to the place where rage and contempt were no more? She told me about the process—or some of it—six months later in a July prison visit.

Power recounted how in late 1997 when she was reflecting on her parole statement, she had felt herself "stuck in an angry place," still enraged that Robert McNamara, General Westmoreland, William

---

*It is worth pointing out that, regarding my notes from those prison visits at which tape recorders were forbidden, I use quotation marks only when I am 100% certain that I have her exact words. These were her exact words.

Calley, and the rest—that none of them had spent a day in prison for their killing. Then something happened. It happened during Sunday Mass. Toward the end of the ceremony the inmate-congregants all joined hands and voiced aloud the Lord's Prayer. "Forgive us our trespasses, as we forgive those who have trespassed against us," they recited.

She had repeated these words tens of thousands of times in her life. This time, though, the words reconfigured themselves in her mind. This time she heard how this prayer made *being* forgiven contingent upon forgiving. She understood that in order to earn forgiveness for herself, she needed to forgive her "enemies" their sins. In a flash, the hatred evaporated, and forgiveness of her enemies flowed into that soft space. She got unstuck.

As described here, this looks like a lightning-bolt epiphany. To the contrary, I believe that this breakthrough was years—decades—in the making. And it appears that my own work, along with the Lord's Prayer, may have unwittingly contributed to this transformation of hers.

As mentioned earlier, Power had read the essay in which I had paired her with Robert McNamara as War Resister and War Maker. There I had reported how in 1967 many observers, including President Johnson, had feared that McNamara was close to breakdown, perhaps even suicide, from the strain of his job. I had quoted the following passage by his (not particularly laudatory) biographer, Deborah Shapley, about how in 1967 McNamara:

> still gave dozens of briefings before the blown-up maps of Vietnam, with chart and pointer. But now his voice sometimes broke, and he put his hand up to his mouth, apparently to cough but really to catch the confused tide of emotions surging within.[24]

Interesting, I thought when I first read this, reserving my doubts about the specific nature of the "confused tide of emotions." Maybe he was just worried about being fired, I thought—knowing that when McNamara "resigned" soon after, it was widely rumored that he had actually been fired.

Something else in Shapley's biography I could not shrug off. In 1967, McNamara and William Brehm, a statistical control aide of his, were, in Shapley's words, "computing" an order of ammunition for Vietnam. Shapley's word choice corresponds with the widespread perception of McNamara as the "walking computer" who ran the Vietnam War with all the chilliness of a CEO exporting widgets to the other side of the world.

McNamara and Brehm were doing their computations in a room in which hung a large portrait of James Forrestal, at that time the only previous Secretary of Defense. Forrestal had committed suicide, reportedly from the stress of the position. In my "War Maker and War Resister" essay, I had quoted in full the episode as recounted by Shapley:

> The defense secretary was pacing back and forth on the carpet, between Brehm's chair and the [portrait of the] intense, angular face of Forrestal. "Let's see. That would be two thousand rounds for every enemy infiltrator," McNamara said. "That oughta be enough."
>
> McNamara stopped pacing and looked straight at Forrestal's portrait, which gazed back at him through blank eyes. His body suddenly shivered violently. He was sobbing, Brehm realized, as though he could never stop.[25]

The Robert McNamara revealed here was a man in agony.

I had been deeply moved by this extraordinary episode. So moved that besides including it in my essay, I brought it up with Power in at least one prison visit. In doing so, I had no intention of influencing her (although of course it would be highly unlikely that an interviewer who spent four years with someone would *not*). At the time, I hadn't grasped how central to her ethical state her attitude toward Robert McNamara was.

Research and lived experience alike reveal how uncommon it is for human beings to accommodate information that opposes our prejudices. She could have easily turned away from my sympathetic reading of McNamara's biography. But she didn't. She absorbed it—not, however, without more than one seismic tremor within.

This information shook, for instance, the firstborn and most beloved of her myths: that of her pre-murder antiwar self as pure Goodness and of McNamara and his ilk as pure Evil. When she allowed herself to admit that the War-Maker-in-Chief had wept over his actions, Power was parting with her longstanding view of herself as morally superior to him. And in point of fact, in 1970 she had turned *herself* into a war maker. She was one of Them.

Shapley's report about McNamara also shook the foundations of her moral outrage against the criminal justice system, outrage that had enabled her to rationalize her flight from justice for over twenty years. This information showed that in all likelihood the War Maker had suffered private punishments over his part in the killing. Who knows, perhaps his life after the Vietnam War was as conscience-stricken as hers. Furthermore, unlike any of the other captains of the Vietnam War, he had publicly admitted his mistakes. Yes, his admissions had come late. Like hers.

During those years in prison Power had been quietly taking this information into deep layers of herself, where in the fullness of time, contempt and moral outrage gave way to empathy. When, during that prison Mass, she forgave the flawed, suffering man named Robert McNamara, she achieved something splendid.

***

Katherine Power had no idea when she surrendered how good prison could be for her. Eventually, though, she surrendered, really surrendered, to the criminal justice system—one long known for grinding slowly, but grinding exceeding fine.[26]

In my imagination, I see her in that place for punishment that we call a "penitentiary" and she called "an intensely moral cauldron," sweating, chopping, grinding, and stirring batches of ingredients she kept discovering in herself—bitter, sour, and hard-to-swallow ingredients, along with some savory and sweet ones. It took time, six years of redeeming-time, but in the end her conscience work created a transformed self.

CHAPTER 10

THE PAROLE HEARING:
MAKING HERSELF A MINOR
CHARACTER IN SOMEONE
ELSE'S STORY

IN MARCH 1998, four and a half years into her prison sentence, Power became eligible for early release. To request early release, she would have to appear before the parole board and the Schroeder family and present her case. She went back and forth as to whether she should even try.

In the "Murphy's Law" interview a month after her parole hearing, Power described the events leading up to it. Again, the interviewer is attorney Bob Ahearn:

BA: . . . . I want you to give the people watching the show a sense of what happened [in the parole hearing] and how that went . . . .

KP: This was my first parole eligibility. And it was kind of shockingly early because I had earned "good time." . . . . I participated in education and work and whatever other activities are available for earned good time. And so it was almost a year before I would've otherwise been eligible for parole that my eligibility date came up. And I really didn't think that I was going to get parole. And of course I wanted desperately to go home; there's nobody in prison who doesn't want desperately to go home. So I decided I would approach it as an open-ended process. But it was extraordinarily painful. What you have to do when you appear before parole is that you have to talk about—what you did.

BA: Right. And re-live it again.

KP: You really do. You have to be bare—and radically honest. And I was writing the statement that I had to write for them, and it was excruciating. And I said: Why am I doing this? I don't even have to do this. People aren't even gonna let me go. Why am I doing this? And every time I got to that point, I said: Well, this is my only opportunity to be in the same room with the Schroeder family.

BA: Right.

KP: And show them my *human* face, not mediated by a reporter .... And I decided that I had to go through with the hearing no matter how painful it was. [emphasis is Power's]

Apart from wanting to get out of prison, then, Power was hoping to enact her restorative-justice-based vision of repair. Three years earlier, she had tasked herself with searching out any and all possible avenues for *alleviating the untold suffering she had caused.* "Where can I act? Everywhere that I can act is my responsibility," she had said. This parole hearing was the one place she could see to act, her only opportunity for her victims to see her in person, and hear her in person talk honestly about what she had done that had brought them such sorrow. And, by the way, she would have to stop thinking and talking in such nebulous terms as "what [I] did."

It was Friday, February 6, 1998, and we had just had one of our evening prison visits. Afterwards, I got into my car in the prison parking lot, clicked on the overhead light, and recorded in my notebook that earlier that day Power had delivered a lengthy written statement to the parole board. She felt, she said, that she had finally done the work of taking on full responsibility and expressing full and unreserved remorse with no more "Yes, buts." She looked completely at peace.

Following is Power's parole statement (with only non-substantive materials omitted), which she delivered in person before the Massachusetts Parole Board on March 6, 1998. I can't overstate how much it merits being read in full.

The Parole Statement of Katherine Power

[Introductions]

I want to make it clear that my offenses include not only the events of 1970, when Walter Schroeder was killed during a bank robbery, but also my 23-year flight from justice and my defensive posture at the time of my surrender. I particularly want to acknowledge that the Schroeder family have been victims of my action in each of these three phases.

Phase I: The Robbery and Murder

In the summer and fall of 1970 I was guilty of a series of ethical failures, compulsive rebelliousness, and wrong thinking that resulted in the robbery of the State Street Bank in Brighton and the murder of Walter Schroeder. I know now that my actions were misguided, hurtful, and indefensible. As I review for you the thoughts and feelings that led me to that event, I must emphasize that I intend no justification or defense of any of them. I write about these ideas and feelings in order to show that I recognize them, and having recognized them, I have rejected them as influences on my behavior.

That summer, I was in unbearable pain over the suffering caused by the war in Viet Nam. The war, and its seemingly unstoppable momentum, evoked a blinding rage. My particular sensitivity was a product of events in my personal and family life, but so many people seemed to share that rage that I convinced myself that it was all right to act on it. We were arrogant in our confidence of our moral rightness and in our certainty that it was pure evil that we opposed. I decided that I would try to do acts of sabotage against the war effort. I had no idea what these acts might be, or how they might be done; I had no experience in sabotage. That is no excuse. I set out to find people who knew what to do, and how. Stanley Bond asked me to join a "revolutionary action" group he was forming. I agreed. It seemed like what I had been looking for.

We were not clear about what exactly this group would do. We thought we would be one of many revolutionary groups trying to overturn capitalism and the military/industrial complex. We were drenched with dangerous romanticism and saw ourselves as noble warriors for a great cause. We thought there was glamour in gun-toting violence. Everything had escalated far beyond what I had originally pictured myself doing, but I did not find the courage or the presence of mind to leave. Instead, I went along, riding a high of pent-up anger finally released, the relief that came from feeling finally able to be doing something—anything—to feel useful instead of powerless.

I remember clearly and with deep shame the moment when I realized that some of the people in the group were dangerous in their willingness to use criminal violence, and decided to stay anyway. I thought that I would learn from them, then leave. On the day of my surrender, Kathleen Brannigan of the FBI said to me, "You should have known better." It is precisely because I should have known better, should have known that there is no such thing as a "little bit violent," should have known that if you go around with guns, someone is going to get hurt or killed, that I am responsible in the death of Walter Schroeder. I was active in the group, supporting its operations: renting the apartment which was a base of operation, purchasing used cars, and acting as a lookout during the robbery of the Newburyport Armory. I also provided a sense of comradely loyalty and ideological justification for what we were doing. We were all in agreement that we would finance the group's activities by bank robbery. We all deferred to Stanley Bond's planning the details and assigning the roles in the September 23 robbery.

At about 10:00 that morning I was parked in the "switch" car about one half mile from the State Street Bank. Bond, Valeri, and Saxe went into the bank and held it up at gunpoint. Gilday was supposed to stand watch across the street. Bond, Valeri, and Saxe met me at the switch car, and we returned to the apartment. There, we heard on the radio that a police officer had been shot in the back by a gunman. (We assumed it was Gilday.) I was shocked and angry. But mostly I was sickeningly, shamefully aware that in my immature, romantic, and stupid quest to feel that I was putting my life on the line for a cause, some real person—someone who loved his life and was loved in it—was killed.

In preparing for this hearing, I have had a glimpse at the life of the Brighton community where Walter Schroeder grew up, lived, and worked. I have learned that he was able to plan his patrol so that he could drive past his mother's house, where she watched for him from the front porch, and waved. I now know that she was watching from the porch as his partner drove him, mortally wounded, from the bank to the hospital. I have seen how my act tore a hole in the lives of a whole group of people, of family, friends, neighbors, and fellow officers. I know it is late, and far too little, but today I offer again my sincere and humble apologies to those people.

William Gilday never returned to the apartment, and, as far as I know, none of us ever saw him again. Valeri left the apartment and was arrested at his mother's home. He told the police the names of the other people in the group. By that time Saxe, Bond, and I had left Boston and become fugitives.

Phase II: Flight from Justice

Thus began the second phase of my offense: living as a fugitive, denying justice to the victims of my crime, refusing to answer for my actions to legitimate authorities. I justified this refusal by a combination of terrible shame and a continuation of the compulsive rebelliousness in which I denied that there is such a thing as a legitimate authority. Shame, of course, can be both convenient and morally sleazy, since it takes into account only the feelings of the wrongdoer and not those of the victim of the wrong.

It is true that I tried to reform my life during this period. Publicly I was a good neighbor, a valued co-worker, a loving mother, a helpful friend. My remorse and sorrow over Walter Schroeder's death did dominate my inner life and drive me to re-establish sound ethical standards. It broke through the enchantment of zealous self-righteousness and allowed me to put careful treatment of and right relations with people back into the center of my moral vision. I grew up, into the understanding that the hard work of living peacefully, and not the simplistic glory of war, is the only possible response to the pain of what is around us. It looked as though I had found a place in decent society after all. But it was a fraudulent place because of what it failed to account for, namely my debt to justice and to the family of Walter Schroeder.

My refusal to answer for that obligation had implications in the life I was leading, potentials to harm still more people, which I could not ignore. Every time people invested money in a business with me, they were subject to a risk I was not disclosing, the risk that I would be apprehended, with calamitous results for the business they had invested in. I came to realize that I could not subject people to this fraud. There were many possible solutions to that problem. But the other fraud in my life was not so easily resolved.

I was lying to my son, about my life and about his own family. He did not deserve to be deprived of the family of grandparents, aunts, uncles, and cousins of which he was a part, nor they of him. He was approaching adolescence, that time of life when parents owe their children the honest stories of their lives. I knew that he was learning the values I modeled to him. Did I really want to teach him to lie about and cover up his mistakes?

My refusal to accept public responsibility for my actions had serious consequences for my mental health. Self-disgust, guilt, and the feeling that I was an irredeemable monster caused a depression that ultimately threatened my life and provoked me to seek professional help. I knew that this inner conflict could not be resolved by therapy and that I would have to come forth and accept the legal consequences for those acts, including going to prison.

Phase III: The Surrender Process

I began the process of surrender, the third phase of my offense against the Schroeder family. I meant my surrender to communicate my deep remorse for what I had done. I meant my guilty plea to be an unequivocal admission of responsibility. And yet the Schroeder family and their community were robbed of justice by the way I was presented on my surrender. At the moment when they should have been unequivocally identified as the victims of a terrible loss, press attention was lavished on the story of my family's loss and hardships.

I am sorry for that injury, and I want to acknowledge my part in bringing it about. I contributed to it by my posture of defensiveness, by the way that I called attention to my "limited" legal responsibility and not to the enormity of what my human responsibility was for—that on a September morning Officer Walter Schroeder said goodbye for the day to whoever in his family was awake, that he went out conscientiously to do his job, that he never came home. That he would never come home again; that he would never again come home at the end of a shift with sore feet and an aching back to hear about his children's day. That he would not watch proudly as his children, one by one, graduated and made their way into the world of work, some of them following in his own profession; that Marie Schroeder, his wife, and Clare, Paul, Erin, and his other children would ever after wake up in the morning with that hole in their lives, the place where his love and his fears and his advice and his stories and his whole alive being belong.

When I heard that the Boston Police Headquarters had been named in honor of Walter Schroeder, I thought how even that wonderful honor, the highest honor his city could devise, would for his family be no replacement for what I had helped to take away.

My work in prison has been to peel off the layers of that defensiveness, to get to the point where I could look squarely into the pained accusing faces of the victims of my crime and say, "I was wrong. I was wrong all along. Before God I am sorry. I will always be so sorry."

First, I had to stop turning away (conveniently) from my own acts in shame, had to sit unflinchingly in the presence of the reality that because of my acts another human being was dead.

Then, I had to be willing to look deeply at my distorted relationships with authority, the source of my thinking that living as a fugitive was somehow an all right thing to do. I had to find and reject the source of the "Yes, but..." that the Schroeders heard from me every time I talked about my criminal acts.

. . . . My crime could not really begin to end until this moment when I could stand with no defenses before the people I have wronged, both the family of my victim and the representatives of the justice system, admit my culpability in these events, and accept my responsibility for all the harm that I have caused.

***

Power's surrender and parole hearing are manifestly contrasting moments in the arc of her transformation. Her surrender statement starred Katherine Power. In her parole statement, she made herself, to adopt the phrasing of narrative scholar Gary Morson, "a minor character in someone else's story."[1]

This new chapter in Power's chronicle emerged directly from the conscience work she did in both the private and the public realms. To repair herself and the ongoing damage to the Schroeders, she had some painful reframing to do. She had to stop hiding from herself the worst parts of her very *self.* She had to stop romanticizing herself as an anti-war activist and principled revolutionary and admit that she had made of herself an armed robber—when it comes right down to it, a common criminal. Recasting her overly virtuous conception of herself may have represented Power's most difficult moral challenge. Her parole statement confirms that she met this challenge.

In stark contrast to the self-exonerating rhetoric of the surrender statement, in her parole statement Power admits that several quite distasteful things about her had significantly contributed to her crimes. Having characterized her 21-year-old self in her surrender statement, for instance, as "naive and unthinking," five years later, she replaced those feeble self-assessments with the tougher-minded "immature and stupid."

A more momentous admission of Power's is "compulsive rebelliousness," or "distorted relationships with authority." There had not been the faintest whisper about compulsive rebelliousness in her surrender statement or in any of her conversations with me; here she referred to it three times. It can't have been easy to own up to this personal defect. Compulsive rebelliousness is such a quintessentially adolescent trait, and she was 43 before she gave up her life as a fugitive.

Three years before the parole hearing, Power had set for herself the transformative task of analyzing how she had come to cause such harm, and she had characterized prison as a place for offenders to "take time out to pay attention to the effects their actions, their sicknesses, . . . their brokenness has had on other people." Of course, therapy is also a good place for that, and she did therapy work in prison. Her compulsive rebelliousness was surely to some extent a form of brokenness brought about by familial and religious authorities, with their demands that she always be a good girl, a perfect girl. We might be tempted to view her anarchically destructive rebellion against authority as an acute eruption of sickness. This forbearing impulse is not entirely wrong. Again, however, I am cognizant of the hazard of psychological reductivism. Power said it: the point of paying attention to one's sickness and brokenness, whatever their origins, is to use the resulting self-knowledge as a springboard for taking responsibility for how one has harmed other people. Her parole statement shows her doing just that.

"Moral righteousness" is another unsavory trait of her younger self that she acknowledges. In front of her victims she identifies three harmful components of that moral righteousness, none of which she had acknowledged before, stating that:

> the war in Viet Nam, and its seemingly unstoppable momentum, evoked a *blinding rage* . . . . I convinced myself that it was all right to act on it. We were *arrogant* in our confidence in our moral righteousness and in our *certainty* that it was pure evil that we opposed. [my emphases]

Blinding rage is almost always a tip-off that one's "moral outrage" may have more to do with one's own internal baggage than with the wrongs being perpetrated by others. In Power's case, as she admits here, she spent that outlaw summer "riding a high of pent-up anger." By indulging that rage and the arrogant certainty about her own rightness and the Other's wrongness, she obliterated her better values. She decided armed violence was justified.

As we know, too, Power had originally mythologized her 1970 actions as a form of "holy" war. Here for the first time she publicly reveals distinctly unholy elements of herself that had primed her decision to make war, confessing that she had glamorized "gun-toting violence" and had romanticized the "simplistic glory of war." These admissions dispense with the "deep philosophical and spiritual commitments" rhetoric in the surrender statement with its aura of saintliness. The related myth of noble martyrdom begged for rigorous cross-examination. And it got it, as evinced in her confession that her crimes had their roots in an "immature, romantic, and stupid quest to feel that I was putting my life on the line for a cause."

These and other aspects of herself had helped her shore up for decades a self-righteous conception of who she had been at age 21. Where the surrender statement was long on deflecting responsibility, in her parole statement Power admitted for the first time—and publicly—what it was about *her* that had enabled her crimes and her long fugitive life. It was only near the end of her prison sentence that she was able to put her new self-conception into words: "I began the wrenchingly painful work of looking at myself as a person who really had done something that bad: gone to war, picked up the gun, robbed a bank, destroyed a life, wrecked a family."[2]

This time she finally stopped speaking in abstractions about the "acts of my life," "the events of 23 years ago," "what I'd done in my life," "going to war," and even "callous, blind damaging of other people." She owned up to being a "person who really had done" those specific and odious things.[3] She finally succeeded in an honest reframing of *herself*. I remember how Power had praised Steven Black (after he had put himself through his mock trial) this way: "One of my marks of a moral person is that they're horrified at themselves."

Next, she had those 23 years as a fugitive to deal with. In her surrender statement, Power had excused her fugitive life by an appeal to shame and depression. At her parole hearing, she again spoke about both emotions, but in remarkably different terms than five years earlier.

Close reading of two different uses Power made of an ostensibly trivial locution, the prepositional phrase "of course," reveals her altered perspective on her shame. At the time of her surrender Power had explained her prolonged flight from justice this way: "The depth of shame is unimaginable and my response was, *of course,* to flee." That "of course" rationalizes her flight, as if it had been inevitable, rather than a choice. In her parole statement, she had quite another take on it: "shame, *of course,* can be both convenient and morally sleazy." The first "of course" oozes self-justification; the second breathes self-knowledge. Power's ability to problematize her experience of shame signals a pretty spectacular ethical turnaround.

Similarly, Power wound her way out of the moral wasteland from which she could excuse her fugitive years in terms of depression. She had written in her surrender statement that depression had "prevented my taking this step before." In polar contrast, she wrote in the parole statement: "My refusal to accept public responsibility for my actions had serious consequences for my mental health. Self-disgust, guilt and the feeling that I was an irredeemable monster caused a depression." After five years of conscience work, Power recast her depression while a fugitive as effect, not cause.

Extending her re-thinking of her fugitive years, Power affirmed in her parole statement that she knew that her "inner conflict could not be resolved by therapy and that [she] would have to come forth and accept the legal consequences" for her acts. Just so. No amount of private, internal change—or living one's life as a penitent—would ever suffice.

Recall that a full two years into her prison sentence, Power was declaring to me that the "fraudulent and immoral" criminal justice system had no right to judge her. Thus it is truly remarkable that three more years of conscience work had transformed her to the point where she admitted that she had a "debt to justice" and to "the representatives of the justice system."

Most central of all to private reckoning and external repair, Power accepted personal responsibility for her crimes and their hideous outcome. Averring responsibility for one's crimes in the abstract is easy and not terribly convincing. In her parole statement, Power went far beyond the abstract, laying out specific aspects of her personal responsibility. She admitted to her victims that she had taken active steps to join the group that included three ex-cons. She admitted that she failed to leave the group when she knew she should. And she spelled out in detail things she had done to provide active support to the group.

To arrive here, she had to, among other things, stop blurring what exactly was the outcome of staying with that group. In her surrender statement, the closest she could come was: "his death." Five years later, she named it and him: "the murder of Walter Schroeder."

Furthermore, she showed decisively that she understood why, despite a role in the bank robbery overtly less violent than those of her comrades, she bears responsibility:

> It is exactly because I should have known better, should have known that there is no such thing as "a little bit violent," should have known that if you go around with guns someone is going to get hurt or killed, that *I am responsible in the death of Walter Schroeder.*

Power no longer evaded her responsibility: "I was wrong. I was wrong all along." And: "*Because of my acts* another human being was dead." Gone were the efforts to minimize her responsibility behind the several fortifications she had erected in her surrender statement. Power now characterized her involvement in the robbery and murder as "indefensible." Period.

When all these admissions are taken together, I hear a full admission by Power of her own responsibility. She was done defending the indefensible.

Making Walter Schroeder the starring character in the story she told about herself was absolutely crucial to Power's moral reckoning. She had to gaze upon that murdered face until Walter Schroeder fully inhabited her consciousness. And she did just that. How? By searching out everything she could about Officer Schroeder, his family, and his death. Finally she understood, with painful particularity, the damage she had caused— that *because of her*, "some real person—someone who loved his life and was loved in it—was killed . . . . that he went out conscientiously to do his job, that he never came home." She came to recognize both the depth and the reach of the harm she had perpetrated. "I have seen how my act tore a hole in the lives of a whole group of people, of family, friends, neighbors, and fellow officers." She had made the anguish of the Schroeder family and their community as real to herself as she could.

Power's parole statement enacted the assertion set forth here by scholar of forgiveness Nicholas Tavuchis:

> [I]nterior probing, interrogation, and anguish are not enough to restore an offender to a state of social grace or put things right . . . . Until these inchoate feelings and ruminations surface, purged of all traces of self-pity and, most important, *articulated in the presence of the offended other*, they serve only as soliloquies with little or no consequence or meaning.[4] [my emphases]

After five years of conscience work, Power had transformed the self-justifying, self-pitying, and inchoate thinking reflected in her surrender statement into a coherent and compelling statement of empathic contrition and personal responsibility, which she articulated with no defensiveness in the presence of the Schroeder family.

***

Not even her radically honest parole statement took Power off the hook. She knew her inner conscience work wasn't finished. Now she felt it was incumbent upon her to listen to what her victims had to say about how she had hurt them, to try to take their suffering into her heart, and to consent to the pain of knowing she had caused them so much hurt and suffering.

As mentioned previously, in the local cable TV interview a month after the parole hearing, Bob Ahearn asked Power to describe the hearing for viewers:

> KP: The next part of the hearing is that I sat on the side, and members of the Schroeder family talked to the parole board. And I sat on the side of that room with a really open heart and listened to people talk about their loss and their pain. I would say that I opened myself deliberately to the suffering because that's an obligation you have if you've hurt someone. . . .
>
> They have terrible losses, and they are deeply hurt, and that can't ever be taken away, or what I would think of as fixed. But it can be made better—by some restoring acts. And that includes me *hurting* for how they feel, really feeling it, and knowing that I caused it. [Power's emphases]

Ahearn then prompted Power to tell what happened after the Schroeders spoke:

> BA: . . . and there was a kind of extraordinary act that you did at the parole hearing I wanted you to explain.
>
> KP: Yes. It was clear to me from some of the family members' statements to the parole board that they didn't really believe what I was saying—because it was attached to my request to be paroled and go home to my family. And it became really clear to me that as long as those two things were joined, the communication that I intended to make was not going to be complete.
>
> And so after they spoke, then I returned to face the parole board and was allowed to speak again, and so I said at that time that it was really clear to me that my intended outcome wasn't happening yet—which is that these people would *know* that I *know*

that I hurt them and that I feel *really* bad about that, and that I acknowledge how terribly wrong how I acted was, and that if they couldn't believe that statement because it was connected to my request for parole, then I would withdraw my request for parole. [Power's emphases]

In addition to Power's, there are a number of independent accounts of how she ended her parole hearing. Here is the *Boston Globe*'s report of what happened in that room:

> An hour after making her apology, Power sat in her closed parole hearing on Thursday night as Clare, daughter of the Boston police officer who was her victim, said, "It is only very recently that Ms. Power has expressed her remorse . . . in an unreserved and unqualified manner. Anyone in her position, reasonably intelligent and faced with the possibility of gaining parole, would express similar sentiments."[5]

The authenticity of Power's words was bound to be questioned. After all, she was speaking in the context of a culture of stonewalling, "plausible deniability," non-apologetic "apologies," and phony, agent-free "mistakes-were-made" accounts by public figures. More to the point, those 23 years of flight and the injurious surrender would have impressed themselves on her victims far more deeply than the five-plus years of prison Power had served by then. Then too, in their minds she was now asking to renege on the sentence they had negotiated with her lawyers.

At the parole hearing, Power absorbed the skepticism she heard from the children of Walter Schroeder. In order to disentangle her words from the appearance of self-interest, she tearfully asked to withdraw her parole request.[6] She had herself put back in handcuffs and sent back to her cell at MCI-Framingham for another year and a half. She would serve out the agreed-upon number of years in prison.

The *New York Times* wrote that Power's act of withdrawing her request for parole left the people in the hearing room "stunned."[7] The *Boston Herald*, heretofore reliably hostile toward Power, quoted Clare Schroeder as saying that when Power withdrew her parole request:

"There were several seconds worth of silence . . . [as a] quiet . . . hung over the hearing room."[8] The *Boston Globe* editorial that appeared the day after Power's parole hearing was entitled "A Greater Power."

The headline of another piece in the *Globe* went further, stating: "Schroeders Find Solace in Power's Decision to Back Down on Parole."[9] I know of no evidence to support the inference that they experienced solace, per se. But their words do show appreciation for Power's parole statement and her withdrawal of her request for release. Immediately after the hearing, Erin Schroeder (then a Boston police officer) told the *Globe*: "I was very happy and I was very surprised . . . . It wasn't what I expected. I have to say I respect it."[10] Clare Schroeder agreed, describing the parole hearing to the *Globe* as a "valuable experience for all of us. Katherine got a chance to see and hear the impact of her crimes on other people and I got a window on her personality that I hadn't seen before."[11] Clare elaborated to a *New York Times* reporter:

> I respect what she did . . . And I think it must have been an extremely difficult thing for her to have done. From a personal point of view I think she did the right thing, and I appreciate that . . . I think that Katherine is sincere . . . I think what we heard last night was an unqualified acceptance of responsibility and apology that I have not felt in her statements in the past.[12]

This was new. Erin and Clare Schroeder appear to have finally heard the expression of responsibility and contrition the family needed from her. Perhaps, too, it was these words and that action that softened Clare's heart to the point that for the first time she called Power by her first name rather than by the distancing "Ms. Power." Do these statements of Erin and Clare Schroeder's then indicate forgiveness?

Forgiveness, which used to be the provenance of religion, has recently drawn notice within the ivied walls of secular scholarship. So far no consensus has emerged as to its definition.[13] (I am partial to those definitions that make emotion the centrally defining feature—that is, the cessation of resentment toward someone who has harmed oneself.)[14] However, scholars do generally agree about what forgiveness is *not*. Forgiveness is not forgetting, excusing, condoning, or justifying.

The research that finds that the more we try to forget something, the more it plagues us, also tells us that, whether or not it should, forgiveness cannot require forgetting.[15, 16] Nor can forgiveness mean excusing. If a wrongdoer's act is justified, then there is nothing to forgive.[17]

Generally speaking, the Christian perspective dominant in American culture construes forgiveness as a virtue and non-forgiveness as a fault, if not a sin. Some moral philosophers argue, to the contrary, that forgiveness can be illegitimate, irrational, even morally wrong. Retributive non-forgiveness (i.e., resentment due to the injustice of the maltreatment)—as opposed to malicious or vengeful non-forgiveness—can certainly be legitimate, rational, and moral.*[18] Because this standpoint on forgiveness is so foreign to so many, I will elaborate.

Archbishop Desmond Tutu once provided an example of irrational forgiveness:

> You see, if you have stolen my pen and you say you are sorry, and I forgive you and you still retain my pen, then I must call into question the authenticity of your contrition. I must—as part of the process of reconciliation, of forgiving, of healing, of the willingness to make good—appropriate restitution.[19]

Forgiveness of a wrongdoer who has done nothing to make amends, Tutu is saying, would be irrational and unwarranted.

In *The Sunflower* Simon Wiesenthal recounts an agonizing personal situation regarding forgiveness. In a Ukrainian concentration camp in the 1940s, Karl, an SS soldier, was dying. He called for a Jew to be brought to his deathbed. Simon Wiesenthal is the Jew who happened to be summoned. After describing a particularly horrific atrocity against

---

*An example of an illegitimate and morally wrong act of forgiveness is President Reagan's bestowal of forgiveness in 1985 on the Nazi soldiers buried in Bitburg cemetery in Germany. He didn't understand the truth of 17th-century poet John Dryden's words: that "forgiveness to the injured doth belong." Mr. Reagan was not among the injured, nor was he an appointed representative of the injured.

Jews which he had participated in, the dying SS man told Wiesenthal: "I want to die in peace, and so I need . . . I have longed to talk about it to a Jew and beg forgiveness from him."[20] Wiesenthal suffered the dying Nazi to unburden himself, but he could not grant him forgiveness.

Book Two of *The Sunflower*, "The Symposium," consists of the responses of 53 distinguished scholars and other thoughtful individuals to Wiesenthal's tortured question about what they would have done in this situation. Henry James Cargas, a Catholic theologian of the Holocaust, articulated one of the more frequent objections to forgiving the Nazi:

> Forgiveness is not something we may depend on others for. We must somehow *earn it*. Deathbed conversions are dramatic but in many instances they are too easy. If God chooses to forgive Karl, that's God's affair. Simon Wiesenthal could not, I cannot. For me, Karl dies unforgiven.[21] [emphasis added]

Writer Hans Habes goes further, arguing that it would have been immoral for Wiesenthal to have forgiven the Nazi: "We cannot forgive murderers—so long as the murder is not atoned for . . . An amnesty granted to an unpunished murderer is a form of complicity in the crime."[22] To forgive someone like Karl, so self-indulgently cruel as to ask forgiveness from one's victim without having earned it, would be immoral because such forgiveness would render the forgiver complicit with the crimes.

While Power remained a fugitive, she was refusing to allow justice to mete out its punishment, and she was publicly sending a message that could only be interpreted as the absence of contrition. The unforgiving position of the Schroeder family toward Power while she remained a fugitive would therefore qualify as legitimate, rational, and moral.

When Power finally did give herself up, she wrote a surrender statement riddled with excuses, rationalizations, and deflections of personal responsibility. This rendered her akin to Tutu's hypothetical pen thief. Therefore, the Schroeders' refusal of forgiveness at her surrender was also legitimate, rational, and morally right.

A number of religious and scholarly authorities argue that it becomes legitimate, rational, and moral for victims to forgive only after their perpetrator has taken genuine steps to *earn* forgiveness—admitting responsibility, accepting society's penalties, reforming, reframing, and redressing, for instance. Can we say that when Power withdrew her request for parole she had earned forgiveness—through her admission of personal responsibility, expressions of authentic contrition, and that unstinting act of hers that she hoped would convince the Schroeders that she meant what she said?

If we listen closely to the injured we will note that, for all their favorable reactions to Power's words and acts in the parole hearing, neither spokesperson for the Schroeder family mentioned forgiveness. For now, though, let's leave this as an open question. *If* forgiveness, then shouldn't reconciliation follow?

Thinkers vary in what they mean by reconciliation. Typically it is defined as the establishment of more or less "peaceful relations between opposing parties."[23] At minimum, reconciliation would entail achieving "some measure of interpersonal harmony."[24] At best, it would entail full reunion[25]— that is, an agreement by both parties to associate with one another,[26] to "come together,"[27] or even to come "together to work, play, or live in an atmosphere of trust."[28] As for Power, she would have been grateful, she said, to achieve something even more minimal: namely, a state of "non-enmity" between her and the Schroeders.[29]

The way parole hearings are structured may have helped bring about as much repair as it did. Research finds that perceived equality has the potential to smooth the path toward conciliation between victims and perpetrators.[30] For the members of the Schroeder family to get to speak their minds fully to the parole board while Power had to sit and listen could have provided a meliorating sense of equality to these victims who for more than twenty years had been rendered helpless in the face of Power's disappearance.

But she knew that, intuitively. The first time I talked with Power about Robert McNamara's Vietnam War memoir, I told her about a Vietnam War widow who had stood up in an audience on his book tour and angrily confronted him for the terrible harm his acts had brought to her and her children. "What McNamara has to do," responded Power, "is stand defenseless in front of the people who were angry and hurt, and let them be angry at him." Years later, Power applied this insight to herself. In that hearing room, while the Schroeders spoke, Power sat before them defenseless ("with a really open heart") and listened to them voice their resentment, hurt, anger, and skepticism. What she said in withdrawing her parole request made it clear that she had been listening. She had listened and understood—and chose to do the only thing she could do to redress the suffering she had caused them.

Power was legally entitled to a second parole hearing a year after the first one. She did not pursue this second opportunity for early release. The *Boston Herald* reported Power's decision and Clare Schroeder's reaction, writing that Power had "quietly waived her right to a [second] hearing in a January 22 letter to parole board officials. 'I respect the fact that she opted not to put us through that process again,'" said Clare Schroeder.[31]

***

More of the forgiveness and reconciliation part of Power's story is told in the documentary film *Forgiveness: A Time to Love and a Time to Hate*, which first aired on PBS early in 2011. Power's was one of four stories featured in depth in Part 1 of this film. There filmmaker Helen Whitney interviews Clare Schroeder about the murder of her father. This strong woman—*Sergeant* Clare Schroeder of the Boston Police Department—choked up when speaking about how she wished her father could have lived to see her graduate from college, how she thought it would have meant so much to him, as a father and as a man. Clare is asked at the end of the segment on Power whether she forgives Power. Clare responds with an emphatic no: "What she did was *not* OK, it was not *ever* OK, it will never *be* OK. It's not forgivable." [Clare's emphases] She could not have been clearer.

In the silver-screen version of this story, having done everything she could to earn forgiveness, Power would have been showered with it by one and all. But the poet had more insight than Hollywood about such things; again, "Forgiveness to the injured doth belong." Power's story illustrates the real-world fact that someone who has done serious harm and has "earned" forgiveness through reparation and thoroughgoing moral transformation might still remain unforgiven by the injured.

And yet. Even as Clare Schroeder pronounced Power's acts unforgivable, she also said this: "I hope she can say she redeemed herself and became the person she should have been." Then Clare repeated that sentiment, but with important modifications: she wanted, she said, for "Katherine" to "go on and become the person *she hopes* to become. And that's a great goal. And I wish that for her." [my emphasis] Clare's revision of the sternly backward-looking "the person she should have been" to the generously forward-looking "the person she hopes to become," along with her use of Power's first name, appear to me to evince a certain cessation of resentment toward this woman whose acts she can never forgive. As you will recall, for some scholars, cessation of resentment is the definition of forgiveness.

It appears that Clare understands, and understands correctly, how much Katherine Power hopes to become her best self and how deeply she longs to redeem herself. For Clare to publicly wish her well in realizing these goals and longings seems to me to demonstrate that state of non-enmity that Power had hoped for.

Two years after her surrender I asked Power what she was then wanting from the Schroeder family. Without missing a beat, she responded that she had no right to ask anything of them:

> KP: I will always be open to any kind of reconciliation. But it would be out of line for me to say to them that I *need . . . anything*;

it would be out of line for me to say that they *should . . . anything.*
I need to be respectful of them. [Power's emphases and pauses]

With these words, Power contributes an invaluable correction to
rosy viewpoints on reconciliation and forgiveness. She recognizes that
for her to expect, demand, or ask for anything from the injured would be
to inflict further injury—a recognition that may have its roots in Power's
nuanced attention to the 12-Step Program. As psychologist Sharon
Lamb has asserted, the only thing a wrongdoer is entitled to ask of her
victims is the other-centered question of what they need her to do to
repair the damage.[32]

Power took a parole hearing meant to be an instrument of retributive
justice and turned it into an instrument of restorative justice. Finally she
had allowed Officer Schroeder's death to invade her—as she had invaded
that family, traumatizing them first with his absence and then with hers.
Having allowed the feelings of her victims to rise to the top of her concerns, she conveyed to the Schroeders as much repair as she could. In so
doing, she did a fine thing.

***

In my first interview with her, Power used the word "redemption" or one
of its cousins 13 times. She eschewed the word "guilt," she told me, both
because she felt that the word "implies irredeemability" and because she
didn't "see guilt as transforming." She preferred "to use language that . . .
affirms both the possibility and the requirement of redemption." She does
not want to think of herself as the irredeemable monster she had considered herself for so many years after the killing. Or the irredeemable
shit that she knows many people see in her and other convicts. How very
much Katherine Power wants redemption.

Has she achieved it? I'd prefer not to have to pronounce judgment
on this delicate, fraught, and indeterminate question, but it does seem to
me that Power has now done everything she could to earn redemption.

During those years in prison she searched her heart, followed it all the way down, poured all she had into trying to redeem the time. Her parole hearing some five years after her surrender marked a dramatic and reparative highpoint of those efforts. Finally she was able to express full responsibility for her part in the death of Walter Schroeder. Then when she decided to serve out her entire prison sentence without a fight, she did what the Schroeder family needed, to the point that some family members publicly expressed their appreciation. If redemption means having atoned or made amends for error with one's thoughts, words, and deeds, then Katherine Power has redeemed herself.

Still, redemption remains for me too complicated a matter to support a neat tying up of loose ends. It comes down to my view of the human condition. Most of human existence is, I believe, irreconcilably provisional and ambiguous, with very little of it unequivocally Black or White, Good or Bad. Almost all of human existence is painted in shades of Gray. The most fundamental ambiguity is existential: why we live and what happens when we die. But it's nearly *all* ambiguous: relationships, consciousness, feelings, motivations, words, acts—and morality.

The sad fact is that some mistakes are not expungable, some wounds do not heal, and some damage can never be repaired. "A human life, once lost, is lost forever." When a wrong can never be completely put right, redemption is partial. Furthermore, forgiveness—the if, when, and how of it—rightly belongs only to the injured. And so far, it appears that, although Power may have succeeded in alleviating some of the pain of those she hurt the most, she has not received their forgiveness. Not in so many words. If redemption is defined as paying off a debt in full, then these external restraints on repair and forgiveness make redemption unavoidably incomplete.

There are further limits. A month after Power's parole hearing, attorney and interviewer Bob Ahearn asked her what she would want to say to the Schroeder family if they were present. Without hesitation, she replied:

What I said in the room in parole . . . . I would say it again. That I know I hurt them in their life and I am deeply, deeply sorry for that. And my awareness of that has transformed me as a person . . . . The changed person I am goes with me for all of my life. [my emphases]

Never again could Katherine Power be that person who let righteous anger carry her so far away from her own values that she perpetrated violent criminal acts. Never again could she be that person who for so long ran from accountability for the murder that resulted from her acts. Katherine Power has genuinely and deeply transformed herself.

Even transformation as profound as hers, however, does not end with a whole new and pristine self. Not in this human world. Power understands this: "I will never put behind me what I've done. *It shapes me.*" And: "I tried to forget what I'd done in my life . . . . But you know, we just *can't* forget. *The real work is to incorporate it into who we are.*" Although she is ultimately not reducible to her felonies, they will always be part of who she is (a fact she is confronted with every time she applies for jobs). In this sense, she will always be a mended, repaired, patched-up human being. Not someone who has never broken or been broken. Not someone who has put behind her what she did. Not someone whose past has been erased. Not the shiny new self of Hollywood endings.

I intend no disparagement here. Everyone ends up—at best—salvaged, repaired, patched. Power's transformation story—its belated, discordant, incremental, and limited nature—exemplifies the kind of moral trajectory experienced by most people, a two-steps-forward-one-step-back stagger to self-reform that some, but not all, will find sufficient.

Into her fundamentally good and decent self, Katherine Power has now stitched the part that at long last came forth to plead guilty to armed robbery and manslaughter and to serve out the prison sentence required by her society; the part that fully admitted her personal responsibility for Walter Schroeder's death 28 years after the fact; the part that has been forgiven by her family and her friends; the part that remains unforgiven by her victims; the part that will always be an ex-convict. Power is a walking study in Gray. If redemption can accommodate a belated but thorough atonement for a crime that will always be part of who she is, a crime that helped bring about a death that can never be undone, then Katherine Power has earned redemption.

CHAPTER 11

"I Will Always Be Answerable": Conclusions

At 9:00 a.m. on Saturday, October 2, 1999, Katherine Ann Power walked out of MCI-Framingham, at age fifty a free woman for the first time in her adult life.

The press thronged the prison grounds that crisp autumn morning, but Power neither turned toward nor spoke to the media. In a telling contrast to the dazzling smile that had so affronted the Schroeder family at her arraignment, this time she wore a small smile. She refused scores of interview requests, letting the following exit statement published in the *Boston Herald* speak for her:

> Today marks the payment of my legal debt for my role in the murder of Walter Schroeder. But I will always carry my human responsibility for the sorrow my actions have caused . . . . I do not intend to cultivate media attention to my feelings, to my problems or to what the media see as my "drama." This is a time to acknowledge that a human life, once lost, is lost forever; that the death of a father, husband, and brother is a terrible event, and one for which I will always be deeply sorry.[1]

As Power had said in her parole statement a year and a half earlier, she had come to realize that all the fanfare at her surrender had further wounded the Schroeder family. She was determined not to let that happen again. Of the many people I have spoken with about Power, almost everyone remembers her surrender, no one her release.

For a time, it seemed to me that the pinnacle of the success of Katherine Power's conscience work was her act of withdrawing her request for parole. Now I don't think so. *This* was the true ethical climax: her intentionally undramatic exit from prison and the small written statement accompanying it—as undramatic and definitive as the movement of sap after winter. This quiet act and these remorseful words put the emphasis exactly where it should go—on the death of Walter Schroeder and the suffering it caused a whole family.

***

As Katherine Power found out (to borrow a cliché), the only way to get beyond painful thoughts and feelings is by going through them. The most distressing feelings in particular—the shame, the guilt, the despair—had important things to tell her. But she had to stop and listen. In prison that is what she did. When she opened herself, her mind and her heart, truth took up residence. Radical openness is what took her so far.

To commend the process of sitting with and listening to painful thoughts and feelings is not to recommend a hair-shirt approach to life. It is merely to acknowledge reality: every adult life inevitably includes mistakes, offenses, transgressions, or worse. We might as well take a page from Power's playbook and do that ethically transformative listening.

Much of what Power has to say is not found in the common wisdom or self-help books.* How many of us would recognize on our own that our shame might be "morally sleazy"? Or recognize the moral perils of "moral" outrage, how easily it shapes itself into a gun? Or know that if we've hurt someone, it is incumbent upon us to learn all we can about the specifics of the suffering we've caused? Or realize that a harm-doer has no right to ask, let alone demand, forgiveness from her victims? Or comprehend that personal transformation is as much about profound openness

---

*Prompted by Power, however, I have come to recognize the usefulness of the 12-Step Program and to suspect that there may be other self-help-based pieces of wisdom that I have simply missed.

as it is about active effort? Or understand that ethical transformation depends on changing one's heart as well as one's thoughts? That, in fact, change is above all else a matter of the heart? That the heart has to open, it has to soften, and it has to expand?

In her very first letter, agreeing to talk with me about regret, responsibility, confession, reparation, and transformation, Power wrote that she hoped "to be able to contribute something to thoughtful understanding" of these issues. In that same letter, she expressed a sense of responsibility to speak from her position as a "pivot point between microcosm and macrocosm," writing: "We owe our children the story of the events of Viet Nam, but we haven't finished the process . . . . [of] pass[ing] on the wisdom-gained-from-experience which is the responsibility of the generation of elders." She has more than fulfilled these hopes.

She has brought back from the trenches dispatches about war and about peace. She has brought back the wisdom gained from experience about how crucial it is to keep one's dissent nonviolent. In prison she "grew up, into the understanding that the hard work of living peacefully, not the simplistic glory of war, is the best possible response to the pain of what is around us."*

***

Poet William Stafford once wrote, "Justice will take us millions of intricate moves."**[2] Katherine Power understands better than most of us just what he meant. The conscience work she did in prison, her parole statement, her withdrawing her request for parole, and her humble exit from

---

*On this score, I like to imagine her standing shoulder to shoulder with a fellow with a decidedly British accent and a decidedly American first name, singing with him in two-part harmony: "What's so bloody funny about peace, empathy, and nonviolence? Or so bloody easy?" (Paraphrased from "Peace, Love, and Understanding," a song by Elvis Costello, 1979).

**It's interesting how well Power's story relates to this line from the works of William Stafford, a committed pacifist who went to prison rather than participate in war.

prison manifest the fruition of the self-interrogation, reframing, reform, and repair required of an offender who seeks genuine transformation.

The day after Power's parole hearing, the *Boston Globe* published an editorial which concluded as follows:

> Katherine Power deserves her punishment. But her statement to the Parole Board should be posted in classrooms, government offices, living rooms, boardrooms, hospitals, churches, and everywhere people need reminding of their ability to wreak ruin through a single misdeed, and the power of redemption.[3]

Yes. We all need to be reminded, some of us urgently. And, as the *Globe* recognized, we need to know the whole story—the intricate arc of her crimes and her transformation. Katherine Power's story is deeply relevant not only to this place and time, but everywhere and always.

BY KATHERINE POWER

Many people I've talked with have wanted to know about Katherine Power's post-prison life. So I asked her to send me a brief description of her unfolding life. This is what she wrote:

> The point of the penitential journey is that it ends in redemption, in the invitation to live a full and joyful life.
>
> I am 63 years old now, a mother, grandmother, and (in Massachusetts, at least)[1] a wife. I visit my son, daughter-in-law, and grandsons when I can and share experiences through smartphone photos when I can't.
>
> I walk in the woods, swim in wild waters, eat from nearby farms. I commute farther than is healthy for me or the planet to a job where I manage grant writing for a nonprofit organization. In that role, I work in a concrete way to address suffering, particularly the suffering that results from social and economic inequity.
>
> I haven't given up on social change. I have not stopped paying attention to the suffering wrought by wars and other forms of domination. I have surrendered to this—that we cannot force an end to dominance systems. Yet in my lifetime we have witnessed the collapse of all kinds of oppressive realities. The more I have studied how things change, the more I see that the acts of this moment are hugely powerful, that peace in the moment is the way to peace in the world.

March 12, 2012*

---

*My interviews with Power ended with the completion of her prison sentence in 1999. After that, I felt that she had fulfilled her obligations to my research, so most of our project-related communications came to an end, which explains the date of the epilogue.

APPENDIX

Following is my first letter to Power, which I wrote on University of Michigan letterhead and sent on July 5, 1995. In the interest of transparency, I quote verbatim:

> My current research centers on the topic of how regret and similar emotions are transformed. Paths toward the positive transformation of regret that especially interest me are those that take place out in the broader world—such as reparation and social action. I thought that your experience illustrated these paths to transformation.
>
> I wonder whether you agree with my assessment, and whether you would agree to talk with me further about those aspects of your experiences. If so, I am willing to travel to Massachusetts to talk with you in person. I would like to tape-record our conversations. Or if you are willing and able to talk with me by telephone, mail, or e-mail, I would be happy to do that.
>
> What I am interested in exploring with you is the emotional process you went through, including the events surrounding the death of Officer Schroeder; through the thoughts, feelings, and actions that you underwent during the 23 years you lived as a fugitive; up to and including the point where you are now. Some of my guiding questions are: What is/was it about you that contributed to these experiences? What is/was it about your life circumstances and other people that contributed? Finally, I am interested in how your respective experiences with conventional therapy, New Age approaches, social action, public "confession," and prison have contributed to the emotional experience and its transformation.
>
> I do hope I have not been presumptuous. In the articles that I have read about you (particularly the *New Yorker* piece), you seem so open and articulate about this important experience that I hoped you might not mind talking with me. (Plus, I feel something of a personal connection, as I am a "Catholic girl" about the same age as you; in college I was vehemently opposed to the war and wanted to change the world (still do*); I too lived in Eugene** as an adult; and I can imagine, I think, the impulse you had to give yourself up.)

---

*Given that this project concerns analysis of an activist gone wrong, readers deserve to know that I have been and still am engaged in social and political activism, of a completely nonviolent sort.

**Her restaurant was in Eugene, but she lived in Lebanon, Oregon, a small town north of Eugene.

After some logistical questions, I closed with "Yours with respect."
Power's return letter was dated July 22:

> I would be happy to talk with you about the questions of regret, transforma-
> tion, reparation, and your work. As you concluded from reading the *New
> Yorker,* I am willing to be open about these questions. I hope to be able to
> contribute something to thoughtful understanding of the ways people act,
> what constitutes responsibility, and what is owed to persons, the state, the
> universe as a result of acts that seriously damage. One of my hopes when I
> surrendered is that my willingness to "show up" and declare my responsibility
> could become a challenge to the nation, as an entity and as made up of indi-
> viduals, to do the same. We owe our children the story of the events of Viet
> Nam, but we haven't finished the process. We are collectively sort of in the
> same position as I was with my then-fourteen-year-old son [referring to the
> fact that until just before her 1993 surrender, her son knew nothing about her
> former identity]. I had to bring out from hiding the shameful and terrifying
> "realities"* of my life, digest and understand them, before I could pass on the
> wisdom-gained-from-experience which is the responsibility of the generation
> of elders.
>
>   To make arrangements to see me and be able to take notes and tape record,
> you will need to contact the Superintendent, [NAME DELETED], at this
> same address. Use a copy of this letter as your evidence of my agreement to
> participate. If this does not work out, write to me again, and I'll see what we
> can arrange by correspondence (much less preferable).

---

*I don't quite know what to make of the quotation marks she placed around the
word "realities" in that letter. When I finally perceived it as problematic, it had been
so many years after she wrote the letter that she said she couldn't recall what she had
intended. I am positive that she would not have misused quotation marks to signal
emphasis. And I didn't use any form of "your reality" in my letter, so she was not indi-
cating agreement by quoting me. I hate to think that she would have used the quotation
marks to mean "so-called." There was nothing merely "alleged" about the central realities
she had to bring out of hiding, her participation in the armed robbery in which Walter
Schroeder was murdered. My best guess is that she was challenging the media accounts
that had emphasized the difficulties she and her family suffered during her time on the
lam, thus distorting the full reality (including the difficulties of the Schroeder family).
Or perhaps she was challenging the idea that her crimes represented the *only* realities of
her life, that her life could be reduced to the worst things she had ever done.

ACKNOWLEDGMENTS

THANKS FIRST TO KATHERINE POWER for her openness to making herself a working partner in this investigation of how a decent person can go wrong and how a wrongdoer might go about redeeming herself.

This book, however, definitely embodies the "it takes a village" ethos. Preparation of the earliest drafts of this manuscript was supported by a village fellowship from the National Endowment for the Humanities, a year as a Fellow at the Institute for the Humanities at the University of Michigan, and course releases granted by the Board of Research at Babson College. I am grateful to Brandeis University Archivist Maggie McNeely for digging deep into the archives with me. I thank Michael Bruner, Ron Cohen, Laura Godtfredsen, Laurence Goldstein, James Hoopes, Irv Kurki, Sharon Lamb, David Landau, Jean Manis, Dan McAdams, James Pasto, Mary Price, Jonah Raskin, George Rosenwald, and David Winter for reading individual chapters. I am grateful to David Miller for insightful readings of early proposals and for advice and support. I am supremely indebted to my new friend Fran Danoff and my old friends and colleagues from the Boston University Writing Program: Sarah Madsen-Hardy, the late Tony Wallace, and Chris Walsh. Each of you gave me invaluably detailed, substantive, astute readings of the entire manuscript. For reading the whole thing *twice,* mucho mucho merci, Tony and Chris. Filmmaker Helen Whitney has my gratitude for nudging me gently, in her role as interviewer, to excise as many traces of academese from my speaking as she could, and demonstrating *how,* lessons I've tried to translate to my writing. So many friends (and friends of friends) have lent a hand in ways as specific and as various as you yourselves are: John Barnett, Beryl Burke, Al Cain, Terry Ehret, Kate Farrell, Susan Gunter, Lou Gwendolyn, Mel Manis, Bob Martin, Clark McCauley, Shana Ross, Laz Ross, Rob Sellers, Abby Stewart, Ed Thompson. Over the years I've benefited from writing in coffee shops in at least five different cities. The one I will remember most fondly is the In-House Café in Allston, Massachusetts, where owner Ahmet Floury gave me the personal warmth of his hospitality (and introduced me to those incomparably delicious Moon Flowers). I owe very special thanks to publishers who refused my manuscript before its time, to reviewers whose sharp critiques showed me where to improve it, and to Gordon Anderson and the staff at Paragon House for midwifing this story to the light of day. And then there's Miriam. Because you pushed back on my wish for you to have this book published posthumously, it is coming out in my lifetime. How much better this book is because of your incisive editings, done with all the professionalism of the professional you are and with all the heart and ongoing encouragement of the much-loved daughter you are.

***

NOTES

Prologue

1. Croft, "Hub Officer Shot by Bank Robbers," 52.
2. "'100 Club' to Assist Family of Patrolman," 4.
3. "'100 Club' to Assist Family of Patrolman," 4
4. Murray and Giguere, "Policeman, Father of 9, Shot," 3.
5. Murray and Giguere, "Policeman, Father of 9, Shot," 3.
6. Croft, "Hub Officer Shot," 52.
7. These words of Clare's reassure me that perhaps the Schroeder family might understand my need to visit their father's grave and to begin this book with him.
8. Wilson, "Dubious Sympathies."

Introduction

1. Franks, "Return of the Fugitive," 48.
2. I owe this phrase to Walker Percy, writing in another context in *The Moviegoer.*
3. "A Greater Power," A10.
4. Franks, "Return of the Fugitive," 40-59.

Chapter 1. Meeting Inmate 9309307

1. Daly, "Woman Ends 23 Years as Fugitive," A4.
2. Power, "Sestina for Jaime," 171-172.

Chapter 2. The Crime: Looking for Revolution

1. Croft, "Hub Officer Shot by Bank Robbers," 2.
2. Murray and Giguere, "Policeman, Father of 9, Shot," 3.
3. Creamer and Droney, "Radicals Linked," 3.
4. Murray and Giguere, "Policeman, Father of 9, Shot," 3.
5. "Slay Suspect Slips Dragnet," 5.
6. Franks, "Return of the Fugitive," 54.

7. Franks, "Return of the Fugitive," 54.

8. Mahoney, "'Brilliant' Bond," 4.

9. Franks, "Return of the Fugitive," 49.

10. Kantrowitz, "The Fugitive," 57.

11. Ibid.

12. Mahoney, "'Brilliant' Bond," 1.

13. Mahoney, "'Brilliant' Bond," 4.

14. Franks, "Return of the Fugitive," 52.

15. Franks, 52.

16. Franks, 52.

17. Franks, 52.

18. Hassett, "How Did Five Form Weird Alliance?" 4.

19. Franks, "Return of the Fugitive," 50.

20. "Too Little Contrition, Too Late." *Boston Globe* editorial. September 16, 2011. The occasion for the editorial was the death in prison of William Gilday 41 years after he murdered Officer Schroeder.

21. "Slay Suspect," 5.

22. Blake, "4 Campus 'Radicals,'" A5.

23. Abel, "Apologetic in the End, William Gilday Dies."

24. Murray and Giguere, "Policeman, Father of 9, Shot," 3.

25. Murray and Giguere, "Policeman, Father of 9, Shot," 3.

26. Reinhold, "Students Hunted in Police Killing," 1.

27. Blake, "4 Campus 'Radicals,'" A5.

28. Jacobs and McCarthy, "A Bank Is Robbed, a Cop Is Killed, a Movement Is Hung."

29. Alpert, *Growing Up Underground.*

Chapter 3. Asking Why: Historical Context

1. Markus and Kitayama, "Culture and the Self: Implications for Cognition, Emotion, And Motivation," 246.

2. Ross, "The Intuitive Psychologist and His Shortcomings: Distortions in the Attributional Process."

3. McNamara, preface to *In Retrospect: The Tragedy and Lessons of Vietnam,* xx.

4. Landman, *Michigan Quarterly Review.*

5. http://www.americanforeignrelations.com/O-W/Presidential-Power-Presidential-war-in-vietnam.html.

6. I owe much of the political-historical analysis in this chapter to *The Sixties: Years of Hope, Days of Rage* by Todd Gitlin.

7. "My Lai."

8. Gitlin, *The Sixties: Years of Hope, Days of Rage,* 331.

9. Gitlin, 326, note; Hayden, *Reunion,* 321.

10. Hayden, *Reunion,* 375.

11. Gitlin, *The Sixties,* 410.

12. Viorst, *Fire in the Streets,* 531.

13. Wyckoff, "Jackson State: A Tragedy Widely Forgotten." www.npr.org.

14. Gitlin, *The Sixties,* 410.

15. Rudd, *Underground: My Life with SDS and the Weathermen,* 230.

16. Gitlin, *The Sixties,* 345.

17. Gitlin, *The Sixties,* 348.

18. *Port Huron Statement.*

19. Hayden, *Reunion,* 419.

20. Hayden, 359.

21. Hayden, 358.

22. Garfinkel, "The Vietnam War Is Over. The Bombs Remain."

23. Rudd, *Underground,* 189.

24. Hayden, 359.

25. Rudd, *Underground,* 132.

26. Rudd, *Underground,* 147.

27. Burrough, *Days of Rage,* 87.

28. Ayers, *Fugitive Days,* 242.

29. Staples, "The Oldest Rad," 11.

30. Rudd, *Underground,* 190.

31. Rudd, *Underground,* 190, 191.

32. Allen. "Vietnam: The Last War the U.S. Lost." Alternative radio.org, 2017.

33. Ayers, *Fugitive Days,* 228; Hayden, *Reunion,* 359 (citing figures from the Treasury Department).

34. Gitlin, *The Sixties,* 410.

35. Shapley, *Promise and Power: The Life and Times of Robert McNamara,* 482-483.

Chapter 4: Circumstances that Could Help Explain Her Crimes

1. Belfrage, *Freedom Summer;* Flacks, *Youth and Social Change;* Keniston, *Young Radicals;* McAdam, *Freedom Summer.*

2. Hayden, *Reunion,* 84.

3. Power, personal communication, February 22, 2013.

4. Power, personal communication, February 11, 2013.

5. Power, personal communication, February 22, 2013.

6. Franks, "Return of the Fugitive," 44.

7. Franks, 51.

8. Franks, 48.

9. Power, personal communication, January 31, 2013.

10. Berrigan Brothers.

11. The Catonsville Nine File: Blood to Fire.

12. Evans, *Personal Politics;* Gitlin, *The Sixties,* 362-376.

13. Rudd, *Underground,* 166.

14. Rudd, *Underground,* 166.

15. Power, personal communication, August 17, 2011.

16. Franks, 40.

17. Gitlin, *The Sixties,* 76.

18. Marcuse.

19. Kantrowitz, "The Fugitive," 56.

20. Franks, "Return of the Fugitive," 49.

21. Cohen, J. "The Romance of Revolutionary Violence," 29.

22. Hassett, "How Did Five Form Weird Alliance?" 4.

23. Metzger, "Brandeis: School for Terrorists?" 5-6.

24. Hayden, *Reunion,* 417.

25. Cohen, "The Romance of Revolutionary Violence," 31.

26. Hayden, *Reunion*, 417.

27. Cohen, "The Romance of Revolutionary Violence," 32.

28. Lytle cites two million in *America's Uncivil Wars: The Sixties Era . . .*, 355; Miller cites four million in *Democracy Is in the Streets*, 311.

29. Ayers, 231.

30. Lytle, *America's Uncivil Wars: The Sixties Era*, 355.

31. Hayden, *Reunion*, 416.

32. Jacobs and McCarthy, "A Bank Is Robbed, a Cop Is Killed, a Movement Is Hung."

33. Jacobs and McCarthy, "A Bank Is Robbed, a Cop Is Killed, a Movement Is Hung."

34. Cohen, "The Romance of Revolutionary Violence," 32.

35. Gitlin, *The Sixties*, 410.

36. Marchand, "Kathy 'Used,' Mother Says," 6.

37. Baddeley, *Psychology of Memory*, 78; *Forgetting Curve*.

38. Marcus, *Kluge: Haphazard Construction of the Human Mind*, 31.

39. Baddeley, *Psychology of Memory*, 304.

40. The archivist who steered me to this flyer wondered out loud whether the color of paper stock someone chose for it in 1970—shocking-pink—might indicate that it was made by (and perhaps for) women. And I remembered Gitlin's analysis of how by that time women activists had broken off from the male-dominated movement, even while replicating their machismo.

41. Cohen, "The Romance of Revolutionary Violence," 32.

42. Cohen, "The Romance of Revolutionary Violence," 33.

43. Cohen, "The Romance of Revolutionary Violence," 33.

44. Creamer and Droney, "Radicals Linked," 3.

45. Hassett, "How Did Five Form Weird Alliance?" 4.

46. Hassett, "How Did Five Form Weird Alliance?" 4.

47. Marchand, "Kathy 'Used,' Mother Says," 1.

48. Franks, "Return of the Fugitive," 50.

49. Franks, 50.

50. Franks, 50.

51. Franks, 50.

52. Power, personal communication, February 11, 2013.

53. Cohen, "The Romance of Revolutionary Violence," 29.

54. Power, personal communication, February 11, 2013.

55. Metzger, "Brandeis: School for Terrorists?" 6.

56. Franks, 52.

57. Power, personal communication, February 11, 2013.

58. Spillane, "A 'Radical's' Return," 413.

59. Wolfe, "Radical Chic: That Party at Lenny's."

60. Haidt, *The Righteous Mind*, 47-48.

61. Haidt, *The Righteous Mind*, 85.

62. Franks, 52.

63. Haidt, *The Righteous Mind*, 78, 85, 91.

64. Jacobs and McCarthy, "A Bank Is Robbed, a Cop Is Killed, a Movement Is Hung."

65. Blake, "4 Campus 'Radicals,'" A5.

66. "60's Radical Who Surrendered Pleads Guilty to a Burglary Charge," 7.

67. "Too Little Contrition, Too Late."

68. Cohen, "The Romance of Revolutionary Violence," 33.

69. Rai, "How Could They?" Aeon.com, 15.

Chapter 5: What It Was about Her That Could Help Explain Her Crimes

1. Gitlin, "Return of the Fugitive," *Washington Post*.

2. Bloom, "The Dark Side of Empathy."

3. Jacobs and McCarthy, "A Bank Is Robbed, a Cop Is Killed, a Movement Is Hung."

4. Jacobs and McCarthy, "A Bank Is Robbed, a Cop Is Killed, a Movement Is Hung."

5. Alpert, *Growing Up Underground*, 17-18.

6. Baldwin, "They Can't Turn Back," 628-629.

7. Goldstein.

8. Goldstein.

9. Elkind.

10. McAdams, *The Stories We Live By*, 80.

11. McAdams, 80.

12. Rudd, *Underground*, 218.

13. Linde, *Life Stories;* McAdams, *The Stories We Live By,* 80.

14. Thomas, "Standing Alone," 21.

15. Rai, "How Could They?" 6-7.

16. Franks, "Return of the Fugitive," 51.

17. Thomas, "Standing Alone," 21.

18. Thomas, "Standing Alone," 21.

19. Cohen, "The Romance of Revolutionary Violence," 29.

20. Jacobs and McCarthy, "A Bank Is Robbed, a Cop Is Killed, a Movement Is Hung."

21. Cohen, "The Romance of Revolutionary Violence," 29.

22. Cohen, "The Romance of Revolutionary Violence," 29.

23. Cohen, "The Romance of Revolutionary Violence," 30.

24. Carlson, "The Return of the Fugitive," 61.

25. Cited in Holmstrom, "Conscience Calls a 1970s Radical to Face her Past," 8.

26. Ross, "The Intuitive Psychologist and his Shortcomings," 184, citing 1966 research by Walster.

27. Stoltze, "Ex-Fugitive Sara Jane Olson Sentenced."

28. Flanagan, "Symbionese Liberation Parolee."

29. Stoltze, "Ex-Fugitive Sara Jane Olson Sentenced."

30. Altman, "Sara Jane Olson: American Housewife, American Terrorist."

31. Stoltze, "Ex-Fugitive Sara Jane Olson Sentenced."

32. Altman, "Sara Jane Olson: American Housewife, American Terrorist."

Chapter 6. "I Walked Away and I Kept On": The Fugitive

1. Franks, "Return of the Fugitive," 52.

2. "Slay Suspect," 5.

3. I owe almost all the information about these facts and their chronology to Lucinda Franks's *New Yorker* article.

4. Franks, "Return of the Fugitive," 52.

5. Franks, "Return of the Fugitive," 52.

6. Franks, "Return of the Fugitive," 52.

7. Franks, "Return of the Fugitive," 52.

8. Franks, "Return of the Fugitive," 54.

9.   Franks, "Return of the Fugitive," 54.

10. Franks, "Return of the Fugitive," 55.

11. Franks, "Return of the Fugitive," 55. This last struck one of my readers as an ethical failure strikingly parallel to her crime. Once again, he noted, Power's acts left another family fatherless, and she moved on.

12. Franks, 56.

13. Franks, 57.

14. Franks, 57.

15. Franks, 57.

16. Lambert, "Alice Doesn't Live Here Anymore."

17. Franks, 44.

18. Franks, 58.

19. Franks, 51.

20. Franks, 52.

21. Franks, 54.

22. Power, personal communication, January 15, 2010.

23. Franks, 44.

24. Franks, 54.

25. Franks, 57.

26. Franks, 58.

27. Gouras, "Fugitive Hid 40 Years in Plain Sight."

28. Erikson, *Childhood and Society*, 252-253.

29. Lewis, *Shame and Guilt in Neurosis.*

30. Lewis, 40; Tangney, "Assessing Individual Differences in Proneness to Shame and Guilt."

31. Dostoevsky, *Crime and Punishment*, 509.

32. Franks, 42.

33. Freud, S. "Repression," 84-97.

34. E.g., Pennebaker, "Putting Stress into Words"; Pennebaker, *Opening Up: The Healing Power of Expressing Emotions;* Wegner, "Ironic Processes of Mental Control"; Wegner, *White Bears and Other Unwanted Thoughts.*

35. Franks, 43.

36. Camus, *The Rebel*, 281.

37. Franks, 42.

38. For a more extended comparative analysis of Dostoevsky's fictional radical of the 1860s and this very real radical of the 1960s, see my chapter "The Crime, Punishment, and Ethical Transformation of Two Radicals: Or How Katherine Power Improves on Dostoevsky." In *Turns in the Road: Narrative Studies of Lives in Transition*, 35-66.

39. Franks, 54.

40. Franks, 41.

41. Ryle, quoted in Geertz, *Interpretation of Cultures*, 362.

Chapter 7. Showing Up: The Surrender

1. Franks, 41.

2. Gitlin, "Return of the Fugitive—and the 'Big Chill' Generation," C3.

3. Klieman (with Peter Knobler), *Fairy Tales Can Come True*, 280.

4. "Prodigal Daughter," 18.

5. Power, 1993, Sept. 16, Statement of Vietnam-Era Fugitive, B9.

6. Holmstrom, "Conscience Calls," 8; Egan, "A Conscience Haunted," A1; Bruner, "The Guilt Behind a Tragic Deed," 31.

7. Gitlin, "Return of the Fugitive," C3.

8. "A Clear Voice," A14.

9. Krauthammer, "From People Power to Polenta," 94.

10. Hymowitz and Pollack, "In from the Cold," A1.

11. Cohen, "The Romance of Revolutionary Violence," 28.

12. Krauthammer, "From People Power to Polenta."

13. "Reader Feedback," 26.

14. Wilson, "Dubious Sympathies."

15. Klieman (with Peter Knobler), *Fairy Tales Can Come True*, 279.

16. Kantrowitz, "The Fugitive," 60.

17. Daly, "Woman Ends 23 Years as a Fugitive," A4.

18. Gonzales, M. H., Manning, D. J., and Haugen, J. A., "Explaining Our Sins"; Gonzales, M. H., Haugen, J. A., and Manning, D. J., "Victims as 'Narrative Critics.'"

19. Black, Steven. Personal communication. September 13, 2011.

20. Franks, 41.

21. Krauthammer, "From People Power to Polenta," 94.

22. Wilson, "Dubious Sympathies."

23. "A Clear Voice," A14.

24. Palmer, "For Power, Others, War Protest Was Just the Beginning," 16.

25. Rabinowitz, "A New Eye on American Culture at CBS," A18.

26. Spillane, "A 'Radical's' Return," 413.

27. Gitlin, "Return of the Fugitive," C3.

28. Cohen, "The Romance of Revolutionary Violence," 30.

29. Franks, "Return of the Fugitive," 58.

30. Franks, 54.

31. Franks, 56.

32. Franks, 58.

33. Franks, 59.

34. Franks, 59.

35. I first learned of this event from the 1994 *New Yorker* article, and I interviewed Black about it myself by phone on November 11, 1995.

36. Franks, 45.

37. Franks, 45.

38. Franks, 45.

39. Franks, 45-46.

40. Franks, 46.

41. Franks, 46.

42. Franks, 46.

43. Franks, 46.

44. Franks, 58.

45. E.g., Pennebaker, "Putting Stress into Words"; Roemer and Borkovec, "Effects of Suppressing Thoughts about Emotional Material"; Wegner, "Ironic Processes of Mental Control"; Wegner, *White Bears and Other Unwanted Thoughts*. Wegner, Schneider, Carter, and White, "Paradoxical Effects of Thought Suppression."

Chapter 8. Owning Up: The Guilty Plea

1. Franks, 46.

2. Those who have focused on these legalistic issues have tended to deem her punishment to have exceeded her crimes. Others feel just as strongly that her sentence was too lenient.

3. This idea came from Tony Wallace.

4. Franks, 45.

5. Power's audiorecorded interview with me on August 30, 1995.

6. Whitney, *Forgiveness: A Time to Love and a Time to Hate.*

7. Gitlin, "Return of the Fugitive," C3.

8. Gitlin, "Return of the Fugitive," C3.

9. Power, personal communication, April 18, 2001.

10. Zehr, *Changing Lenses: A New Focus for Crime and Justice,* 211.

11. Zehr, 202.

12. Zehr, 202.

13. Zehr, 202.

14. Forster, E.M. *What I Believe.*

15. Lewis, *Shame and Guilt in Neurosis,* 40; Tangney, "Assessing Individual Differences in Proneness to Shame and Guilt."

16. "Power's Confession a Lucky Break for Prosecutors," A1.

17. If interested in more discussion of this point, you may want to refer to my essay "The Confessions of the War Maker and the War Resister," which appeared in the Summer 1995 issue of the *Michigan Quarterly Review.*

18. Franks, 41.

19. Daly, "Woman Ends 23 Years as a Fugitive, A4.

20. "Felony-Murder Rule."

21. Hymowitz and Pollock, "In from the Cold," A1.

22. "Reader Feedback," 26.

23. "Accessory."

24. "Accomplice."

25. "Aiding and Abetting."

26. "Manslaughter."

Chapter 9. Redeeming Time: The Prison Years

1. Eliot, T.S. "The new years walk, restoring/ Through a bright cloud of tears, the years, restoring/ With a new verse the ancient rhyme. Redeem/the time. Redeem / The unread vision in the higher dream / While jeweled unicorns draw by the gilded hearse." 64.

2. Franks, "Return of the Fugitive," 58.

3. Franks, 59.

4. Franks, 59.

5. Landman and Dawes, "Psychotherapy Outcome."

6. North, "The 'Ideal' of Forgiveness: A Philosopher's Exploration."

7. North, "The 'Ideal' of Forgiveness: A Philosopher's Exploration," 30.

8. North, 30.

9. North, 30.

10. North, 32.

11. North, 32.

12. Power, personal communication, April 18, 2001.

13. Franks, "Return of the Fugitive," 48.

14. Power, personal communication, April 18, 2001.

15. King, "Letter from Birmingham Jail," 269.

16. Peters, "Education of the Emotions."

17. Erikson, *Childhood and Society;* Lewis, *Shame and Guilt in Neurosis;* Tangney: "Assessing Individual Differences in Proneness to Shame and Guilt"; "Proneness to Shame, Proneness to Guilt, and Psychopathology"; "Situational Determinants of Shame and Guilt in Young Adulthood."

18. Power, "Murphy's Law" cable TV interview.

19. Cohen, Ron, "Provocations of Restorative Justice."

20. Power, "Out of Shame, Into Forgiveness."

21. Power, "In a Convict's Heart."

22. Franks, "Return of the Fugitive," 42.

23. Franks, 42.

24. Shapley, *Promise and Power,* 408.

25. Shapley, *Promise and Power,* 415.

26. von Logau, Friedrich. (1604-1655). The allusion is a line from the poem "Retribution": "Though the mills of God grind slowly, yet they grind exceeding small," which is often translated as: "Though the wheels of justice grind slowly, yet they grind exceeding fine."

Chapter 10. The Parole Hearing: Making Herself a Minor Character in Someone Else's Story

1. Morson, *Narrative and Freedom*, 74.

2. Power, "Out of Shame, Into Forgiveness."

3. Gitlin had referred to the phrase "picked up the gun" as one of the "repellent terms of the time" (Gitlin, "Return of the Fugitive.")

4. Tavuchis, *Mea Culpa: A Sociology of Apology and Reconciliation*, 120-121.

5. Canellos, "Katherine Ann Power Halts Bid for Parole," B1.

6. Canellos, "Schroeders Find Solace in Power's Decision," B1.

7. Goldberg, "Sorrowful Outlaw Radical Abandons Bid for Parole," A6.

8. Ford, "Power Withdraws another Parole Bid," 8.

9. Camellos, "Schroeders Find Solace in Power's Decision," B1.

10. Canellos, "Katherine Ann Power Halts Bid for Parole," A1.

11. Canellos, "Schroeders Find Solace in Power's Decision," B1.

12. Goldberg, "Sorrowful Outlaw Radical Abandons Bid for Parole," A6.

13. McCullough, Parmagent, and Thoresen, *Forgiveness: Theory, Research, and Practice*, 7.

14. E.g., Butler, 1726, cited in Murphy and Hampton, *Forgiveness and Mercy*, 15; Downie, "Forgiveness"; Ewing, *The Morality of Punishment*; Hughes, "Forgiveness"; Lamb, *The Trouble with Blame*; Moore, *Pardons: Justice, Mercy, and the Public Interest*; Murphy, in Murphy and Hampton, *Forgiveness and Mercy*; Smedes, *Forgive and Forget*.

15. E.g., Pennebaker, "Putting Stress into Words"; Roemer and Borkovec, "Effects of Suppressing Thoughts about Emotional Material"; Wegner, "Ironic Processes of Mental Control"; Wegner, *White Bears and Other Unwanted Thoughts.* Wegner, Schneider, Carter, and White, "Paradoxical Effects of Thought Suppression."

16. E.g., Minow, *Between Vengeance and Forgiveness*; Smedes, *Forgive and Forget*; Soyinka, *The Burden of Memory, the Muse of Forgiveness*; Tutu, Foreword to *Exploring Forgiveness*, xiv.

17. Enright, Freedman, and Rique, "The Psychology of Interpersonal Forgiveness";

Haber, *Forgiveness;* Hampton, in Murphy and Hampton, *Forgiveness and Mercy;* Murphy, in Murphy and Hampton, *Forgiveness and Mercy.*

18. Murphy and Hampton, *Forgiveness and Mercy;* Haber, *Forgiveness.*

19. Tutu, Foreword to *Exploring Forgiveness,* xiv.

20. Wiesenthal, *The Sunflower,* 54.

21. Cargas, in Wiesenthal, 125.

22. Habes in Wiesenthal, 160-161.

23. Bar-On, "From Intractable Conflict," 352.

24. North, "The 'Ideal' of Forgiveness: A Philosopher's Exploration," 33.

25. E.g., North, "The 'Ideal' of Forgiveness: A Philosopher's Exploration," 34; Pawlikowski, in Wiesenthal, *The Sunflower,* 221.

26. Hampton, in Murphy and Hampton, *Forgiveness and Mercy.*

27. Enright, Freedman, and Rique, "The Psychology of Interpersonal Forgiveness," 49.

28. Exline and Baumeister, "Expressing Forgiveness and Repentance," 136.

29. Power's view coincides with that of moral philosopher Susan Dwyer: "Reconciliation should not be touted as aiming at the happy and harmonious coexistence of former enemies." (See Dwyer, "Reconciliation for Realists," 96.)

30. Maoz, "Participation, Control and Dominance."

31. Ford, "Power Withdraws another Parole Bid," p. 004.

32. Lamb, *The Trouble with Blame,* 163.

Chapter 11. "I Will Always Be Answerable": Conclusions

1. Mueller, "'Deeply Sorry' Power Starts Over," 1.

2. Stafford, "Thinking for Berky," 64-65.

3. "A Greater Power," A10.

Epilogue by Katherine Power

1. In 2012, Massachusetts was one of a handful of states that had legalized same-sex marriage.

WORKS CITED

"'100 Club' to Assist Family of Patrolman." *Boston Herald Traveler,* 27 Sept 1970: 4.

"60's Radical Who Surrendered Pleads Guilty to a Burglary Charge." *New York Times,* 25 Sept. 1993: 7, 9.

"9 Children to Get Full Scholarships." *Boston Herald Traveler,* 27 Sept. 1970: 4.

Abel, David. "Apologetic in the End, William Gilday Dies." *Boston Globe,* 16 Sept. 2011. http://www.bostonglobe.com/metro/2011/09/15/apologetic-end-william-gilday-dies/6ld7fXPXPifZmozCvzt1qN/story.xml.

Abu-Lughod, Lila, and Catherine A. Lutz, "Introduction: Emotion, Discourse, and the Politics of Everyday Life." In *Language and the Politics of Emotion.* Eds. Catherine A. Lutz and Lila Abu-Lughod. New York: Cambridge University Press, 1990. 1-23.

"Accessory." http://definitions.uslegal.com/a/accessory.

"A Clear Voice." Editorial. *Wall Street Journal,* 8 Oct. 1993: A14.

"Accomplice." http://definitions.uslegal.com/a/accomplice.

"A Greater Power." Editorial. *Boston Globe,* 7 March 1998: A10.

"Aiding and Abetting." www.ask.com/question/legal-definition-of-aiding-and-abetting.

Allen, Joe. "Vietnam: The Last War the U.S. Lost." Alternative radio.org, 2017.

Alpert, Jane. *Growing Up Underground.* New York: Citadel Underground, 1990.

Altman, Alex. "Sara Jane Olson: American Housewife, American Terrorist." http://www.time.com/time/nation/article/0,8599,1885965,00.html.

Aucoin, Don. "The Ascent of Rikki Klieman, Legal-TV Star." *Boston Globe,* 3 May 1998: F4-5.

Augsburger, David W. *The Freedom of Forgiveness.* Chicago: Moody Institute, 1988.

Ayers, Bill. *Fugitive Days: A Memoir.* Boston: Beacon, 2001.

Baddeley, Alan D. *The Psychology of Memory.* New York: Basic, 1976.

Baldwin, James. "They Can't Turn Back." *Collected Essays.* New York: The Library of America, 622-637.

Bar-On, Daniel. "From Intractable Conflict through Conflict Resolution to Reconciliation: Psychological Analysis." *Political Psychology* 21 (2000): 351-365.

Bates, Tom. *Rads: The 1970 Bombing of the Army Math Research Center at the University of Wisconsin and its Aftermath*. New York: HarperCollins, 1992.

Baumeister, Roy F., Julie Juola Exline, and Kristin L. Sommer. "The Victim Role, Grudge Theory, and Two Dimensions of Forgiveness." *Dimensions of Forgiveness*. Ed. Everett L. Worthington, Jr. Philadelphia, Penn: Templeton, 1998. 79-104

Belfrage, Sally. *Freedom Summer*. New York: Viking, 1965.

"Berrigan Brothers." www.encyclopedia.com.

Blake, Andrew F. "4 Campus 'Radicals' Hunted in Boston Police Slaying." *Washington Post*, 26 Sept. 1970: A5.

Bloom, Paul. "The Dark Side of Empathy: How Caring For One Person Can Foster Baseless Aggression Towards Another." *The Atlantic*, 25 Sept. 2015. http://www.the-atlantic.com/science/archive/2015/09/the-violence-of-empathy/407155/?utm_source=pocket&utm_medium=email&utm_campaign=pockethits.

Braithwaite, John. *Crime, Shame, and Reintegration*. New York: Cambridge University Press, 1989.

Braungart, M. M., & Braungart, R. G. "The Life Course Development of Left- and Right-wing Youth Activist Leaders from the 1960s." *Political Psychology* 11 (1990): 243-282.

Bruner, Fred. "The Guilt behind a Tragic Deed." *Macleans*, 1 Nov. 1993: 31.

Buruma, Ian. *The Wages of Guilt: Memories of War in Germany and Japan*. New York: Farrar Straus and Giroux, 1994.

Camus, Albert. *The Myth of Sisyphus and Other Essays*. 1955. Trans. J. O'Brien. New York: Vintage International, 1983.

Camus, Albert. *The Rebel: An Essay on Man in Revolt*. New York: Knopf, 1956.

Canellos, Peter S. "Katherine Ann Power Halts Bid for Parole: Ex-Radical: 'I Was Wrong All Along.'" *Boston Globe*, 6 March 1998: A1.

Canellos, Peter S. "Schroeders Find Solace in Power's Decision to Back Down on Parole." *Boston Globe*, 7 March 1998: B1.

Carlson, Margaret. "The Return of the Fugitive." *Time*, 27 Sept. 1993: 60-62.

Carmichael, Stokely, and Charles V. Hamilton. "The Concept of Black Power." *The Social Rebel in American Literature*. Eds. Robert H. Woodward and James J. Clark. New York: Odyssey, 1968. 100-105.

"The Catonsville Nine File: Blood to Fire." www.http://mdch.org.

"Cauldron." http://www.thefreedictionary.com/cauldron.

Collins English Dictionary—Complete and Unabridged, HarperCollins, 1991, 1994, 1998, 2000, 2003.

Cohen, Jacob. "The Romance of Revolutionary Violence." *National Review,* 13 Dec. 1993: 28-33.

Cohen, Ronald L. "Provocations of Restorative Justice." *Social Justice Research* 14 (2001): 209-232.

Cole, Elizabeth R., and Stewart, Abigail. "Meanings of Political Participation among Black and White Women: Political Identity and Social Responsibility." *Journal of Personality and Social Psychology* 71 (1996): 130-140.

Creamer, Bob and Jim Droney. "Radicals Linked to Police Slaying." *Boston Herald Traveler,* 25 Sept.1970: 3.

Croft, George. "Hub Officer Shot by Bank Robbers." *Boston Evening Globe,* 23 Sept. 1970: 32, 52.

Daly, Christopher B. "Woman Ends 23 Years as a Fugitive." *Washington Post,* 16 Sept. 1993: A1, A4.

"David Dellinger." http://web.ncf.ca/fl512/book/authors_david_dellinger.htm.

Dostoevsky, Fyodor. *Crime and Punishment.* 1865-66. Trans. D. McDuff. London: Penguin, 1991.

Downie, R. S. "Forgiveness." *Philosophical Quarterly* 15 (1965): 128-134.

Dwyer, Susan. "Reconciliation for Realists." *Ethics and International Affairs* 13 (1999): 81-98.

Eco, Umberto. "The Revolt Against the Law." *Turning Back the Clock.* Trans. Alistair McEwen. New York: Harcourt, 2007. 180-189.

Egan, Timothy. "A Conscience Haunted by a Radical's Crime." *New York Times,* 17 Sept. 1993: A1, A22.

"Egoism." https://philosophyterms.com/egoism/.

"Egotism." https://philosophyterms.com/egoism/.

Eliot, T. S. "Ash Wednesday." *The Complete Poems and Plays 1909-1950.* New York: Harcourt, Brace & World. 1971. 64.

Enright, Robert D., and Joanna North, eds. *Exploring Forgiveness.* Madison: University of Wisconsin Press, 1998.

Enright, Robert D., Suzanne Freedman, and Julio Rique. "The Psychology of Interpersonal Forgiveness." *Exploring Forgiveness.* Eds. Robert D. Enright and Joanna North. Madison: University of Wisconsin Press, 1998. 46-62.

Erikson, Erik. *Childhood and Society*. 2nd ed. New York: Norton, 1963.

Epps, Garrett. "Judicial Order Cause for Alarm." *Oregon Lawyer,* Spring 2000: 8-10.

Evans, Sara. *Personal Politics: The Roots of Women's Liberation in the Civil Rights Movement and the New Left*. New York: Knopf, 1979.

Ewing, Alfred C. *The Morality of Punishment*. Montclair, NJ: Patterson-Smith, 1970.

Exline, Julie J., and Roy F. Baumeister. "Expressing Forgiveness and Repentance: Benefits and Barriers." *Forgiveness: Theory, Research, and Practice*. Eds. Michael E. McCullough, Kenneth I. Pargament, and Carl Thoresen, 2000. 133-155.

"Felony-Murder Rule." 2007. http://law.jrank.org/pages 6835/Felony-Murder-Rule. html.

Flacks, Richard. *Youth and Social Change*. New York: Markham, 1971.

Flanagan, Caitlin. "Symbionese Liberation Parolee." *New York Times,* 22 March 2009. http://www.nytimes.com/2009/03/22/opinion/22Flanagan.html.

Ford, B. "Power Could Be Freed in '99 with Good Behavior." *Boston Herald,* 7 March 1998: 8.

Ford, B. "Power Withdraws another Parole Bid." *Boston Herald,* 9 March 1999: 4.

"Forgetting Curve." http://www.utdallas.edu/counseling/docs/ForgettingCurve.pdf.

Forster, E. M. *What I Believe*. London: Hogarth, 1939.

Frank, Arthur W. *The Wounded Storyteller: Body, Illness, and Ethics*. Chicago: U of Chicago Press, 1995.

Franks, Lucinda. "The Return of the Fugitive." *New Yorker,* 13 June 1994: 40-59.

Franzen, Jonathan. *Farther Away: Essays*. New York: Farrar, Straus and Giroux, 2012.

Freeland, Richard M. *Academia's Golden Age: Universities in Massachusetts 1945-1970*. New York: Oxford, 1992.

Freud, Sigmund. Freud, S. "Repression." *Sigmund Freud: Collected Papers*. Vol 4. 1915. New York, NY: Basic. 84-97.

Gao, Yuan. *Born Red: A Chronicle of the Cultural Revolution*. Stanford, CA: Stanford University Press, 1987: 85-86.

Garfinkel, Ariel. "The Vietnam War Is Over. The Bombs Remain." 20 March 2018. https://www.nytimes.com/2018/03/20/opinion/vietnam-war-agent-orange-bombs. html.

Geertz, Clifford. *The Interpretation of Cultures*. New York: Basic, 1973.

Gertner, Nancy. *In Defense of Women: Memoirs of an Unrepentant Advocate*. Boston: Beacon, 2011.

Gitlin, Todd. *The Sixties: Years of Hope, Days of Rage.* New York: Bantam, 1987.

Gitlin, Todd. "Return of the Fugitive—and the 'Big Chill' Generation." *Washington Post,* 26 Sept. 1993: C3.

Goldberg, Carey. "Sorrowful Outlaw Radical Abandons Bid for Parole." *New York Times,* 7 March 1998: A6.

Goldstein, Dana. "The Teenage Brain of the Boston Bomber." https://www.themarshall-project.org/2015/01/08/the-teenage-brain-of-the-boston-bomber?_hp=3-111.

Gonzales, Marti H., Debra J. Manning, and Julie A. Haugen. "Explaining Our Sins: Factors Influencing Offender Accounts and Anticipated Victim Responses." *Journal of Personality and Social Psychology* 62 (1992): 958-971.

Gonzales, Marti H., Julie A. Haugen, and Debra J. Manning. "Victims as 'Narrative Critics': Factors Influencing Rejoinders and Evaluative Responses to Offenders' Accounts." *Personality and Social Psychology Bulletin* 20 (1994): 691-704.

Gouras, Matt. "Fugitive Hid 40 Years in Plain Sight." 15 June 2010. http://www.topix.com/forum/city/arizona-city-az/TBABKIE9M53UAHJO8.

Gurovitch, Philip. *We Wish to Inform You that Tomorrow We Will Be Killed with our Families.* New York: Picador, 1998.

Haber, Joram G. *Forgiveness.* Savage, Maryland: Rowman and Littlefield, 1991.

Haidt, Jonathan. *The Righteous Mind: Why Good People Are Divided by Politics and Religion.* New York: Pantheon, 2012.

Hamilton, William. "Former Student Radical's Journey from Depression Led to Surrender." *Washington Post,* 18 Sept. 1993: A3.

Harrington, Walt. "Beginning in Narrative." *Telling True Stories.* Eds. Mark Kramer and Wendy Call. New York: Plume, 2007. 228-230.

Hart, Jordana. "Ex-Fugitive Finally Can Face Past: Katherine Power Finds Peace in Prison." *Boston Globe.* Reprinted in *Denver Post,* 24 July 1994: A21.

Hassett, Robert I. "How Did Five Form Weird Alliance?" *Boston Sunday Herald Traveler,* 27 Sept. 1970: Section 1:1; Section 2: 4-5.

Hayden, Tom. *Reunion: A Memoir.* New York: Random House.

Holmstrom, D. "Conscience Calls a 1970s Radical to Face her Past." *Christian Science Monitor,* 20 Sept. 1993: 8.

Hughes, M. "Forgiveness." *Analysis* 35 (1975): 113-117.

Hymowitz, C., and E. J. Pollock. "In from the Cold: A Confession Was Start of a Long, Strange Trip for Katherine Power." *Wall Street Journal,* 6 Oct. 1993: A1.

"Inmate Nation." Cover story. *Time,* 13 Sept. 1982.

"Involuntary Manslaughter." http://www.massmurderdefense.com/pages/manslaughter-in.html

Jacobs, Scott A., and Michael B. McCarthy. "A Bank Is Robbed, a Cop Is Killed, a Movement Is Hung." Harvard *Crimson,* 5 Oct. 1970.

Jensen, Frances E. *The Teenage Brain.* New York: HarperCollins, 2015.

"John Brown." pbs.org/wgbh/aia/part4/4p1550.html.

Johnson, Denis. *Already Dead.* New York: Harper Perennial, 1998.

Kantrowitz, Barbara. Cover Story. "The Fugitive." *Newsweek,* 27 Sept. 1993: 54-60.

Kaufman, Michael T. Obituary. "David Dellinger, of Chicago 7, Dies at 88." 27 May 2004, http: www.nytimes.com/2004/05/27/national.

Keniston, Kenneth. *The Young Radicals: Notes on Committed Youth.* New York: Harcourt, Brace, World, 1968.

"Kent State." http://www.may4.org.

King, Martin Luther, Jr. "Letter from Birmingham Jail." 1963. *The Best American Essays of the Century.* Eds. Joyce Carol Oates and Robert Atwan. New York: Houghton Mifflin, 2000. 263-279.

Klieman, Rikki. (With Peter Knobler). *Fairy Tales Can Come True*: *How a Driven Woman Changed Her Destiny.* New York: Regan, 2003.

Krauthammer, Charles. "From People Power to Polenta." *Time,* 4 Oct. 1993: 94.

Kunen, James Simon. *The Strawberry Statement*: *Notes of a College Revolutionary.* New York: Avon, 1968.

Lamb, Sharon. *The Trouble with Blame*: *Victims, Perpetrators, and Responsibility.* Cambridge, Mass: Harvard University Press, 1996.

Lamb, Sharon, and Jeffrie G. Murphy. Eds. *Before Forgiving*: *Cautionary Tales of Forgiveness in Psychotherapy.* New York: Oxford University Press, 2002.

Lambert, Pam. "Alice Doesn't Live Here Anymore." *People,* 4 Oct. 1993.

Landman, Janet. *Regret: The Persistence of the Possible.* New York: Oxford, 1993.

Landman, Janet. "The Confessions of the War Maker and the War Resister." *The Michigan Quarterly Review* 38 (1999): 393-423.

Landman, Janet. "The Crime, Punishment, and Ethical Transformation of Two Radicals: Or How Katherine Power Improves on Dostoevsky." *Turns in the Road: Narrative Studies of Lives in Transition.* Eds. Dan P. McAdams, Ruthellen Josselson, and Amia Lieblich. Washington, DC: American Psychological Association, 2001. 35-66.

Landman, Janet, and Robin Dawes. "Psychotherapy Outcome: Smith and Glass's Conclusions Stand up under Scrutiny." *American Psychologist 37* (1982): 504-516.

"Legacies of Loss." *Boston Globe,* 8 March 1998: D3.

Leonard, John. *Reading for my Life*: *Writings 1958-2008.* New York: Penguin, 2012.

Lewis, Helen Block. *Shame and Guilt in Neurosis.* New York: International Universities Press, 1971.

Linde, Charlotte. *Life Stories*: *Creation of Coherence.* New York: Oxford, 1993.

Lytle, Mark H. *America's Uncivil Wars: The Sixties Era from Elvis to the Fall of Richard Nixon.* New York: Oxford, 2006.

Mahoney, James. "'Brilliant' Bond Seen as Founder of Gang." *Boston Herald Traveler,* 26 Sept. 1970: 1, 4.

Malcolm, Janet. "Easy Time." *New Yorker,* 16 Oct. 1995: 99.

Malcolm, Janet. *The Silent Woman*: *Sylvia Plath and Ted Hughes.* New York: Vintage, 1995.

"Manslaughter." http://www.massmurderdefense.com/pages/manslaughter-in.html.

Maoz, Ifat. "Participation, Control and Dominance in Communication between Groups in Conflict: Analysis of Dialogues between Jews and Palestinians in Israel." *Social Justice Research* 14 (2001): 189-208.

Marchand, Earl. "Katherine 'Used,' Mother Says." *Boston Herald Traveler,* 26 Sept. 1970: 1.

Marcus, Gary. *Kluge: The Haphazard Construction of the Human Mind.* New York: Houghton Mifflin, 2008.

Marcuse, Herbert. http://www.brandeis.edu/cges/news/upcomingevents/Adorno.html, March 2009 issue.

Markus, Hazel R., & Shinobu Kitayama, S. "Culture and the Self: Implications for Cognition, Emotion, and Motivation." *Psychological Review* 98.2 (1991): 224-253.

McAdam, Douglas. *Freedom Summer.* New York: Oxford, 1988.

McAdams, Dan P. *The Redemptive Self: Stories Americans Live By.* New York: Oxford, 2006.

McAdams, Dan P. *The Stories We Live By*: *Personal Myths and the Making of the Self.* New York: William Morrow, 1993.

McCullough, Michael E., Julie Juola Exline, and Roy Baumeister. "An Annotated Bibliography of Research on Forgiveness and Related Concepts." *Dimensions of Forgiveness: Psychological Research and Theological Perspectives.* Ed. Everett L. Worthington. Philadelphia, Penn: Templeton, 1998.

McCullough, Michael E., Kenneth I. Pargament, and Carl Thoresen, eds. *Forgiveness: Theory, Research, and Practice*. New York: Guilford, 2000.

McNamara, Robert S. (with Brian VanDeMark). *In Retrospect: The Tragedy and Lessons of Vietnam*. New York: Times Books, Random House, 1995.

Metzger, H. Peter. "Brandeis: School for Terrorists?" *Outpost,* Oct. 2008: 5-6.

"Militant." http://dictionary.oed.com/cgi/entry/00064394.

Minow, Martha. *Between Vengeance and Forgiveness: Facing History after Genocide and Mass Violence*. Boston: Beacon, 1998.

Moore, Kathleen Dean. *Pardons: Justice, Mercy, and the Public Interest*. New York: Oxford, 1989.

Morson, Gary S. *Narrative and Freedom: The Shadows of Time*. New Haven, Conn: Yale University Press, 1994.

Mueller, Mark. "'Deeply Sorry' Power Starts Over." *Boston Herald,* 2 Oct. 1999: 1.

Murphy, Jeffrie G., and Jean Hampton. *Forgiveness and Mercy*. New York: Cambridge University Press, 1988.

Murphy, Jeffrie G. "Moral Epistemology, the Retributive Emotions, and the 'Clumsy Moral Philosophy' of Jesus Christ." *Philosophical Studies* 89 (1998): 215-236.

Murray, Tom, and Paul Giguere. "Policeman, Father of 9, Shot in Bank Holdup." *Boston Herald Traveler,* 24 Sept. 1970: 1, 3.

"My Lai." http://www.law.umkc.edu/faculty/projects/ftrials/mylai/Myl_intro.html.

Nims, John Frederick. *Western Wind: An Introduction to Poetry*. 2d ed. New York: Random House, 1983.

North, Joanna. "The 'Ideal' of Forgiveness: A Philosopher's Exploration." *Exploring Forgiveness*. Eds. Robert D. Enright, and Joanna North. Madison: U of Wisconsin Press, 1998. 15-34.

Opatow, Susan. "Moral Inclusion and the Process of Social Reconciliation." *Social Justice Research* 14 (2001): 149-170.

Ottley, Ted, "Timothy McVeigh and Terry Nichols: Oklahoma Bombing." http://www.trutv.com/library/crime/serial_killers/notorious/mcveigh/dawning_1.html.

Pacheco, Dan. "Fugitive Gives Up 16 Years Later." *Denver Post,* 7 Aug. 1994: C1.

Palmer, Jr., Thomas C. "For Power, Others, War Protest Was Just the Beginning." *Boston Globe,* 17 Sept. 1993: 16.

Pennebaker, James W. "Putting Stress into Words: Health, Linguistic, and Therapeutic Implications." *Behavior Research and Theory* 31 (1993): 539-548.

Pennebaker, James W. *Opening Up: The Healing Power of Expressing Emotions*. New York: Guilford, 1997.

Percy, Walker. *The Moviegoer*. 1961. New York: Vintage International, 1998.

Peters, R. S. "The Education of the Emotions." *Feelings and Emotion: The Loyola Symposium*. Ed. Magda B. Arnold. New York: Academic, 1970. 187-203.

Pogrebin, Letty Cottin. Afterword. "A Dance to John." *John Leonard, Reading for my Life: Writings 1958-2008*. New York: Penguin, 2012.

Port Huron Statement: Students for a Democratic Society. 1962. Chicago: Charles H. Kerr Publishing, 1990.

Power, Katherine A. "Statement of Vietnam War-Era Fugitive." *New York Times*, 16 Sept. 1993: B9.

Power, Katherine Alice. "Sestina for Jaime." *The Best American Poetry 1996*. Ed. Adrienne Rich. New York: Scribner, 1996. 171-172.

Power, Katherine A. Statement to the Parole Board, 6 March, 1998.

Power, Katherine A. "Murphy's Law" Interview, Milton, Massachusetts Cable TV. 5 April 1998.

Power, Katherine A. "Forgive Us Our Trespasses." Unpublished essay, Summer 1999.

Power, Katherine A. "In a Convict's Heart." Unpublished essay, 16 November 1998.

Power, Katherine A. "Out of Shame, Into Forgiveness." Unpublished essay 1999.

Power, Katherine A. "My Journey to Nonviolence." Glavin Chapel, Babson College, Wellesley, Massachusetts. 5 October 1999. Non-public Lecture.

"Power's Confession a Lucky Break for Prosecutors." *Portland Oregonian*, 6 June 1994: A1.

"The Prodigal Daughter." Editorial. *New York Times*, 18 Sept. 1993: 14, 18.

Prose, Francine. *Reading like a Writer*. New York: Harper Perennial, 2007.

"Psychopath." http://wiki.answers.com/Q/What_is_the_difference_between_a_sociopath_and_a_psychopath.

Rabinowitz, Dorothy. "A New Eye on American Culture at CBS." *Wall Street Journal*, 23 Feb. 1994: A18.

Rai, Tage. "How Could They?" *Aeon*, 18 June 2015. http://aeon.co/magazine/philosophy/people-do-violence-because-their-moral-codes-demand-it/.

Randall, Gene, and Bill Delaney. "One-time Campus Radical Katherine Ann Power Released from Prison." *CNN Saturday*, 2 Oct. 1999.

"Reader Feedback." *Boston Globe*, 23 September 1993: 26.

"Reform," http://dictionary.oed.com/cgi/entry/00064394.htlm.

Reinhold, Robert. "Students Hunted in Police Killing." *New York Times,* 26 Sept. 1970: 1.

Rieff, Philip. *The Triumph of the Therapeutic.* New York: Harper, Row, 1966.

Rimer, Sara. "60's Radical, Linked to a Killing, Surrenders after Hiding 23 Years." *New York Times,* 16 Sept. 1993: A1, B9.

Robinson, John A., and Linda Hawpe. "Narrative Thinking as a Heuristic Process." *Narrative Psychology: The Storied Nature of Human Conduct.* Ed. Theodore R. Sarbin. New York: Praeger, 1986. 111-125.

Roemer, L., and Thomas D. Borkovec. "Effects of Suppressing Thoughts about Emotional Material." *Journal of Abnormal Psychology* 103 (1994): 467-474.

Ross, Lee. "The Intuitive Psychologist and his Shortcomings: Distortions in the Attributional Process." *Advances in Experimental Social Psychology.* Vol. 10. Ed. Leonard Berkowitz. New York: Academic Press, 1977. 173-214.

Rudd, Mark. *Underground: My Life with SDS and the Weathermen.* New York: HarperCollins, 2009.

Scheer, Robert. "McNamara's Evil Lives On." *The Nation,* 20 July 2009.

Scobie, E. D., and G. E. W. Scobie. "Damaging Events: The Perceived Need for Forgiveness." *Journal for the Theory of Social Behaviour* 28 (1998): 373-401.

Schönbach, Peter. *Account Episodes: The Management and Escalation of Conflict.* Cambridge: Cambridge University Press, 1990. Quoted in Marti H. Gonzales, Julie A. Haugen, and Debra J. Manning. "Victims as 'Narrative Critics': Factors Influencing Rejoinders and Evaluative Responses to Offenders' Accounts." *Personality and Social Psychology Bulletin* 20 (1994): 691-704.

Shapley, Deborah. *Promise and Power: The Life and Times of Robert McNamara.* New York: Little, Brown, 1993.

"Slay Suspect Slips Dragnet." *Boston Herald Traveler,* 26 Sept. 1970: 1, 4, 5.

Smedes, Lewis B. *Forgive and Forget.* San Francisco: Harper, Row, 1984.

Soyinka, Wole. *The Burden of Memory, the Muse of Forgiveness.* New York: Oxford, 1999.

Spillane, Margaret. "A 'Radical's' Return." *Nation,* 18 Oct. 1993, 413.

Spinoza, Baruch. *Ethics.* Trans. Samuel Shirley. Indianapolis: Hackett, 1991.

Stafford, William. "Following the *Markings* of Dag Hammarskjold: A Gathering of Poems in the Spirit of his Life and Writings: Prologue." *Stories that Could Be True.* New York: Harper, Row, 1977. 133.

Stafford, William. "Thinking for Berky." *Stories that Could Be True.* New York: Harper, Row, 1977. 64-65.

Staples, Brent. "The Oldest Rad." Rev. of *Fugitive Days: A Memoir*, by Bill Ayers. *New York Times Book Review*, 30 Sept. 2001: 11.

Steinem, Gloria. Afterword. "A Dance to John." *John Leonard, Reading for my Life*: *Writing, 1958-2008*. New York: Penguin, 2012.

Stoltze, Frank. "Ex-fugitive Sara Jane Olson Sentenced to 20 Years to Life." 18 January: 2002.   http://news.minnesota.publicradio.org/features/200201/18_stoltzef_ olsonsentence/.

Tangney, June P. "Assessing Individual Differences in Proneness to Shame and Guilt: Development of the Self-Conscious Affect and Attribution Inventory." *Journal of Personality and Social Psychology* 59 (1990): 102-111.

Tangney, June P., Patricia Wagner, and Richard Gramzow. "Proneness to Shame, Proneness to Guilt, and Psychopathology." *Journal of Personality and Social Psychology* 101 (1992a): 469-478.

Tangney, June P. "Situational Determinants of Shame and Guilt in Young Adulthood." *Personality and Social Psychology Bulletin* 18 (1992b): 199-206.

Tavuchis, Nicholas. *Mea Culpa: A Sociology of Apology and Reconciliation*. Stanford, Calif: Stanford University Press, 1991.

Thomas, Louisa. "Standing Alone." Rev. of *Beautiful Souls*, by Eyal Press. *New York Times Book Review*, 11 March 2012: 21.

Thoreau, Henry David. *Civil Disobedience and Other Essays*. 1849. Mineola, NY: Dover, 1993.

Todd, Elizabeth. "The Value of Confession and Forgiveness According to Jung." *Journal of Religion and Health*, 24 (1985): 39-48.

Tutu, Desmond. Foreword. *Exploring Forgiveness*. Eds. Robert D. Enright and Joanna North. Madison: University of Wisconsin Press, 1998. xiii-xiv.

Viorst, Milton. *Fire in the Streets: America in the 1960's*. New York: Simon & Schuster, 1979.

Wegner, Daniel M. "Ironic Processes of Mental Control." *Psychological Review* 101 (1994a): 34-52.

Wegner, Daniel M. *White Bears and Other Unwanted Thoughts: Suppression, Obsession, and the Psychology of Mental Control*. New York: Guilford, 1994b.

Wegner, Daniel M., David J. Schneider, Samuel R. Carter, and Teri L. White. "Paradoxical Effects of Thought Suppression." *Journal of Personality and Social Psychology* 53 (1987): 5-13.

Whitney, Helen. *Forgiveness: A Time to Love and a Time to Hate*. Produced, directed, and written by Helen Whitney. Clear View Productions. 2010. Docurama Films, 2011. DVD.

Wiesenthal, Simon. "The Sunflower." *The Sunflower: On the Possibilities and Limits of Forgiveness*. Book One. Eds. Harry J. Cargas and Bonny V. Fetterman. New York: Schocken, 1998.

Wilson, Bradford P. "Dubious Sympathies." *On Principle* 1(3) Oct. 1993. www.ashbrook.org/publicat/onprin/v1n3/wilson.html.

Wiman, Christian. *My Bright Abyss: Poems*. New York: Farrar, Straus and Giroux, 2013.

Wolfe, Tom. "Radical Chic: That Party at Lenny's." *New York Magazine,* 8 June 1970. http://nymag.com/news/features/46170/.

Wyckoff, Whitney Blair. "Jackson State: A Tragedy Widely Forgotten." 3 May 2010. http://www.npr.org.

Yeats, William B. "The Second Coming." *The Collected Works of W. B. Yeats*. Vol.1: *The Poems* Revised. Ed. Richard J. Finneran. New York: Macmillan. 187.

Zaretsky, Robert. *Albert Camus: Elements of a Life*. Ithaca, NY: Cornell University Press, 2010.

Zehr, Howard. *Changing Lenses: A New Focus for Crime and Justice*. Scottdale, Penn: Herald Press, 1995.

INDEX

Symbols

12-Step Program 37, 156, 157, 159, 197, 202

A

Alice Metzinger 1, 12, 93, 97, 102, 121, 124, 126
Alpert, Jane 20, 41, 82
Ayers, Bill 30

B

Berrigans 45-47
Black Liberation Army 28, 30, 31
Black Panthers 1, 17, 18, 25, 27-30, 50-53, 58, 59, 66, 67, 69, 91
Black, Steven 5, 98, 114, 119, 123-125, 129, 132, 136, 143, 145, 185
bombings 20, 29, 31, 92, 93
Bond, Stanley 15-18, 57, 63-69, 72, 73, 96, 99, 100, 118, 179-181
Boston Globe 2, 111, 117, 118, 145, 190, 191, 204
Boston Herald vi, 171, 190, 195, 201
Brandeis University 1, 5, 16, 17, 44-46, 48-57, 61-63, 69, 71, 81, 82, 90, 91
  Archives 90
Brown, John 73
Buddhist 37, 150, 154

C

Calley, William 136, 139, 174
Cambodia 27-29, 52, 53, 57, 58, 86
Catholic guilt 10, 42, 129, 130-132, 147, 155
Catholicism 37, 40, 41, 43, 45, 48, 50, 84, 100, 120, 125, 126, 130-132, 134, 154, 170
Chicago 1968 26, 27, 60
Chicago Seven 27, 52
Cohen, Jacob 48, 51, 52, 54, 58, 61, 65, 73, 90, 91, 110, 116, 118
conscience work 6, 7, 75, 141, 149, 150, 152, 155, 157-159, 163, 172, 176, 183, 186-188, 202

D

Davis, Angela 34, 49
Dellinger, David 27, 47

E

empathy 79, 80, 87, 167, 171-173, 176, 203

F

FBI's Most Wanted 1, 49, 93
felony murder 1, 21, 144-146
forgiveness 5, 101, 126, 131, 135, 137, 156, 170, 174, 188, 191-198, 202
Franks, Lucinda 3, 9, 42, 64, 99, 100, 104, 120, 124, 125, 153
fundamental attribution error 21-24, 93

G

Gilday, William Lefty 1, 15, 16, 18, 19, 68, 69, 72, 75, 99, 111, 118, 145, 146, 180, 181, 212
Gitlin, Todd 28, 29, 58, 79, 110, 118, 138, 213, 215
good time 2, 12, 177
group dynamics 62, 68, 70, 91

guilt 3, 11, 98, 100, 102, 103, 110, 135,
        136, 140-142, 153, 168, 169,
        182, 186, 197, 202
guilty plea 2, 84, 99, 108, 114, 129-
        136, 139, 143, 144, 146, 147,
        157, 182, 199

H

Hayden, Tom 27, 29, 51, 52, 54

I

interpersonal influence 62, 68, 71

J

Jackson State 27, 28, 60
Johnson, Lyndon 24-26, 174
Judge Banks, Robert 115-117, 136, 168

K

Kennedy, John F. 37, 40
Kennedy, Robert 45
Kent State 17, 27, 28, 53, 56, 60
King, Martin Luther 27, 45, 166
Klieman, Rikki 98, 108, 112, 113
Krauthammer, Charles 110, 115, 129,
        130

L

Lamb, Sharon 197
Lebanon, Oregon 119, 207

M

manslaughter 2, 16, 84, 99, 121, 130,
        139, 144-146, 157, 199
    definition 145, 146
Mao Tse Tung 71, 85, 86
McAdams, Dan 85
MCI-Framingham 9, 12, 99, 152, 173,
        190, 201

McNamara, Robert 5, 23-25, 31, 136-
        138, 172-176, 195
    my interview 5, 23, 24, 173
moral psychology 67

N

National Strike Information Center
        52, 53, 55-58, 62, 63, 68, 69
New Age 110, 118, 129, 207
Newsweek 48, 72, 107, 108, 110-112
New Yorker 3, 9, 42, 48, 63, 95, 100,
        107, 118, 120, 171, 207, 208
New York Times 107-110, 117, 190,
        191
Nixon, Richard 25, 27, 31, 52, 116
North, Joanna 159-164, 171

P

parole statement 5, 172, 173, 179, 183-
        188, 191, 201, 203
Power's husband 38, 97, 102, 109, 135,
        153, 154, 171
Power's son 13, 14, 97, 99, 109, 119-
        121, 170, 171, 181, 205, 208
prison sentence 2, 63, 99, 111, 137,
        140, 145, 165, 168, 171, 198, 221
probation 2, 140, 168

R

radical chic 66, 67
redemption 2, 7, 141, 154-156, 169,
        197, 198, 200, 204, 205
regret 3-5, 7, 11, 23, 37, 98-100, 102,
        141, 159, 161, 164, 168, 169,
        171, 207, 208
release from prison 2, 201
remorse 3, 98, 114, 129, 159, 168, 169,
        179, 181, 182, 190, 202
restorative justice 139, 140, 142, 160,
        167, 178, 197
retributive justice 140, 167, 197

revolutionary 1, 10, 18, 19, 31, 41, 47, 49, 60, 63, 65, 68, 70- 72, 74, 75, 79, 82, 83, 86, 87, 90, 94, 104, 117, 137, 157, 165, 179, 180, 183
Rudd, Mark 30, 31, 41, 46

S

Saxe, Susan 15, 16, 49, 51, 57, 61, 65, 68, 96, 97, 104, 144, 145, 180, 181
Schroeder, Clare 5, 111, 112, 116, 117, 182, 190, 191, 195, 196, 198, 211
Schroeder, Erin 182, 191, 198
Schroeder family 2, 19, 83, 100, 111, 112, 116, 126, 127, 143, 157, 160, 161, 171, 172, 177-183, 188,-191, 193-196, 198, 201, 202, 211
Schroeder, Marie 83, 111, 182
Schroeder, Walter vi, 1, 7, 15, 19, 57, 62, 63, 75, 83, 92, 94, 99, 102, 106, 108, 109, 111, 113, 115, 117, 118, 129, 130, 135, 137, 146, 160, 161, 165, 168, 171, 172, 179-182, 187, 188, 197, 199, 201, 202, 207
SDS 29, 31, 34
Seale, Bobby 27, 51, 53, 54, 57, 71
self-radicalization 49, 50, 79, 90-92, 94
sentencing vi, xv, 2, 81, 111, 114, 115, 143, 168
Sestina for Jaime 12, 13, 121, 170
shame 3, 11, 67, 77, 85, 87, 98, 102, 103, 109, 118, 122, 127, 142, 167-170, 180-182, 186, 202, 208
Shapley, Deborah 174-176
social psychology 22, 23, 67, 69, 70
special condition vi, 2, 136, 140
Spinoza 167, 168, 172, 173
suicide 41, 105, 170, 174, 175

surrender statement 5, 9, 42, 83, 84, 108-110, 113-116, 118, 126, 127, 135, 161, 171, 183-187, 188, 193

V

Valeri, Robert 15, 16, 18, 19, 68, 69, 72, 75, 180, 181
victim statement xv, 111
Vietnam War 4, 5, 16, 22-29, 31, 34, 35, 37, 41, 45, 52, 54, 56-58, 64, 72-74, 79, 86, 89, 90, 104, 108, 116, 117, 123, 124, 136, 138, 139, 142, 165, 172, 176, 179, 184, 195

W

Walters, Barbara 102, 108, 117
Washington Post 19, 71, 107, 110, 138
Weather Underground 25, 29-31, 34, 46, 50, 71, 73, 86, 90, 91, 97
Westmoreland, General William 136, 138, 173
Whitney, Helen 5, 195